JavaScript 1.5

BY EXAMPLE

201 West 103rd Street
Indianapolis, Indiana 46290

Adrian Kingsley-Hughes and Kathie Kingsley-Hughes

JavaScript 1.5 by Example

International Standard Book Number: 0-7897-2499-5

Library of Congress Catalog Card Number: 00-110226

Printed in the United States of America

First Printing: January 2001

03 02 01 4 3 2

Trademarks

All terms mentioned in this book that are known to be trademarks or service marks have been appropriately capitalized. Que cannot attest to the accuracy of this information. Use of a term in this book should not be regarded as affecting the validity of any trademark or service mark.

Warning and Disclaimer

Every effort has been made to make this book as complete and as accurate as possible, but no warranty or fitness is implied. The information provided is on an "as is" basis. The authors and the publisher shall have neither liability nor responsibility to any person or entity with respect to any loss or damages arising from the information contained in this book.

Acquisitions Editor
Todd Green

Development Editor
Dean Miller

Managing Editor
Thomas F. Hayes

Project Editor
Karen S. Shields

Copy Editor
Megan Wade

Indexer
Aamir Burki

Proofreader
Jeanne Clark

Technical Editor
Jim O'Donnell

Team Coordinator
Cindy Teeters

Media Developer
Jay Payne

Interior Designer
Karen Ruggles

Cover Designer
Rader Design

Layout Technicians
Ayanna Lacey
Heather Miller
Stacey Richwine-DeRome

Contents at a Glance

Table of Contents

About the Author

Adrian and Kathie Kingsley-Hughes have been writing about the subject of Web development for more than three years. Their titles include *Intro to Web Style Sheets Part 1 and Part 2*, *VBScript Part 1 and Part 2*, and *Databinding and Scriptlets* (all published by Active Path/ZDEducation). They have been coauthors on Wrox Press's *VBScript Programmer's Reference* and *XML Applications*. Adrian also contributed to Sybex's *HTML Complete, Second Edition*.

They are both consultants for a U.K. Web development and training company, designing and delivering training courses in Web development and programming. They both teach online at ElementK.com and SmartPlanet.com, and before that they taught at ZDU.

Dedication

To our families, especially Joyce and Bruce, for their unshakeable faith and indefatigable support; Nain and Taid, for wisdom and strength—we miss you; and lastly, but never least, our great kids, Katie, Amy, and Tina, for their patience while we write and for all the happiness and joy they bring to us every single day.

Acknowledgments

No project of this scale can ever be credited entirely to the one or two people with their names on the cover. Our sincerest thanks to all the editors and staff we've had the pleasure of working with to produce a product that actually works! It has been fun, and we hope to have the pleasure of working with each of you again in the future.

Many thanks to Todd Green for the great idea and shaping the product into this fine format, keeping us happy, providing prompt answers to many long-winded emails, and for giving us great suggestions as to how to make this product better.

A big thanks to Victoria Elzey for all her hard work at the beginning of this project, honing the initial outline from a bunch of bullet points into a firm foundation for us to work from—thanks!

Big thanks is also due to Dean Miller, Cindy Teeters, and Karen Shields for keeping the project moving along over the weeks it took to write it, and also thanks to Megan Wade for here fine work on the copy edit—thanks!

Also, thanks to Jim O'Donnell for reading through the initial manuscript and making sure we were all on the right track—great work there and many thanks!

Finally, a big "Thank you" to all those other people who worked behind the scenes on this project, the people who we never got the opportunity to meet! Your efforts have not gone unnoticed.

Adrian and Kathie Kingsley-Hughes, Dec 2000

Tell Us What You Think!

As the reader of this book, *you* are our most important critic and commentator. We value your opinion and want to know what we're doing right, what we could do better, what areas you'd like to see us publish in, and any other words of wisdom you're willing to pass our way.

As an Associate Publisher for Que, I welcome your comments. You can fax, email, or write me directly to let me know what you did or didn't like about this book—as well as what we can do to make our books stronger.

Please note that I cannot help you with technical problems related to the topic of this book, and that due to the high volume of mail I receive, I might not be able to reply to every message.

When you write, please be sure to include this book's title and authors as well as your name and phone or fax number. I will carefully review your comments and share them with the authors and editors who worked on the book.

Fax: 317.581.4666

E-mail: feedback@quepublishing.com

Mail: Associate Publisher
Que
201 West 103rd Street
Indianapolis, IN 46290 USA

Introduction

The *by Example* Series

There are two distinct advantages in learning JavaScript when it's done *by Example*. First, by completing the examples as you read through each chapter, the concepts are reinforced for you immediately, much more so than just reading about a technique.

Second, with the JavaScript examples that will be available for download from the Web, *JavaScript 1.5 by Example* gives you a great position on the cutting edge of Web development, all the while enabling you to practice your new skills on today's sites. How? As you work through the examples, you can edit them to suit your immediate needs, enabling you to have a working JavaScript-enabled Web site in no time.

Who Should Use This Book

This book teaches how to write and create JavaScript script to new JavaScript programmers, people who may have never even seen a JavaScript statement. The key concepts of the JavaScript scripting language are described, such as input and output, variables and data types, expressions, conditions, statements, functions, and objects. No experience with JavaScript is assumed (although knowledge of HTML is assumed), and everything is covered from the beginning, step by step, and *by Example*!

If you've never heard of JavaScript until this morning, or in the past have looked at examples longingly, wishing you could write JavaScript like that, then this is the book for you!

This Book's Organization

This text focuses on how to write correct JavaScript by teaching you all the techniques and skills you need. You'll start with simple examples and build on your knowledge and understanding, one example at a time, one concept at a time. You won't be rushed into creating a "super-example" in Chapter 1 or be introduced to script libraries for you to cut and paste into your Web pages. What you will find here is a solid grounding in JavaScript that will enable YOU to move on and use the language in the way that you want to!

JavaScript 1.5 by Example teaches you what you need to know about the language to be able to use it. As well as learning the actual ins and outs of the language, you'll learn tips and warnings, gain some ideas as to how you could put JavaScript to good use, and get to know a little of the history behind what has become the most important and exciting scripting language the Web has ever seen.

Not only is learning JavaScript rewarding in its own right, it also can serve as a springboard for you if you want to progress onto other computer languages, such as Java, C++, Perl, VB, C, and so on, because of the similarities between them all.

In this book, you will come across examples of how people are actually putting JavaScript to work on their Web sites. These examples will be fully documented, and you will have plenty of opportunities to hone your JavaScript skills by experimenting with and expanding on the examples presented in these chapters.

Please visit the *by Example* Web site for code examples or additional material associated with this book. They can be found at `http://www.quecorp.com/series/by_example`.

Conventions Used in This book

This book uses the following typeface conventions:

Typeface	Meaning
Italic	Variables in "pseudocode" examples and terms used the first time
Bold	Text the reader types in
Computer type	Commands, filenames, HTML tags, and JavaScript language, as well as URLs and addresses of Internet sites, newsgroups, and mailing lists

EXAMPLE

This icon tells you when a JavaScript example is about to be presented.

OUTPUT

This signals what should appear on your screen after you create and run an example. Please note that minor variations might occur, depending on the browser you are running.

NOTE

Notes provide additional information related to a particular topic.

TIP

Tips provide quick and helpful information to assist you along the way.

What's Next

The best place to start learning any computer language is at the beginning, so the first chapter takes you on a journey of the history of JavaScript. Along the way, you'll also find out what you need in the way of software to become a JavaScripter (don't worry—you won't need to buy anything!).

So, get ready to learn JavaScript—*by Example*!

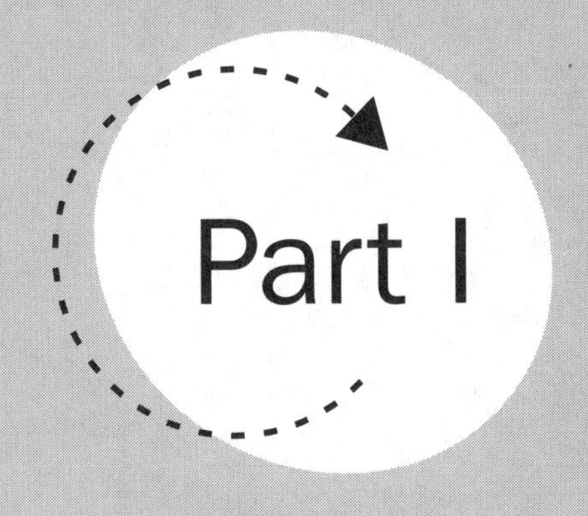

Welcome to JavaScript

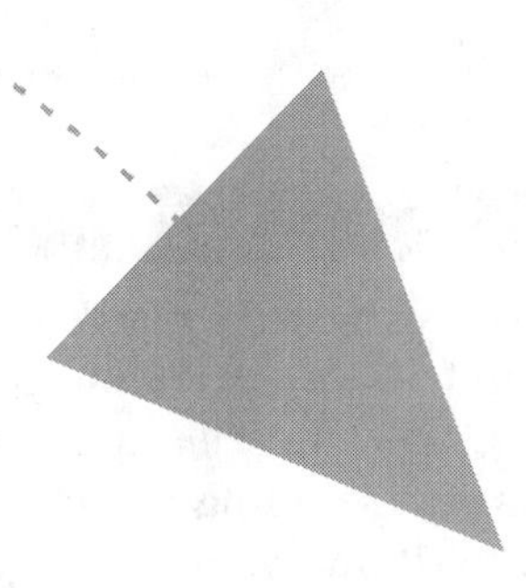

1

Getting into JavaScript!

JavaScript is a scripting language that enables you to add a new level of interactivity and function to Web pages. After you learn JavaScript, your Web development will take on an entirely new level. In this, the first chapter, you discover why being able to write JavaScript is nowadays almost as important as knowing how to use HTML. You will also get a bit of background on JavaScript before you begin writing JavaScript in earnest in the next chapter.

From this point on, your Web pages will never be the same again!

This chapter teaches you about the following:

- Why you need to learn JavaScript
- The origins and history of JavaScript
- Some of the differences between a scripting language and a programming language
- The tools you will need to write JavaScript

JavaScript Is Everywhere

Take a look at some of the sites you visit on a regular basis. What do you see? The pages probably all have text on them, and also a load of images, right? But take a closer look; what else do you see? Do you see anything else? Maybe a clock telling you the time or a message scrolling in the browser status bar? Perhaps the site has a form to fill in: Notice when you omit some information, a message pops up telling you that a problem exists. On some of the pages, you might see images that move across the screen or text that changes when you click it. With each of these features and effects, there is a good chance that you are seeing JavaScript in action! These are the kinds of things that someone with a good knowledge of JavaScript can do. Quickly and easily.

TIP

It's a really good idea to keep an eye out for what other developers, like yourself, are doing with JavaScript. This is a great way to find out What's Hot and What's Not!

Throughout this book, you will not only be learning how JavaScript works (as opposed to just learning how to cut and paste scripts into your Web pages), but you'll also get plenty of ideas for new and exciting applications you can create for yourself using JavaScript.

Why You Need to Learn JavaScript

It is because JavaScript is used so much on the Web that you really need to know how to use it. Because so many Web sites add script to their pages (for a variety of reasons, as you will find out), sites that don't use script can look bland, or even boring, in comparison. So, even if your content is otherwise great, your visitors are less likely to return. Of course, every Web site needs good content, but spicing it up with some JavaScript can not only make it clearer, but can also add some useful functionality—making it more memorable.

TIP

Remember, sometimes the only thing that separates successful from unsuccessful Web sites is how they look and feel. Invariably, the site that gives the visitor the best browsing experience is the most popular.

CAUTION

Be wary of cut-and-paste JavaScripts that you can find on the Web. Many are poor-quality scripts, but worse still is the fact that you can find the same script used on literally thousands of Web sites. Learning JavaScript frees you from this and enables you to give your visitors a totally unique—and memorable—experience.

Plenty of other practical reasons exist for learning and using JavaScript, too. For example, a few lines of script can be used to direct the visitor to the page appropriate to his browser type and settings, or it can automate a task for the visitor, such as totaling up columns in an online order form. These tasks might not be visually stunning or outwardly impressive, but they are the sign of a professional developer who cares for her visitors.

JavaScript History

JavaScript (or Livescript as it was called back then) was invented by Brendan Eich of Netscape Communications, and its name was changed only when *Java* became a very fashionable Web term.

The first browser to support JavaScript was Netscape Navigator 2.0. It was then that Microsoft saw how useful a Web scripting language would be and released its own variant, called JScript 1.0, with the Internet Explorer 3.0 browser and Internet Information Server software. Microsoft's JScript 1.0 was pretty much compatible with Netscape's JavaScript 1.0, which meant that JavaScript written for one of the browsers had a very good (but not always 100%) chance of working as expected in the other browser.

Later, Netscape released JavaScript 1.1 with Netscape Navigator 3.0 browser and LiveWire Web server software. This version had all the features of JavaScript 1.0 plus many new features and capabilities. Microsoft responded to this by upgrading its own JScript but decided not to include all the features included in JavaScript 1.1. This was the beginnings of *browser incompatibility*, in which HTML and scripts written for one browser wouldn't work properly when viewed in the competitor's browser.

Netscape made the JavaScript definition public (that is, they attempted to make their version the most popular by being open with everyone about what they were doing). Shortly thereafter, Netscape agreed with, among others, Microsoft to create a neutral standard. The European Computer Manufacturing Association (ECMA), a Swiss standards body, began developing the standard in November 1996. In July 1997, they released the standard, calling the language *ECMAScript*. While all this was happening over in Switzerland, Netscape released JavaScript 1.2 with their Netscape Navigator 4.0 browser, and Microsoft released JScript 2.0 for the Internet Explorer 3.0 browser. Neither JavaScript 1.2 nor JScript 2.0 was 100% compliant with the ECMAScript standard (which is sometimes also referred to as *ECMA-262*).

Those times are now generally looked back upon as being very hard on Web developers the world over. Not only did they need to remember what worked for each browser version, but they also had to somehow create Web pages that worked for both Internet Explorer and Netscape Navigator.

Many believed that things wouldn't get any better and that the standards would continue to drift further apart, while others optimistically clung to the hope that the ECMA standard would catch on and that the standards would once again become compatible.

Thankfully, a lot of this chaos has now given way to a closer adherence to the standards by both parties, with both JavaScript 1.5 and JScript 5.5 being (barring a few minor exceptions retained for backward-compatibility and extensions added by Microsoft and Netscape in anticipation of becoming standards) 100% ECMAScript Edition 3 compliant. This means that, in theory at least, you can write JavaScript that will work equally well in both browsers. However, as you will later discover, other differences in the browsers still mean that it isn't always as easy as perhaps it could be. Tables 1.1 and 1.2 chart the history of JavaScript through the browsers.

CAUTION

Standards are great if everyone is using the latest version of the browser. However, as you probably already know, this isn't the case. Plenty of people are still surfing the Net with version 4, 3, and in some cases even version 2 or older browsers. If you have visitors using these browsers, you still must accommodate them—you will find out how to do this later.

Table 1.1: JavaScript Through the Browsers—Netscape JavaScript Versions

Browser	Version
Netscape 2.0	1.0
Netscape 3.0	1.1
Netscape 4.0	1.2
Netscape 4.5	1.3/1.4
Netscape 6.0	1.5

Table 1.2: JavaScript Through the Browsers—Internet Explorer JScript Versions

Browser	Version
Internet Explorer 3.0	1.0/2.0
Internet Explorer 4.0	3.0
Internet Explorer 5.0	5.0
Internet Explorer 5.5	5.5

JavaScript Today

JavaScript 1.5 and JScript 5.5 represent the latest in Web scripting languages, giving you an awesome amount of power over both how the page looks and how it behaves. When you take JavaScript and combine this with other cutting-edge technologies present in the latest browsers—technologies such as the comprehensive browser Document Object Model and Cascading Style Sheets (which will be covered later in the book)—you have almost complete control over everything that happens on a Web page. By using JavaScript and the Object Model of the browser, you can create Web pages that respond to a user's clicks and keyboard strokes. On the other hand, combining JavaScript and Cascading Style Sheets enables you to do things such as hide or display text at will, move images across the page, control the browser window, and much, much more.

TIP

Don't worry if the previous sounds a little disheartening—it's not as bad as it sounds!

With these technologies, you don't just create Web pages, you create an *environment* for the visitor that can look, feel, and respond just like any other application on her computer. Later in this book, you will find out how to do this.

The Future of JavaScript

With the ECMA standard bringing JavaScript and JScript together, the future of JavaScript on the Web is guaranteed. Both Netscape and Microsoft (who has another Internet Explorer–only scripting language based on its Visual Basic language called VBScript) have pledged that they will continue to both support and develop JavaScript in the future. In addition to Netscape and Microsoft's involvement, Opera Software has joined in by adding JavaScript support for their Opera browser since version 3.

This means that JavaScript is future-proof—you can learn how to write it today confident in the fact that it's not going to disappear in the near future.

What Is the Difference Between a Script and a Program?

This is a commonly asked question by those who are new to scripting and even those who have been using script for a while. The technical (read "gear head") answer is that a *script* is a sequence of instructions (or sometimes even another program) that is interpreted or carried out by another program rather than by the computer's processor. What does this mean in the real world? Well, first off, to create a program you need another program (a compiler at the very least), whereas to write script the least that you want is a text editor (more on this in a minute). This means that scripts are easier and generally faster to write than programs are because they are written in more structured and compiled languages, such as C and C++.

However, a script does take longer to run than a compiled program because each instruction in the script is being handled by another program first (which requires additional programs to be loaded and more instructions carried out), rather than directly by the processor. However, this drawback is more than compensated for by the fact that a script can be written using a free text editor, whereas a C++ program can require software worth hundreds of dollars!

What About the Difference Between a Scripting Language and a Programming Language?

You might have heard things in the past like "Oh yes, JavaScript is just like C++," or "JavaScript and Java are just the same thing." Well, in reality, neither of these statements is true. JavaScript is a third-generation language, which means it is a cousin to C, Pascal, and BASIC (if you have difficulty visualizing what this means, don't worry about it!). Similarities do exist, but so do some important differences. Here are a few:

- JavaScript is free-formatted. This means that careful formatting is optional.
- JavaScript is an interpreted language. This means that it is processed by a separate program on the computer.
- JavaScript is highly portable and hardware independent. This means that, similar to Java, it can run anywhere.
- JavaScript embeds easily into other software, like browsers (try doing that with C++!).

What this all means is that if you have some C, C++, Pascal, BASIC, Java, FORTRAN, or Perl experience, you might find that some aspects of JavaScript seem familiar. However, don't expect to be able to create JavaScript using any of them—to write JavaScript you have to use JavaScript!

Tools for the JavaScripter

As you already know, JavaScript doesn't require you to go to your software retailer and buy expensive software to write JavaScript. However, two different kinds of software exist that will let you do the job. Let's look at these now.

The Simple Text Editor

Probably the best option is choosing a simple text editor (such as faithful old Windows Notepad) and typing in the code this way. Writing JavaScript this way might be the "hard way" to write JavaScript, but it has some cracking advantages:

- It's cheap!
- You don't need to learn how to use a complex piece of software.

- You actually learn JavaScript, as opposed to learning how a software package works.
- It frees you from the JavaScript techniques built into the software package. By writing the code yourself, you can do anything and everything that JavaScript enables you to do.
- You're free to format and add notes and comments to the JavaScript as you see fit. You know how it all works, so making changes to the JavaScript is easy.
- You can keep all the little snippets of JavaScript that you write, building up your own JavaScript library.
- You have the satisfaction that the JavaScript is all your own work, and you can take all the credit for it!

CAUTION

Don't be tempted to use a rich text editor (such as Microsoft Word or Windows Write) to write JavaScript, because problems can result. A common problem is quote marks. JavaScript requires plain quotes (' or ''), whereas certain rich text editors have a tendency to use curly "smart quotes." These simple, curly smart quotes can cause big problems. The best way to avoid these problems is to use a simple text editor.

Throughout this book, we will use Windows Notepad (as shown in Figure 1.1) for all the examples.

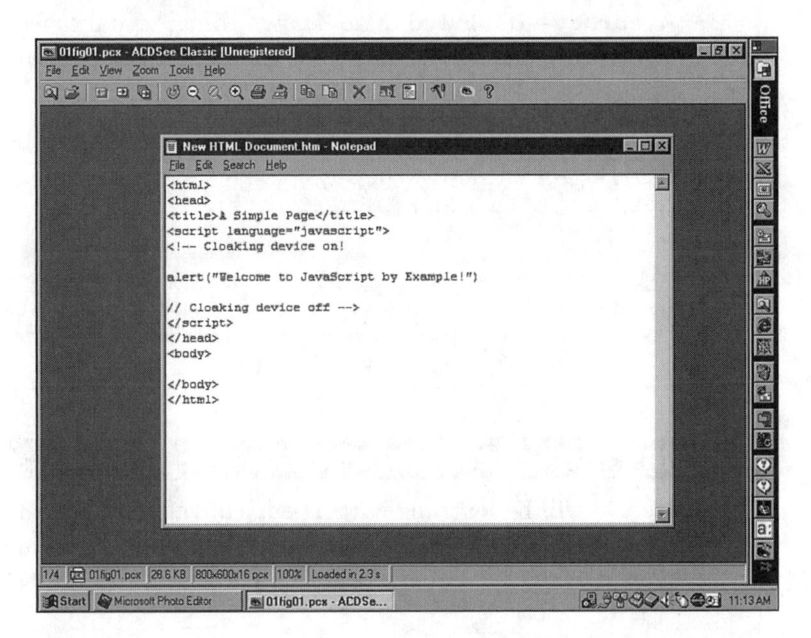

***Figure 1.1:** JavaScript displayed in Windows Notepad.*

Using Visual Tools

Visual tools for writing JavaScript are usually HTML editors/creators that enable you to drop into the Web page simple scripts to perform simple tasks. Examples of such tools include Microsoft FrontPage, Macromedia Dreamweaver, and Adobe GoLive.

Usually, you don't even have to look at or type in any JavaScript at all, which on the face of it might seem like a good idea. But what they offer in terms of ease of use, they lose in terms of flexibility. Each tool is usually limited to a few JavaScript tricks in its repertoire, so the scope for creativity is somewhat limited. Another drawback is that the JavaScript outputted by these visual tools is usually so long and complicated that even professional developers find it difficult to read, let alone make changes to or edit, the script. It is not unusual for one small edit to cause the whole JavaScript to stop working and throw up errors—not a good thing to show the visitors to your site!

However, there might be times when you need to or have to use a visual tool. That's OK. The main thing is that you will be able to write your own JavaScripts when you want to and not have to rely solely on the built-in scripts in the software.

However, some advantages do exist to using visual tools:

- **Speed**—They are much faster to use than manual typing.
- **Accuracy**—If allowed to do its own thing, visual tools output JavaScript that works (however, this might not be the case once you start to modify it!).
- **Special features**—Features such as color coding of the HTML make the HTML and JavaScript more readable.

TIP

Throughout this book, we encourage you to actually type out the examples for yourself. Although this might seem tedious and time-consuming, it is by far the best way to learn how to write and, more importantly, how to think, in JavaScript. This enables you to get a feel for how the language actually comes together.

Having the Latest Browsers

Because you will be learning cutting-edge JavaScript here, it is important that you have the latest browsers available to take advantage of this. We suggest you have at least Netscape Navigator 4.0 and Microsoft Internet

Explorer 5.5 installed. Internet Explorer 5.5 and Netscape Navigator 6 Preview Release 2 are shown in Figures 1.2 and 1.3, respectively.

TIP

Both browsers can be downloaded free of charge from the Web. Go to `http://www.microsoft.com/ie` for the latest on Internet Explorer and `http://www.netscape.com` for the latest on Netscape Navigator.

NOTE

The only other browser capable of running JavaScript is Opera Software's Opera (currently at version 4.5). This browser isn't available free of charge but can be purchased and downloaded from `http://www.opera.com`.

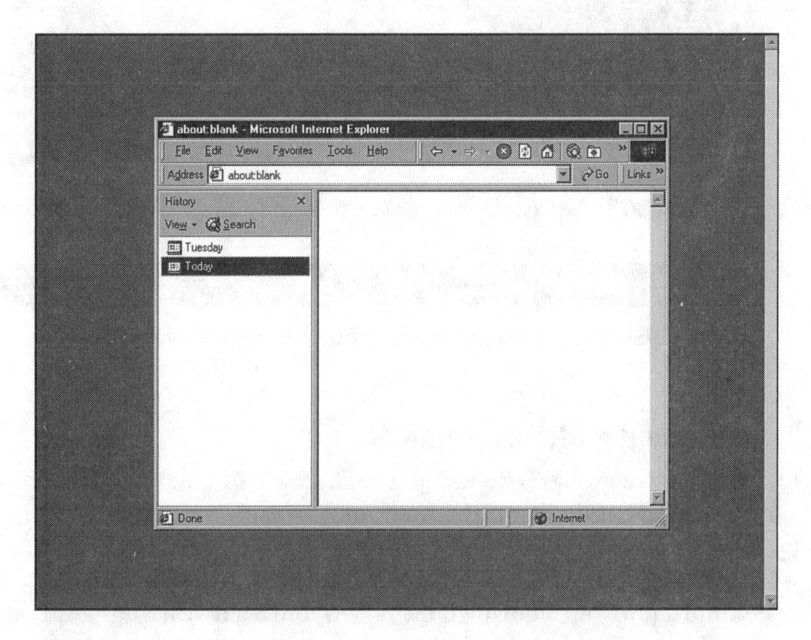

Figure 1.2: Microsoft Internet Explorer 5.5.

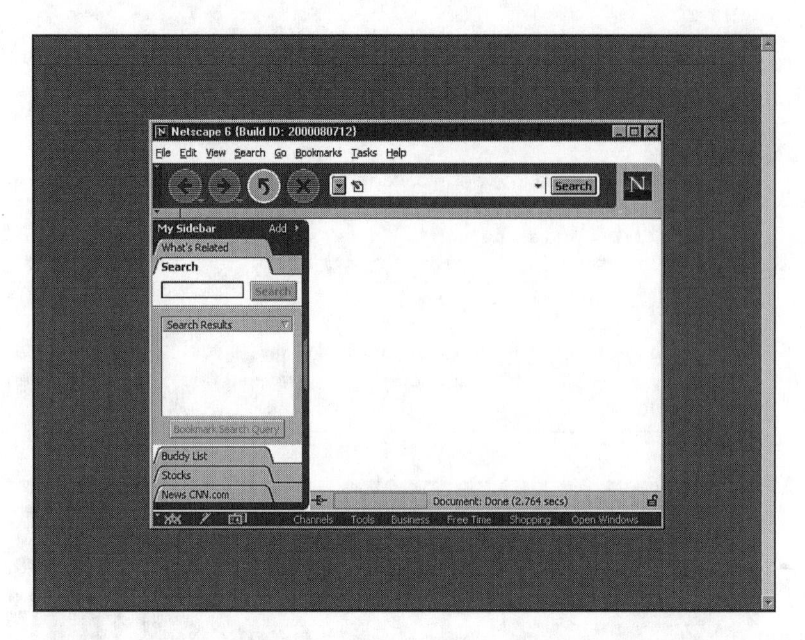

Figure 1.3: *Netscape Navigator 6 (this is the Preview Release 2 version).*

Other Tools

What else can you do to make your life as a JavaScripter easier? Here are a couple of ideas.

Creating an HTML Template

EXAMPLE

If you are going to be using a text editor to create your Web pages, it makes sense to cut down on the amount of repetitive typing you have to do. One way you can do this is by using an HTML template. A *template* is a text file containing the skeleton HTML that goes into every page. It can be customized to suit your own situation, but as a starting point, the following might suffice:

```
<html>
<head>
<title>HTML Template Page</title>
<script language="javascript">
<!--

// -->
</script>
</head>
<body>

</body>
</html>
```

This template has been customized a little to accommodate the fact that you're going to be learning how to write JavaScript, but don't worry if you don't understand something in it. You will be looking at it in more detail in the next chapter!

After you have created this template (shown in Figure 1.4), you can save it in a convenient location on your hard drive, such as your Windows desktop or your current project folder. Just remember to rename the file before you save it after you've started working on it.

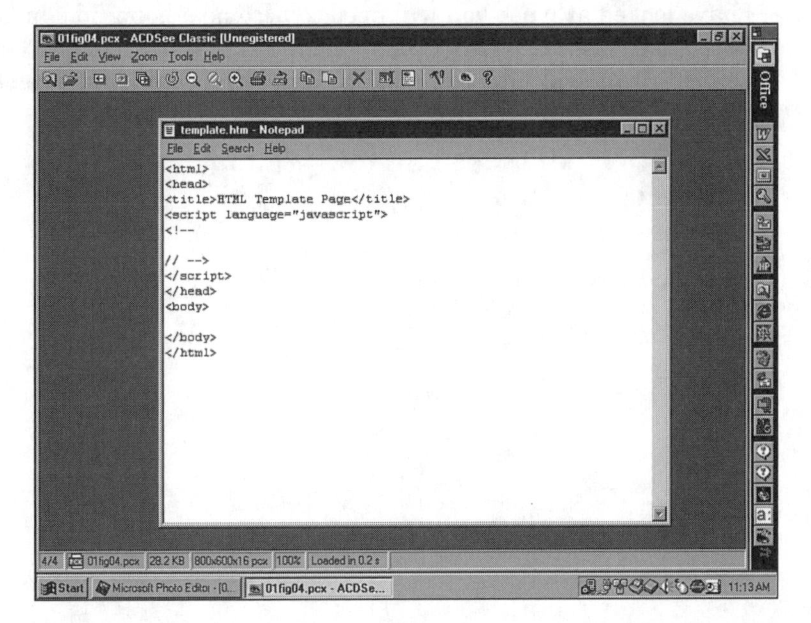

Figure 1.4: *Your HTML template displayed in Windows Notepad.*

NOTE

If you have a standard layout for the HTML of your pages, you can add this to the template.

Keeping a Script Library

As you learn to write JavaScript, one thing you can do that will be an enormous timesaver is to create your own JavaScript library. This need be nothing more than a bunch of text files in a folder. (Give them meaningful names, though, because going through them all looking for a script you need can be more time-consuming than typing it out!)

If you really want to build a great library, you can create a database of JavaScript snippets, giving each a title and including some notes about each of them. This can make finding and retrieving the right script very easy.

TIP

By keeping a JavaScript library, you not only make future programming easier and less time-consuming, but you also make tracking your progress and watching just how much you have improved easy.

What's Next

Now that we've covered the origins, history, and future of JavaScript and have looked at what you will need to become a bona fide JavaScripter, you are ready to start writing some script! After you've completed the next chapter, you will understand how JavaScript and HTML come together in a Web page.

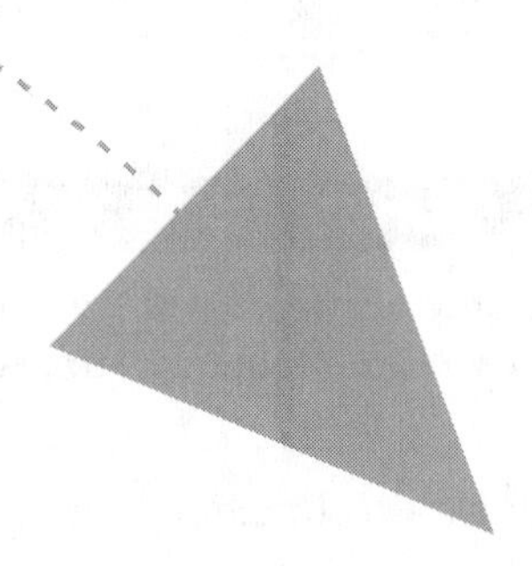

2

Combining JavaScript and HTML

The first thing you need to understand if you want to learn how to write JavaScript is how the JavaScript and HTML of a Web page come together. In this chapter, you will learn just that.

This chapter teaches you about the following:

- How JavaScript is added to the HTML of a Web page
- The importance of the `<head>` tag
- What the `<script>` block is and how to add it to a Web page
- How to hide JavaScript from older, non–JavaScript-enabled browsers

Meeting of Worlds—HTML and JavaScript

So, you know how HTML works, and you now know a little about JavaScript. The next step is to look at how the two come together and work in harmony on a Web page.

Because HTML and JavaScript are entirely separate technologies, rules exist as to how JavaScript can be slotted in to the HTML of a Web page. There are, in fact, several ways to add JavaScript to a Web page, but to get you started we are initially going to concentrate just on the most commonly used and arguably the most flexible method. In this method, JavaScript is inserted in a script *block* into the `<head>` tag.

Let's take a look at how we can do this.

The HTML Skeleton

EXAMPLE

Before moving on, you must be familiar with the anatomy of an HTML page. Here is the HTML code for the very basic Web page displayed in the browser shown in Figure 2.1:

```
<html>
<head>
<title>A Simple Page</title>
</head>
<body>
<p>A very simple Web page indeed!</p>
</body>
</html>
```

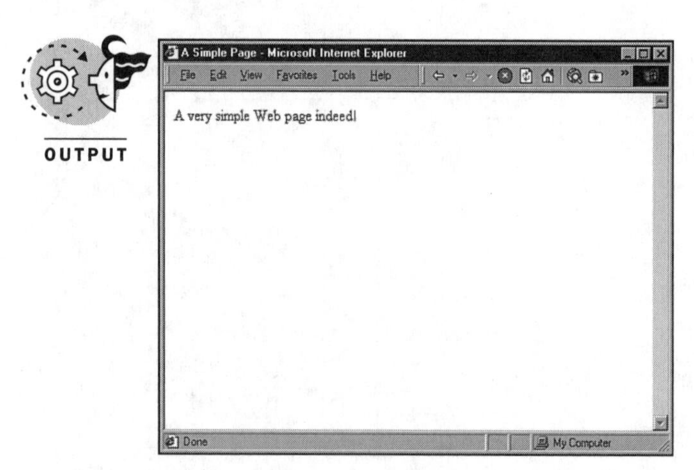

Figure 2.1: *A simple HTML Web page displayed in Internet Explorer.*

The part of this page you need to be aware of from a JavaScript point of view is the HTML block beginning with the opening tag `<head>` and closing with `</head>`. This is the `<head>` block of the page, also known as the *header* of the Web page, and it is here that you will be placing your JavaScript.

However, you can't just place the code directly into the `<head>`. There's something else you must do first!

The <script> Block

To place the JavaScript inside the `<head>` tags, you must add a new HTML block to the `<head>`. This block is the `<script>` block. The purpose of this script block is to tell the browser that whatever is contained within its opening and closing tags is a script—and it should deal with it as such.

This block can be added anywhere inside the `<head>` block but is normally added at the end, before the closing `</head>` tag:

```
<html>
<head>
<title>A Simple Page</title>
<script>

</script>
</head>
<body>
<p>A very simple Web page indeed!</p>
</body>
</html>
```

CAUTION

One reason the `<script>` block is put in the header is that by placing it here you guarantee that it is loaded before anything else, which dramatically reduces the scope for errors. If this doesn't make any sense to you now, don't worry, you'll be covering it in greater detail later in this book.

Before you can add JavaScript to the `<script>` block, you must do a few more things. The first of these tasks is to tell the browser which type of script is contained within the `<script>` block tags. This is because JavaScript isn't the only Web scripting language you could use. Another widely used scripting language is Microsoft's VBScript. So, to tell the browser that the language you are using is JavaScript, you first must add the `language` attribute to the `<script>` tag as follows:

```
<html>
<head>
<title>A Simple Page</title>
<script language="">
```

```
</script>
</head>
<body>
<p>A very simple Web page indeed!</p>
</body>
</html>
```

You declare that the language used is JavaScript by typing `JavaScript` inside the quotes:

```
<html>
<head>
<title>A Simple Page</title>
<script language="JavaScript">

</script>
</head>
<body>
<p>A very simple Web page indeed!</p>
</body>
</html>
```

NOTE

If, for example, you wanted to write a script in VBScript, the language would be set to `vbscript`:

```
<script language="vbscript">
```

You have just covered two points about that.

First, quotes. On some occasions, you might look at some JavaScript code and see the language declared with no quotes used to surround the word. Everything seems to work just fine, so why bother typing them in? Well, again it is one of those times when it is better to be absolutely correct. Even though both Internet Explorer and Netscape Navigator browsers understand the language with or without the quotes, the proper form is to use the quotes, so that is why it is shown as such here. There might come a time when the browsers demand that HTML be written correctly. By writing well-formed HTML now, you are ensuring your skills are future-proof!

The second point is one of case sensitivity. Take a look at the following:

- `<script language="javascript">`
- `<script language="JavaScript">`
- `<script language="JAVASCRIPT">`

What is the difference? Right, they are each written with various forms of capitalization. Throughout this book we will be using "JavaScript," but when creating your Web pages, by far the best to use is all lowercase. Not only is this quicker, it is far less prone to typos.

Now again, if you look at scripts written on the Web, you sometimes notice that the `language` attribute is omitted. Well, again this works fine. The reason behind this is that, because JavaScript was the first scripting language to appear, it is considered to be the default. However, to maintain properly formed Web pages, it is best to include it. This again ensures that the skills you learn today are future-proof.

More on the `language` Attribute

There is more to the `language` attribute than meets the eye. Although just plain old JavaScript is the default, you read in the previous chapter that quite a few versions or flavors of JavaScript exist. JavaScript 1.0, JavaScript 1.1, JScript, and so on are all available. You can actually use the `language` attribute to specify exactly which version you have written for. Which version you specify really depends on the browser and JavaScript version you want to run the script as. This sounds a bit complicated, but let's look at a few examples, which will help.

If you use `<script language="JavaScript">`, you are telling the browser it is just JavaScript and to use your JavaScript engine (the program that actually interprets the JavaScript) to run it. This is the default. However, if you want the JavaScript to just run on Microsoft's Internet Explorer, the best way to do this is to define the JavaScript you have written as JScript, as follows:

```
<script language="JScript">

</script>
```

Now, any JavaScript contained in the `<script>` block runs in only the Internet Explorer browser.

What if you wanted to target Netscape Navigator 3.0 users? From the previous chapter, you might remember that this browser had version 1.1 of JavaScript. This means that if you used the following language settings, only Netscape Navigator 3.0 would run your JavaScript:

```
<script language="JavaScript1.1">

</script>
```

This point is brought up to give you the full picture. Later in the book we will revisit this again and show you some tricks that you can perform with it!

CAUTION

Remember that the default is `language="JavaScript"`, and a majority of the examples in this book use this language (if we want you to set it to something else, we'll make a note of it). Be careful not to inadvertently set the language to something else because this will cause the script not to run in the new browsers, and sometimes spotting this mistake can be tricky!

Hiding JavaScript from Older Browsers

Browsers prior to Netscape Navigator 2.0 cannot run JavaScript at all, and if they come across JavaScript in a Web page, it causes them to generate some really ugly errors. To avoid the possibility of such errors, hide any script you place on the page by putting HTML comment tags inside the `<script>` block. This is quick and simple to add, and even though older browsers are pretty rare nowadays, inserting the comment tags into your HTML template so that they appear on every Web page that contains JavaScript is still worthwhile.

These comment tags are easy to add. Inside the `<script>` tags, insert another pair of tags, `<!--` and `-->`. All the code you write goes in between these tags and is then ignored by any browser that doesn't understand what the `<script>` tags mean.

NOTE

It might seem strange to place anything you want the browser to use inside comment tags because these are what is used to prevent text on the page from being displayed. But the fact is that all the browsers that understand script also know to ignore these comment tags and proceed as though they weren't there.

To make the comment tags more obvious, oftentimes developers place some (sometimes entertaining!) comments inside these HTML comment tags telling others who might view the code what they do:

```
<script language="JavaScript">
<!-- Cloaking device on!

// Cloaking device off -->
</script>
```

The page now looks like the following:

```
<html>
<head>
<title>A Simple Page</title>
<script language="JavaScript">
<!-- Cloaking device on!
```

```
// Cloaking device off -->
</script>
</head>
<body>
<p>A very simple Web page indeed!</p>
</body>
</html>
```

NOTE

Believe it or not, you've just come across your first small bit of JavaScript! This is the JavaScript comment tag (//). These are different from HTML comment tags; in the next chapter, you will see how these work and much more.

What's Next

You've now learned all that you need to know about how JavaScript fits into an HTML Web page, and you are ready to start writing JavaScript! In the next chapter, you learn how to write a few simple lines of JavaScript, which will show you how to get JavaScript to display outputs and accept inputs.

Language Tour

JavaScript in Action

Handling Data with Variables

JavaScript Arrays and Escape Characters

Expressions, Conditions, Operators, and More Strings and Numbers

Using Statements in JavaScript

Writing Better JavaScript Scripts by Using Functions and Events

Getting the Most Out of Objects

Bugs—How to Find Them and Kill Them

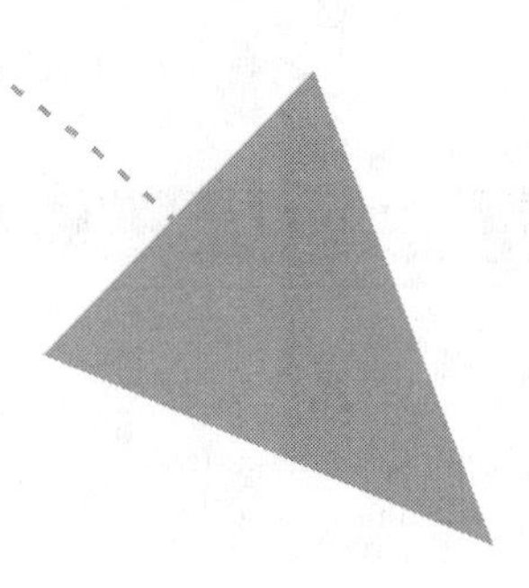

JavaScript in Action

In this chapter, you get your first opportunity to write JavaScript! This chapter introduces you to JavaScript properly. In addition, this chapter is a big hands-on chapter in which you really start to learn the fundamentals of JavaScript ... by example!

This chapter teaches you about the following:

- Some of the fundamentals of JavaScript, such as syntax, layout, commenting code, and so on
- Some of the terminology of JavaScript and also why it is known as an object-oriented language
- How to practice reading and writing JavaScript on a Web page
- How you can use JavaScript to create inputs and outputs

Exploring JavaScript Inputs and Outputs

NOTE

This chapter uses many small examples of JavaScript. I suggest you work through each example for yourself, actually typing out the code. The purpose of this is for you to get plenty of practice with JavaScript basics before moving on to more complex JavaScript examples.

Repetition is the key to JavaScript success.

Not only are JavaScript inputs and outputs great for being able to write JavaScript code that will communicate two-way with the user, but exploring this area of JavaScript is also a great place to begin your journey to proficiency!

Computing is all about inputs and outputs. Data goes in and data comes out. Without inputs and outputs, nothing would happen and nothing would get done. A word processor doesn't begin to do anything until it receives input from the user (usually in the form of characters generated by keystrokes), and this then leads to an output (it is outputted onto the screen and subsequently to paper or electronically).

Here, we are going to use JavaScript to control inputs and outputs in the form of various types of message boxes (guaranteed, if you've been surfing the Web for more than a few minutes, you've seen these message boxes before!).

Three types of message boxes can be conjured up using JavaScript. Figures 3.1, 3.3, and 3.5 show the Internet Explorer message boxes, whereas Figures 3.2, 3.4, and 3.6 show the message boxes of Netscape Navigator.

- **Alert**—This is for outputting information.

Figure 3.1: *An alert box displayed by Internet Explorer.*

Figure 3.2: *An alert box displayed by Netscape Navigator.*

- **Confirm**—This outputs information and allows the user to input a choice in the form of a yes/no question.

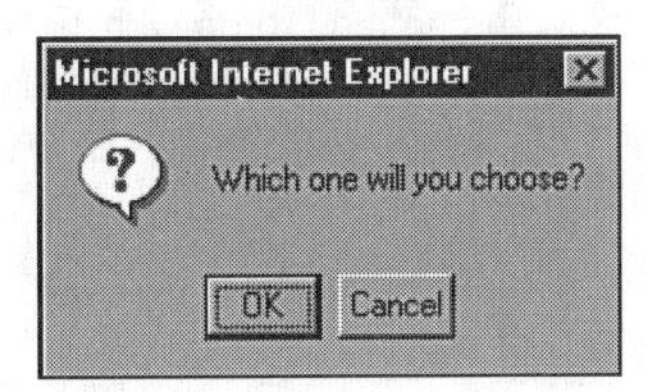

Figure 3.3: *A confirm box displayed by Internet Explorer.*

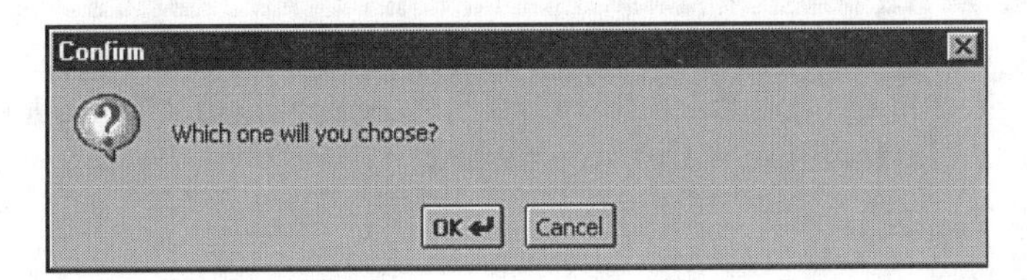

Figure 3.4: *A confirm box displayed by Netscape Navigator.*

- **Prompt**—This outputs some information and enables the user to type in a response to the output.

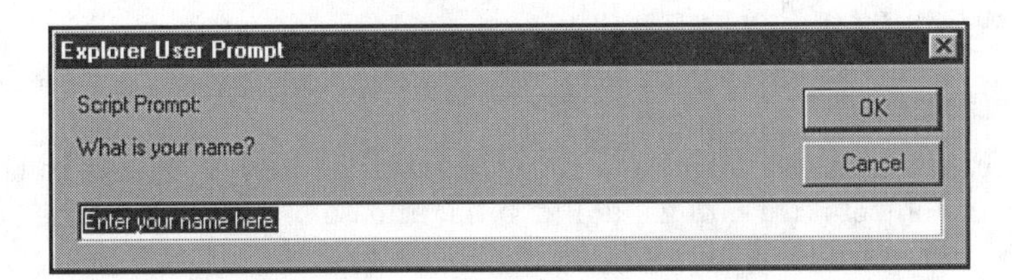

Figure 3.5: *A prompt box displayed by Internet Explorer.*

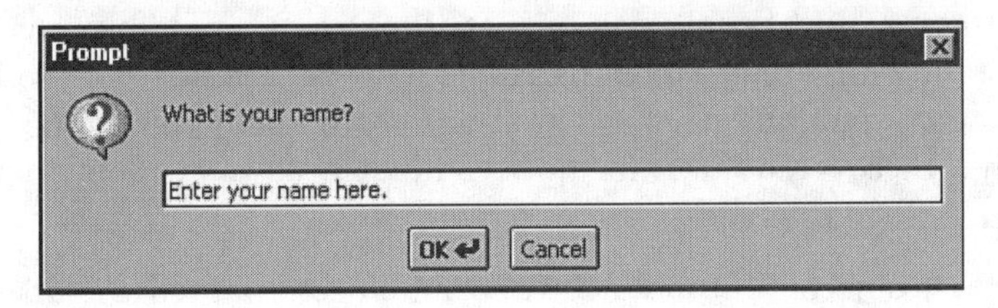

Figure 3.6: *A prompt box displayed by Netscape Navigator.*

NOTE

Why do the message boxes in Internet Explorer look so different from the message boxes in Netscape Navigator? This actually has nothing to do with JavaScript—they are different because the alert, confirm, and prompt windows are generated by the browser. These boxes are only triggered by JavaScript. Because of this, each browser adds its own uniqueness to the look.

`alert()`, `confirm()`, and `prompt()` are actually all methods of the browser's Window object.

Objects, Methods, ... and Even Properties

One thing you've probably heard about JavaScript is that it is an object-oriented language. But what does this really mean? To understand this, you need to be familiar with three terms:

- Objects
- Methods
- Properties

What follows is a brief look at the three. After you have used JavaScript for a little while, you'll find yourself using them a lot more, so we can leave the detailing of them until later.

Objects

Put simply, an *object* is a thing, anything. Just as things in the real world are objects (cars, dogs, dollar bills, and so on), things in the computer world are regarded as objects, too.

To JavaScript, its objects all live in the Web browser. These are things like the browser window itself, forms, and parts of forms such as buttons and text boxes. JavaScript also has its own group of intrinsic, or built-in, objects as well, which relate to things such as arrays, dates, and so on. At the moment, you don't need to think too much about these objects because they'll be covered later; for now you just need to get some of the necessary terminology in place.

But it is objects that make JavaScript object-oriented. JavaScript is organized around objects rather than actions; to put it another way, it's organized around data rather than the logic of the programming. Object-oriented programming takes the viewpoint that what you really care about are the objects you want manipulated and not the logic required to manipulate them. One of the benefits of this is that—because you are freed from the logic of the programming—not only is the process of programming (or scripting) easier, but there are also many ways to perform a particular operation.

Methods

Methods are things that objects can do. In the real world, objects have methods. Cars move, dogs bark, dollars buy, and so on. `alert()` is a method of the Window object, so the Window object can alert the user with a message box. Examples of other methods are that windows can be opened or closed and buttons clicked. The three methods here are `open()`, `close()`, and `click()`. Note the parentheses. Look out for these because they signal that methods are being used, as opposed to properties.

Properties

All objects have *properties*. Cars have wheels and dogs have fur. For JavaScript, things such as the browser have a name and version number.

TIP

It might help you to think of objects and properties as *things* and methods as *actions*.

Using the alert() Method

`alert()` is the easiest of the three methods to use. You can use it to display textual information to the user in a simple, concise way. When the user is finished reading the message, she simply must click OK to get rid of it.

First, open your template HTML page in your favorite text editor and save it with a new name in a convenient location on your hard drive:

```
<html>
<head>
<title>A Simple Page</title>
<script language="JavaScript">
<!-- Cloaking device on!

// Cloaking device off -->
</script>
</head>
<body>

</body>
</html>
```

NOTE

Remember to save it with the file extension HTM or HTML; otherwise, things won't work as planned.

WARNING

At this stage, it is probably worth knowing that JavaScript is a *case-sensitive* language. You'll study this in much greater detail in future chapters, but for now, note that it is best to follow the choice for upper- and lowercase letters for all JavaScript, apart from text strings that you want to use.

To conjure the alert message box, type in the following:

```
<html>
<head>
<title>A Simple Page</title>
<script language="JavaScript">
<!-- Cloaking device on!
alert();
// Cloaking device off -->
</script>
</head>
<body>

</body>
</html>
```

NOTE

The semicolon at the end of the `alert()` method is called a *line terminator* and is required to make your JavaScript ECMA compliant (although it will work properly without it). You will see this a lot over the next few chapters; in Chapter 4, "Handling Data with Variables," you find out exactly when and where it is used.

Now, for the message that you want displayed. This is placed inside quote marks inside the parentheses:

```
<html>
<head>
<title>A Simple Page</title>
<script language="JavaScript">
<!-- Cloaking device on!
alert("An alert triggered by JavaScript!");
// Cloaking device off -->
</script>
</head>
<body>

</body>
</html>
```

Save the page, load it into the browser, and watch the message appear (see Figure 3.7)!

***Figure 3.7:** An alert box complete with a custom message displayed by Internet Explorer.*

Making a second alert appear is just as simple as making the first one appear—just add `alert()` to the `<script>` block underneath the first and add your own message surrounded by quotes:

```
<html>
<head>
<title>A Simple Page</title>
<script language="JavaScript">
<!-- Cloaking device on!
alert("An alert triggered by JavaScript!");
alert("A second message appears!");
// Cloaking device off -->
</script>
</head>
<body>

</body>
</html>
```

Save the file in the text editor and refresh the browser. This time notice that two messages come up. But more importantly, notice how they are displayed separately, instead of one on top of the other. What this shows is that the JavaScript stopped between each and didn't just blindly run to the end of the script. It waited patiently until the user clicked OK on the first box before going on to display the second.

TIP

Remember to resave the file before viewing the changes you've made. You wouldn't believe the number of users who forget this step and think they have done something wrong!

EXERCISE

As an exercise, go back to the template and, from scratch, create a new JavaScript to trigger an alert box with a message of your choice.

After you have done that, add a second alert box, following the same format. Next, add the `alert()` method on a new line and then, inside the parentheses and in quotes, add the message you want displayed.

Adding Comments to JavaScript

Professional JavaScripters strive to make it easy to reread their code when they come back to it (maybe many months later). One of the things they use to help them is the JavaScript comment tags, one of which you've already come across in the previous chapter—the single-line comment.

Single-Line Comments

Here is an example of single-line comment tags in action:

```
<html>
<head>
<title>A Simple Page</title>
<script language="JavaScript">
<!-- Cloaking device on!
// The first alert is below
alert("An alert triggered by JavaScript!");
// Here is the second alert
alert("A second message appears!");
// Cloaking device off -->
</script>
</head>
<body>

</body>
</html>
```

If you run this JavaScript, you won't notice any difference at all. That is because the comment tags have done their job and hidden the comments from the browser's view.

Multi-Line Comments

Sometimes you need to add multiple-line comments to your scripts, and although you could go round placing slashes (//) at the beginning of each line, it isn't really convenient. This is where the multi-line comment tags come into their own.

Multi-line comment tags consist of the open comment tag (/*) and then the comments themselves followed by the closing comment tag (*/).

Here is an example of a multi-line comment:

```
<html>
<head>
<title>A Simple Page</title>
<script language="JavaScript">
<!-- Cloaking device on!
/*
```

```
Below two alert() methods are used to
fire up two message boxes - note how the
second one fires after the OK button on the
first has been clicked
*/
alert("An alert triggered by JavaScript!");
alert("A second message appears!");
// Cloaking device off -->
</script>
</head>
<body>

</body>
</html>
```

Adding meaningful comments to a script is something that only comes with practice. At first, it might seem tedious or even unnecessary, but not only does it make your JavaScripts easier to understand, in the early stages it helps you get a clearer idea of how your scripts work. Take every opportunity possible to comment your scripts!

EXERCISE

For the example you created for the previous exercise, comment your code using single-line and multi-line comments.

Using the confirm() Method

The confirm() method works similarly to alert(), but this box is used to give the user a choice between OK and Cancel. You can make it appear in pretty much the same way, with the only difference being that instead of using the alert() method, you use the confirm() method.

NOTE

The Cancel button needs more JavaScript behind it than you have covered so far to make it work. Fear not, though; it will be covered!

EXAMPLE

So again, following the same routine as for the alert() method, you begin by adding the confirm() method to the script block as follows:

```
<html>
<head>
<title>A Simple Page</title>
<script language="JavaScript">
<!-- Cloaking device on!
confirm();
// Cloaking device off -->
```

```
</script>
</head>
<body>

</body>
</html>
```

And again, the message you want to appear in the box is typed inside the parentheses, contained in quotes:

```
<html>
<head>
<title>A Simple Page</title>
<script language="JavaScript">
<!-- Cloaking device on!
confirm("Which one will you choose?");
// Cloaking device off -->
</script>
</head>
<body>

</body>
</html>
```

Save the file (again under a different name from the template and remembering to use the HTM or HTML file extension) and load it into the browser (see Figure 3.8).

Figure 3.8: *A confirm box complete with a custom message displayed by Internet Explorer.*

Now notice the buttons on the box—OK and Cancel. However, at the moment nothing happens when you click them except that the box disappears and the JavaScript continues to run again. Before you can use the buttons on the confirm box, you will need a few more JavaScript skills, after which you will revisit the `confirm()` method.

EXERCISE

Practice adding the `confirm()` method to a Web page. Add your own messages.

Add a couple of separate `confirm()` methods to a Web page and note the result.

Using the prompt() Method

The prompt() method is a little different from the other two you have looked at in the course of this chapter. This is the only one that either allows the user to type in his own response to the question, instead of the script just processing information it already has (as with the alert() method), or allows the user to choose OK or Cancel (available using the confirm() method).

You add the prompt() method in much the same way as the other two. To begin with, add the prompt() method to the <script> block:

```
<html>
<head>
<title>A Simple Page</title>
<script language="JavaScript">
<!-- Cloaking device on!
prompt();
// Cloaking device off -->
</script>
</head>
<body>

</body>
</html>
```

The prompt() method now starts to differ from the other two methods because two pieces of text must be added within the parentheses. The first is the message you want to appear.

This is done in exactly the same way as before. Again, the text goes inside the parentheses and inside quotes:

```
<html>
<head>
<title>A Simple Page</title>
<script language="JavaScript">
<!-- Cloaking device on!
prompt("What is your name?");
// Cloaking device off -->
</script>
</head>
<body>

</body>
</html>
```

Save this page and view it in the browser. Notice that the prompt appears, asking the user for his name (see Figure 3.9). You can type it in and proceed by clicking OK, or you can click Cancel.

OUTPUT

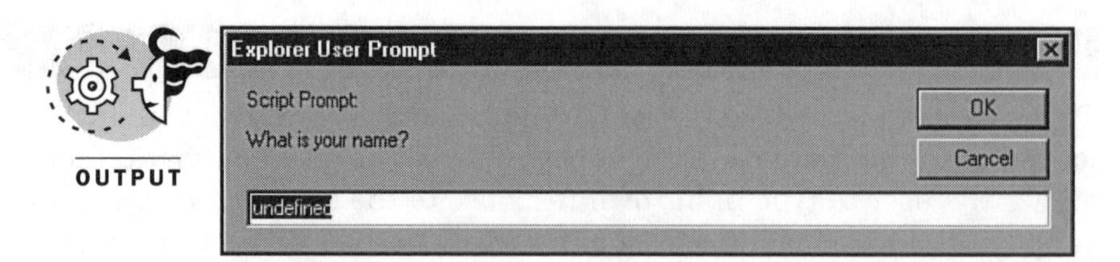

Figure 3.9: *A prompt box with a custom message displayed by Internet Explorer.*

Note the word `undefined` in the input box. This is an Internet Explorer feature; Netscape Navigator simply leaves the box blank (see Figure 3.10).

OUTPUT

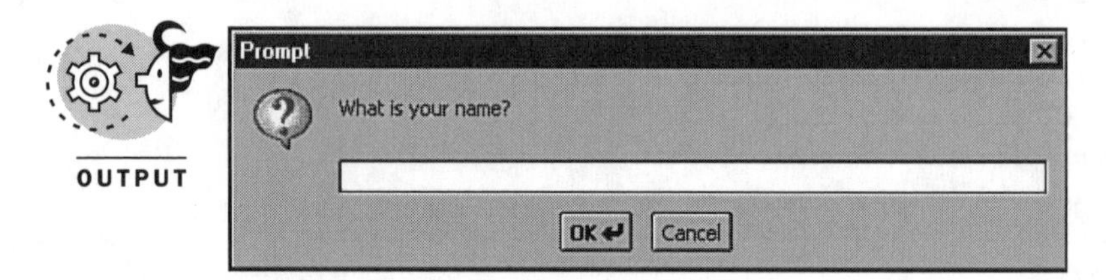

Figure 3.10: *The same prompt box in Netscape Navigator; note that no text appears in the input box.*

At the moment, nothing really happens no matter what you do, but by the end of this chapter you'll be able to put this to work with a little more JavaScript!

EXAMPLE

Another piece of text we can add is the default text to appear in the actual input box of the prompt. Adding this is simple and gets rid of the ugly looking "undefined" that Internet Explorer displays. Here is what you need to do. After the first piece of text inside the parentheses, place a comma outside the quotes, and after that place a second piece of text (again in quotes). Here is an example of this in action:

```
<html>
<head>
<title>A Simple Page</title>
<script language="JavaScript">
<!-- Cloaking device on!
prompt("What is your name?","Enter your name here.");
// Cloaking device off -->
</script>
</head>
<body>

</body>
</html>
```

Save the page again and refresh the browser. Notice how the once-empty input box now contains the text from the second set of quotes (see Figure 3.11).

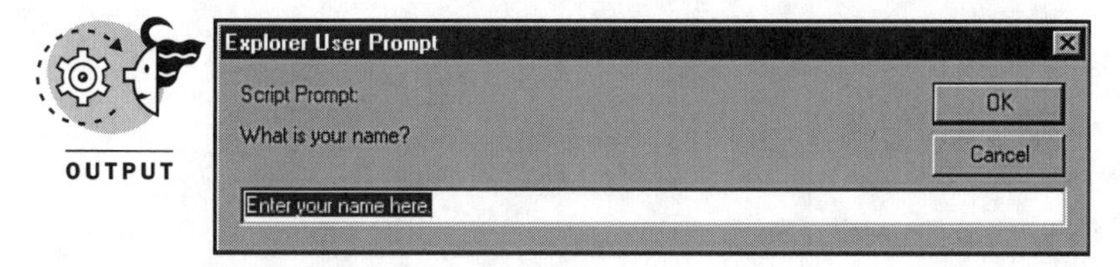

Figure 3.11: *A prompt box with a custom message and default input box text displayed by Internet Explorer.*

EXERCISE

Practice adding the `prompt()` method to a Web page. Add your own messages and default text for the input box.

Add a couple of separate `prompt()` methods to a Web page and note the result.

Add some comments (single- and multi-line) to your pages explaining what happens and what each part is.

What's Next

So far you've seen how to display three kinds of message boxes using JavaScript. In the next chapter, you learn how to make these message boxes and other JavaScripts really work by exploring two of the most important areas of JavaScript—handling data with variables and arrays.

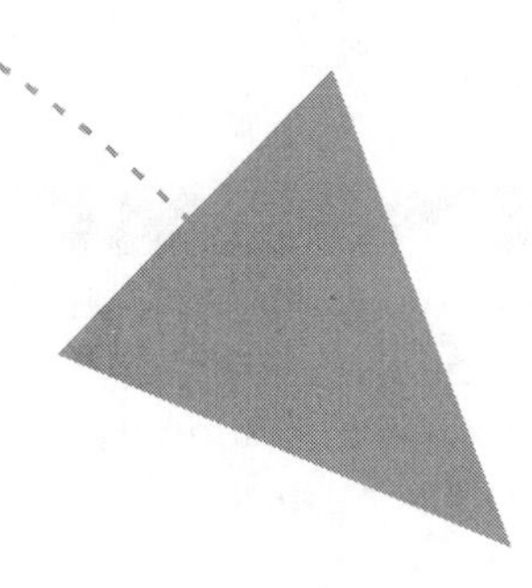

4

Handling Data with Variables

In the previous chapter, you saw how to use JavaScript to generate three types of message boxes that you can use for the purposes of inputting and outputting decisions and text. However, the JavaScript you've seen so far isn't very flexible. You type the JavaScript, complete with the messages you want displayed, with no room for anything else. In addition, any text typed into the prompt box is simply lost as soon as OK or Cancel is clicked. In this chapter, you learn how to change this to make JavaScript really work for you!

This chapter teaches you about the following:

- Values
- Variables
- How to use them within JavaScript

JavaScript Values

Information is everything, and in JavaScript every piece of information is known as a *value*. Because many kinds of information exist in the world, there are many kinds of values to choose from. However, to simplify things, the simplest building blocks of all information in JavaScript are known as *primitive types*.

The three main primitive types are

- String
- Number
- Boolean

Strings

Probably the most common value is a string. A *string* is a chain of characters that can include letters, punctuation marks, and numerals, which are literally strung together. In JavaScript, strings usually represent text.

The following are all examples of strings:

```
Hello and welcome!
Who are you?
I am 6 feet tall
```

Strings can be included in your JavaScript by surrounding them in matching pairs of double or single quotes, like so:

```
"Hello and welcome!"
```

The reason for this flexibility is so that double quotes (`"`) can be contained within your strings by surrounding the string with single quotes (`'`). Conversely, single quotes can be contained by surrounding the whole string with double quotes:

```
"I'm 6 feet tall."
'"Who are you?" he asked.'
```

An interesting point to note is that a string doesn't have to contain any characters at all. When this is the case, it is called an *empty* string and is signified by empty quotes:

```
""
```

Numbers

JavaScript recognizes two types of numbers. These are *integers* and *floating-point* numbers.

INTEGERS

Integers are whole numbers that include positive numbers, such as

```
1
2
3
```

negative number, such as

```
-1
-2
-3
```

and zero:

```
0
```

Although most numbers used in JavaScript are written in decimal (base 10), they can also be written in octal (base 8) and hexadecimal (base 16).

NOTE

We use decimal base 10 throughout this book.

FLOATING-POINT VALUES

Floating-point values can either be whole numbers with a decimal portion, such as

```
3.14159265358979323846264338327 95
```

or be expressed in scientific notation:

```
3.76e2
```

NOTE

When writing in scientific notation, an uppercase or lowercase "e" is used to represent "ten to the power of."

A number that begins with a single zero and contains a decimal point is interpreted as a decimal floating-point number.

WARNING

A number that begins with "00" and contains a decimal point (such as 005.5) generates an error.

Numbers, Numbers, Numbers ...

Table 4.1 contains some examples of JavaScript numbers to help you get more comfortable with them.

Table 4.1: JavaScript Numbers

Number	Description	Decimal Equivalent
91	Integer	91
4.56e2	Floating-point number	456
0.001	Floating-point number	0.001
00.001	Generates an error	
0.001 .001 1e-3 1.0e-3	Four equivalent floating-point numbers	0.001

How Big a Number? How Small?

> **NOTE**
>
> Unless you are into some very heavy math, you probably won't need to worry about the size of the numbers you use.

Numbers can be very large or very small in JavaScript. By very large we mean up to about 10^308 (that's a 1 with 308 zeros after it), and by small we mean 10^-308 (that is a 0. followed by 307 zeros and then a 1).

Boolean

Boolean values differ from strings and numbers because they can have only two values: `True` and `False`.

> **NOTE**
>
> Boolean is named after George Boole (1815–1864), an English mathematician.

The following are examples of Boolean values:

```
Dogs bark = true
Dogs have five legs = false
```

You'll revisit Boolean later in Chapter 6, "Expressions, Conditions, Operators, and More Strings and Numbers," when you look at expressions and conditions. For now, all you need to know is that it exists and it is a possible value type in JavaScript.

Special Data Types: Numbers, Nulls, and Undefined

Along with the three types you've looked at so far, there are a few more, less obvious, primitive data types available. These are the four special number values:

- Positive infinity
- Negative infinity

- Positive and negative 0
- NaN

Two special types also exist:

- Null
- Undefined

Briefly, as far as the four special number values are concerned, there is no possible way for you to type them in (do you want to try to type in an infinite number?). NaN stands for Not a number, and it is usually generated as a result of a mathematical operation that doesn't make sense (such as dividing any number by zero). The values relating to infinity result from the 10^308 or 10^-308 barrier being broken (say, multiplying 1.0e300 by itself), so again they aren't very useful to you (apart from telling you that something has probably gone wrong!).

The null type has only one value, `null`. Null means nothing—no data—and it is just used to tell you that nothing useful in the way of information or data is available.

Undefined is a little more difficult to understand. Again, it has one value (`undefined`) that, more often than not, is the same as `null`. In all but the most extreme cases, `undefined` (especially if displayed to the visitor) is a bad sign, and its presence tells you that something has gone wrong with your JavaScript.

JavaScript Variables

Now that you are aware of JavaScript values, you are ready to enter the world of JavaScript *variables*.

Variables are important, not only in the context of JavaScript but in all computer programming languages. Without variables very little can happen. With variables, you unleash a tremendous amount of power and the capability to move, change, and work with all kinds of data.

Put in its simplest terms, a variable is a container, to which you assign a name, for a value (which always has a particular type) held in the memory of the computer running the JavaScript. This statement actually might make variables sound more complicated than they really are, because in the real world, they are very easy to use.

Creating Variables

Creating variables in JavaScript is easy. To give you a quick and simple introduction to variables, let's return to your standard HTML template:

```
<html>
<head>
<title>A Simple Page</title>
<script language="JavaScript">
<!-- Cloaking device on!

// Cloaking device off -->
</script>
</head>
<body>

</body>
</html>
```

The first thing to do is create a variable. You can do this two ways: by declaring them and on-the-fly. To start with, let's look at variables that are declared before being used. Later in this chapter, we'll look at creating them on-the-fly.

To declare (create) a variable, you use the JavaScript statement `var` (which stands for variable) followed by the name you want to assign the variable. So, the following line of JavaScript creates a variable called `msg`:

```
<html>
<head>
<title>A Simple Page</title>
<script language="JavaScript">
<!-- Cloaking device on!
var msg;
// Cloaking device off -->
</script>
</head>
<body>

</body>
</html>
```

NOTE

A statement is the equivalent of a complete sentence in English. More on this in Chapter 7, "Using Statements in JavaScript."

Here are a few things you need to know about variable names:

- Variable names can contain uppercase characters, lowercase characters, or a mixture of both.
- Until initialized, the value of a variable is `undefined`.

- The first character cannot be a digit.
- Variable names cannot contain spaces; if you want to string together two or more words, you should use the underscore character (_).
- You should avoid using the dollar symbol ($) in a variable name because Internet Explorer 3.02 (with JScript 1.0) and Netscape Navigator 2.02 cannot handle it.
- You should avoid using variable names that differ only in case (for example, `msg` and `MsG`) because JScript 1.0 cannot distinguish between the two.

The following are all valid variable names:

```
msg
Hello_There
Msg1
Msg_1
```

The following variable names are all either invalid or best avoided:

`1msg`	Starts with a digit
`hello there`	Contains a space
`var`	A JavaScript reserved word
`dollar$`	Best avoided because it contains a $
`msg` and `Msg`	Best to avoid both together because they differ only in case

If you want to assign a value to your newly created variable, you can either do the creating and assigning all in one line:

```
<html>
<head>
<title>A Simple Page</title>
<script language="JavaScript">
<!-- Cloaking device on!
var msg = "Welcome to JavaScript variables!";
// Cloaking device off -->
</script>
</head>
<body>

</body>
</html>
```

Or, you can do the creating and assigning on separate lines:

```
<html>
<head>
<title>A Simple Page</title>
<script language="javascript">
<!-- Cloaking device on!
var msg;
msg = "Welcome to JavaScript variables!";
// Cloaking device off -->
</script>
</head>
<body>

</body>
</html>
```

If, instead of wanting to assign the variable a string, you wanted to assign it a number, you would do as follows:

```
<html>
<head>
<title>A Simple Page</title>
<script language="JavaScript">
<!-- Cloaking device on!
var msg = 22;
// Cloaking device off -->
</script>
</head>
<body>

</body>
</html>
```

CAUTION

When assigning numbers to variables, remember to leave out the quotes because they signify that the value is a string instead of a number.

EXERCISE

Create a sample page on which you create a variable and assign a string value to it. Then, create a new page on which you assign a number. Also, practice creating the variable and assigning the value on the same line and on separate lines. As in the previous chapter, don't forget to add appropriate comments.

Creating Multiple Variables

You'll probably find yourself needing more than one variable at some point in your JavaScript career (very soon in fact!), so you'll need to be able to create multiple variables.

One way to do this is by creating each on a separate line in the JavaScript:

```
<html>
<head>
<title>A Simple Page</title>
<script language="JavaScript">
<!-- Cloaking device on!
var msg1;
var msg2;
var num1;
var num2;
// Cloaking device off -->
</script>
</head>
<body>

</body>
</html>
```

This works just fine, but it makes the code a little difficult to read. A far better way to do this is by declaring it all on one line, as follows:

```
<html>
<head>
<title>A Simple Page</title>
<script language="JavaScript">
<!-- Cloaking device on!
var msg1, msg2, num1, num2;
// Cloaking device off -->
</script>
</head>
<body>

</body>
</html>
```

The line begins with var, and then the name for each variable you want to create is added after it, with a comma separating each variable name. At the end of the line is the semicolon line terminator.

WARNING

Omitting the comma results in errors!

If you want, you can create the variable and assign the values all in one line:

```
<html>
<head>
<title>A Simple Page</title>
<script language="JavaScript">
```

```
<!-- Cloaking device on!
var msg1 = "Hello", msg2 = "There", num1 = 6, num2 = 52;
// Cloaking device off -->
</script>
</head>
<body>

</body>
</html>
```

EXERCISE

Practice creating multiple variables, preferably assigning values to them at the same time. Remember to separate the variable names with commas.

Add comments to your JavaScript as you see fit.

Displaying the Contents of a Variable

So, you've created variables and assigned string and numerical values to them. Now, you can make them work for you!

The first thing you can do is prove that all this variable stuff actually works. So, in this short example you are going to use the `alert()` method to display the value of variables.

So, again, you can begin this by declaring a couple of variables called `msg1` and `num1` and assigning values to them, `"Hello there"` (a string) and 22 (a number):

```
<html>
<head>
<title>A Simple Page</title>
<script language="JavaScript">
<!-- Cloaking device on!
var msg1 = "Hello there", num1 = 22;
// Cloaking device off -->
</script>
</head>
<body>

</body>
</html>
```

Next, you add the `alert()` method to the page—make sure it is below the variables:

```
<html>
<head>
<title>A Simple Page</title>
<script language="JavaScript">
```

```
<!-- Cloaking device on!
var msg1 = "Hello there", num1 = 22;
alert();
// Cloaking device off -->
</script>
</head>
<body>

</body>
</html>
```

Finally, you must get the `alert()` method to read the value of the variable. Remember when you generated an alert box with text in it? The text was placed in quotes. This was done to show that it was a string. However, getting the alert box to display the value of a variable is easier. All you need to do is place the variable name inside the parentheses (no quotes, nothing):

```
<html>
<head>
<title>A Simple Page</title>
<script language="JavaScript">
<!-- Cloaking device on!
var msg1 = "Hello there", num1 = 22;
alert(msg1);
// Cloaking device off -->
</script>
</head>
<body>

</body>
</html>
```

Save the page and load it into the browser to see your work in action (see Figure 4.1)!

Figure 4.1: An alert box displaying the value of the variable `msg1`.

Moving on to the second variable, you can now display that in a second alert box:

```
<html>
<head>
<title>A Simple Page</title>
```

```
<script language="JavaScript">
<!-- Cloaking device on!
var msg1 = "Hello there", num1 = 22;
alert(msg1);
alert(num1);
// Cloaking device off -->
</script>
</head>
<body>

</body>
</html>
```

Save the page again and refresh the browser to see the changes you have made. This time two alert boxes appear, one after the other, with the second alert box displaying the number 22 (see Figure 4.2).

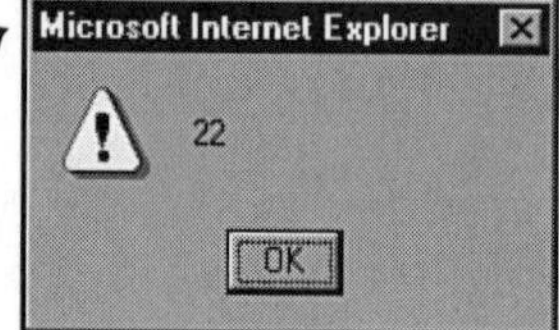

Figure 4.2: *The second alert box displaying the value of the variable* `num1`.

EXERCISE

To help consolidate what you've learned so far in this chapter, you can now create a couple of similar examples based around what you have learned. Create a couple of variables and assign them values of various types; then use the `alert()` method to display the variables' values.

You'll get much more out of it if you start these pages from scratch using just your template. Don't just cut and paste from the examples we've already worked on!

Use comments to make your JavaScript easier to read and follow.

Troubleshooting!

What is wrong with the following examples?

Example 1

```
<html>
<head>
<title>A Simple Page</title>
<script language="JavaScript">
```

```
<!-- Cloaking device on!
var msg1 = "Hello there", num1 = 22;
alert(msg11);
alert(num1);
// Cloaking device off -->
</script>
</head>
<body>

</body>
</html>
```

ANSWER: The first `alert()` method is displaying a variable that hasn't been created or had a value assigned to it (`msg11`). This is an example of an `undefined` value.

Example 2

```
<html>
<head>
<title>A Simple Page</title>
<script language="JavaScript">
<!-- Cloaking device on!
var msg1 = "Hello there" num1 = 22;
alert(msg1);
alert(num1);
// Cloaking device off -->
</script>
</head>
<body>

</body>
</html>
```

ANSWER: No comma separates the variables in the line

```
var msg1 = "Hello there" num1 = 22;
```

Example 3

```
<html>
<head>
<title>A Simple Page</title>
<script language="JavaScript">
<!-- Cloaking device on!
var 1msg = "Hello there", num 1 = 22;
alert(1msg);
alert(num 1);
// Cloaking device off -->
```

```
</script>
</head>
<body>

</body>
</html>
```

ANSWER: Both variable names are illegal. The first is illegal because it begins with a digit, and the second is illegal because it contains a space.

Using the `prompt()` Method to Assign a Value to a Variable

So far, you've seen examples of how to assign values to variables directly in the JavaScript. Sometimes, though, you can't do this. For example, if you ask the user a question, such as her name, you have no possible way to know what the answer might be (unless perhaps you have only one person visiting your site!).

Fortunately, assigning values to variables in mid-script is easy. The following example shows you how to use the `prompt()` method to accomplish this.

You once again begin with your blank HTML template page and into the `<script>` block add the `prompt()` method:

```
<html>
<head>
<title>A Simple Page</title>
<script language="JavaScript">
<!-- Cloaking device on!
prompt();
// Cloaking device off -->
</script>
</head>
<body>

</body>
</html>
```

Next, you add the message and default text you want displayed:

```
<html>
<head>
<title>A Simple Page</title>
<script language="JavaScript">
<!-- Cloaking device on!
prompt("What is your name?","Type your name here ...");
// Cloaking device off -->
</script>
```

```
</head>
<body>

</body>
</html>
```

Next, you need a way to assign the text the user types to a variable you can use later. This is surprisingly easy to do. All you need to do is type in the variable name at the beginning of the line, followed by an equal sign (=):

```
<html>
<head>
<title>A Simple Page</title>
<script language="JavaScript">
<!-- Cloaking device on!
yourname = prompt("What is your name?","Type your name here ...");
// Cloaking device off -->
</script>
</head>
<body>

</body>
</html>
```

Notice here how we have created the variable on-the-fly without using the var statement. Many times it is useful to create a variable on-the-fly, especially if you are going to use that variable in only a simple manner (say, to hold a small string or a number). But, if you actually want to work with the variable (say, for instance, to do some math), you should use the var statement because your variables will be easier to keep track of. Additionally, if you want to use a variable that has been created using the var statement, it is exactly the same—you just need to create it first!

Now, all that is left to do is take the value of the variable yourname and display it in an alert box:

```
<html>
<head>
<title>A Simple Page</title>
<script language="JavaScript">
<!-- Cloaking device on!
yourname = prompt("What is your name?","Type your name here ...");
alert(yourname);
// Cloaking device off -->
</script>
</head>
<body>

</body>
</html>
```

Save the page and load it into the browser. The first thing you will see is the prompt box being displayed, as shown in Figure 4.3.

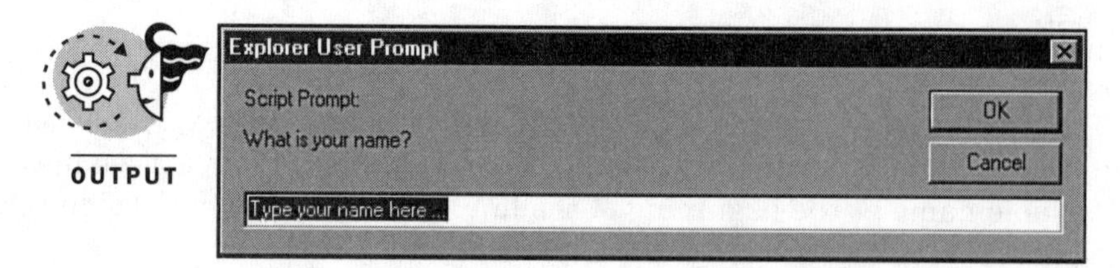

Figure 4.3: *The prompt box displaying default text.*

Type your name in the input box (see Figure 4.4).

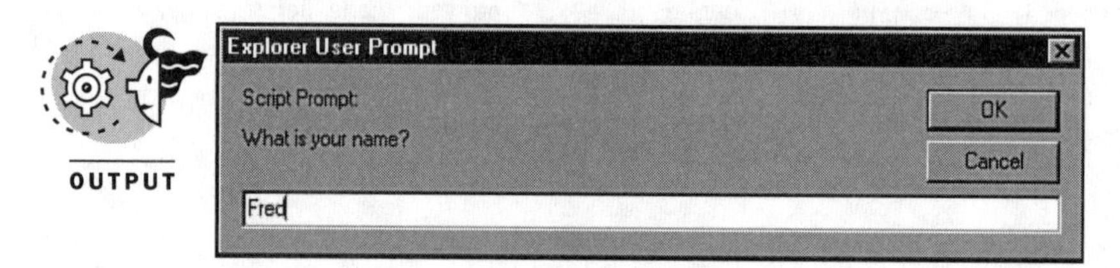

Figure 4.4: *The prompt box with added text in the input box.*

Next, click the OK button and watch the alert box appear with your name displayed in it (see Figure 4.5).

Figure 4.5: *An alert box showing the value of the* `yourname` *variable.*

If you click the Cancel button, the value of `yourname` is set to `null`, which is displayed in the alert box (see Figure 4.6).

Figure 4.6: *A* `null` *value displayed in the alert box.*

Note, too, that you can easily redisplay the value of a variable (as the following example demonstrates) because the value is retained until it's changed or cleared:

```
<html>
<head>
<title>A Simple Page</title>
<script language="JavaScript">
<!-- Cloaking device on!
yourname = prompt("What is your name?","Type your name here ...");
alert(yourname);
alert(yourname);
// Cloaking device off -->
</script>
</head>
<body>

</body>
</html>
```

To demonstrate that you can change the value of a variable, add another `prompt()` method to give you the opportunity to change it again:

```
<html>
<head>
<title>A Simple Page</title>
<script language="JavaScript">
<!-- Cloaking device on!
yourname = prompt("What is your name?","Type your name here ...");
alert(yourname);
yourname = prompt("Type something different in","Something different ...");
alert(yourname);
// Cloaking device off -->
</script>
</head>
<body>

</body>
</html>
```

Save the page and try it out in the browser. The text you enter into the second prompt box is stored in the same variable, and the old value is silently lost.

NOTE

No way exists to recover the previous value of the variable; after it's changed, it's lost.

Passing Variable Values to Another Variable

If, for some reason, you want to retain the value of the variable, you can pass the value onto a different variable. So, before the value of `yourname` is changed, you could pass it on to a new variable called `yourname2`, like so:

```
yourname2 = yourname
```

This creates a new variable on-the-fly called `yourname2` and gives it the same value as `yourname`. So in effect, both variables have the same value at this point. Remember that you must do this before you change the value of the first variable!

The following code demonstrates this:

```
<html>
<head>
<title>A Simple Page</title>
<script language="JavaScript">
<!-- Cloaking device on!
yourname = prompt("What is your name?","Type your name here ...");
alert(yourname);
yourname2 = yourname
yourname = prompt("Type something different in","Something different ...");
alert(yourname);
alert(yourname2);
// Cloaking device off -->
</script>
</head>
<body>

</body>
</html>
```

EXERCISE

Practice using `prompt()` to assign values to variables created both on-the-fly and using variables created using the `var` statement.

Practice passing variable values to other variables and reusing variables.

As always, add comments so you understand every step and to make your code easier to read!

What's Next

In the next chapter, you learn about a different kind of variable that is capable of holding more than one value—the array.

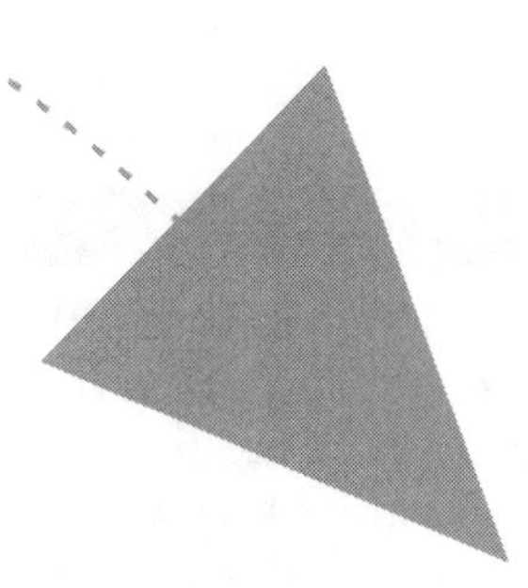

JavaScript Arrays and Escape Characters

In the previous chapter, you looked at how to use variables. This chapter builds on this by introducing you to arrays.

This chapter teaches you about the following:

- Using arrays
- Creating arrays
- Creating array elements
- Using escape characters

Using Arrays

Arrays are a powerful feature of most programming languages, and they are also available to the JavaScripter! An *array* enables you to store several separate values within a single variable. Usually, all these values have a connecting theme (such as days of the week). Arrays are great because when you know how to use them they can really simplify your code—saving you from having to create a bunch of separate variables with similar names.

So, let's look at how to create and use arrays. The example here will be used to hold the seven days of the week.

The first thing you need to do is to bring the array into existence:

```
<html>
<head>
<title>A Simple Page</title>
<script language="JavaScript">
<!-- Cloaking device on!
var days_of_week = new Array(7);
// Cloaking device off -->
</script>
</head>
<body>

</body>
</html>
```

WARNING

Note the parentheses (`()`) at the end of `new Array`. A common error is to place square brackets here!

This single line of JavaScript has accomplished several different things:

- First, it creates a variable called `days_of_week`.
- Second, you use `new Array()` to define the new variable as an array.
- Third, it has defined the size of the array (in this case, `7`).

What you have in effect created is seven empty cells, or *elements*, ready to accept values (see Figure 5.1).

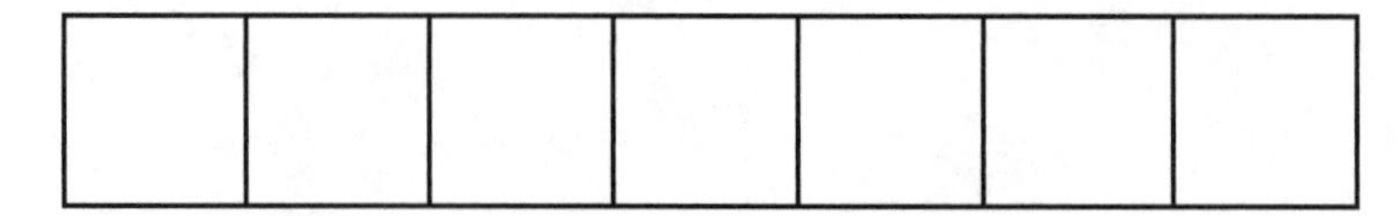

***Figure 5.1:** Representation of an empty, seven-element array.*

Entering the values is equally easy—just remember to keep track of what you want to go where.

```
days_of_week[x]
```

In the previous code, x is the position of the element.

The first thing you must notice is how JavaScript counts arrays. This is done using the following method.

When dealing with arrays, JavaScript doesn't look at the first array as being number 1; instead, it is 0 (zero). So, the days of the week example will have elements 0–6, rather than 1–7. Take a look at Figure 5.2 to see how this works.

0	1	2	3	4	5	6

***Figure 5.2:** Seven elements numbered 0–6.*

So, to place the appropriate value (Sunday in this case) in the first element of the array, you would do as follows:

```
<html>
<head>
<title>A Simple Page</title>
<script language="JavaScript">
<!-- Cloaking device on!
var days_of_week = new Array(7);
days_of_week[0] = "Sunday";
// Cloaking device off -->
</script>
</head>
<body>

</body>
</html>
```

Following this format, you can now fill the array with the appropriate values:

```
<html>
<head>
<title>A Simple Page</title>
<script language="JavaScript">
<!-- Cloaking device on!
var days_of_week = new Array(7);
```

```
days_of_week[0] = "Sunday";
days_of_week[1] = "Monday";
days_of_week[2] = "Tuesday";
days_of_week[3] = "Wednesday";
days_of_week[4] = "Thursday";
days_of_week[5] = "Friday";
days_of_week[6] = "Saturday";
// Cloaking device off -->
</script>
</head>
<body>

</body>
</html>
```

Figure 5.3 provides a visual representation of this array.

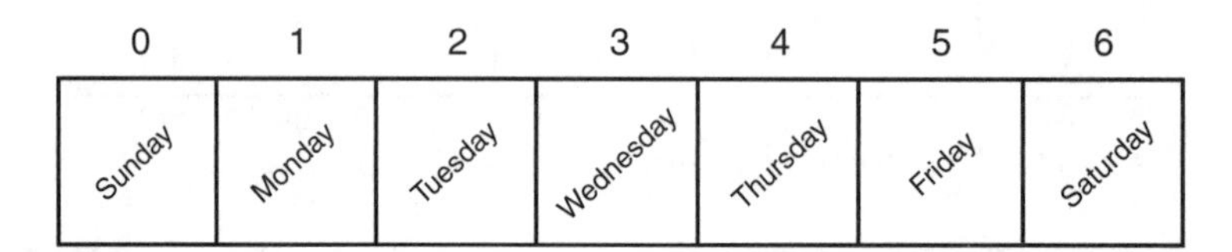

***Figure 5.3:** State of the array after values have been added.*

Now you are ready to retrieve the values of the elements in the array. Just as you assigned the values by using the format or variable name (in this case `days_of_week`) followed by a set of square brackets containing the element number (for example, `days_of_week[2]`), this format is used to retrieve the values. So, to place the value of the third element into an alert box, you would do the following:

```
<html>
<head>
<title>A Simple Page</title>
<script language="JavaScript">
<!-- Cloaking device on!
var days_of_week = new Array(7);
days_of_week[0] = "Sunday";
days_of_week[1] = "Monday";
days_of_week[2] = "Tuesday";
days_of_week[3] = "Wednesday";
days_of_week[4] = "Thursday";
days_of_week[5] = "Friday";
days_of_week[6] = "Saturday";
alert(days_of_week[2]);
// Cloaking device off -->
```

```
</script>
</head>
<body>

</body>
</html>
```

Figure 5.4 shows the output of this script.

Figure 5.4: *Alert box displaying the value for element number 2.*

NOTE

Remember the convention to begin counting at 0!

Here is another way that the same result can be accomplished:

```
<html>
<head>
<title>A Simple Page</title>
<script language="JavaScript">
<!-- Cloaking device on!
var days_of_week = new Array(7);
days_of_week[0] = "Sunday";
days_of_week[1] = "Monday";
days_of_week[2] = "Tuesday";
days_of_week[3] = "Wednesday";
days_of_week[4] = "Thursday";
days_of_week[5] = "Friday";
days_of_week[6] = "Saturday";
var x = 2;
alert(days_of_week[x]);
// Cloaking device off -->
</script>
</head>
<body>

</body>
</html>
```

Here, you see an example in which a variable, `x`, is created and the number `2` assigned as its value. The variable `x` is then placed in square brackets, and the result is that element 2 from the array is returned.

EXERCISE

Create an array to hold the months of the year and use both methods of retrieving the values of variables to display the months of February and August. (That you'll comment your code effectively goes without saying from here on in!)

Creating an Array in a Hurry!

Here is a much faster way to create the exact same array that you have in the previous example—this time, all in one line:

```
<html>
<head>
<title>A Simple Page</title>
<script language="JavaScript">
<!-- Cloaking device on!
var days_of_week = new Array("Sunday","Monday","Tuesday","Wednesday","Thursday",
➥"Friday","Saturday");
// Cloaking device off -->
</script>
</head>
<body>

</body>
</html>
```

The advantage of creating the array in this way is that you don't need to worry about how many elements there are in advance. Using this method, an array with the appropriate number of elements is created automatically.

This array behaves functionally in the same way as in the previous example, and its elements can be accessed in exactly the same way.

The Length of an Array

Earlier, you read that the length of an array is hidden away within the property `length`. `length` is a property of the array, and though it may be hidden, it isn't beyond your reach.

To find out how many elements are in the `days_of_week` array, you can use the following:

```
days_of_week.length
```

In the following example, an alert box is used to show this value:

```
<html>
<head>
<title>A Simple Page</title>
<script language="JavaScript">
```

```
<!-- Cloaking device on!
var days_of_week = new

Array("Sunday","Monday","Tuesday","Wednesday","Thursday","Friday","Saturday");
alert(days_of_week.length);
// Cloaking device off -->
</script>
</head>
<body>

</body>
</html>
```

The output from this example is shown in Figure 5.5.

Figure 5.5: *Alert box displaying the number of elements in the array* `days_of_week`.

EXERCISE

Use the `length` property to count the elements in the months of the year example you created previously.

Showing All Elements

Finally, let's look at a quick and simple way to list the values of all the elements in an array. This is done by simply using the name of the array. Therefore, to return all the elements of `days_of_week` and place them in an alert box, you can use the following (see Figure 5.6 for output):

```
<html>
<head>
<title>A Simple Page</title>
<script language="JavaScript">
<!-- Cloaking device on!
var days_of_week = new Array("Sunday","Monday","Tuesday","Wednesday","Thursday",
➥"Friday","Saturday");
alert(days_of_week);
// Cloaking device off -->
</script>
```

```
</head>
<body>

</body>
</html>
```

OUTPUT

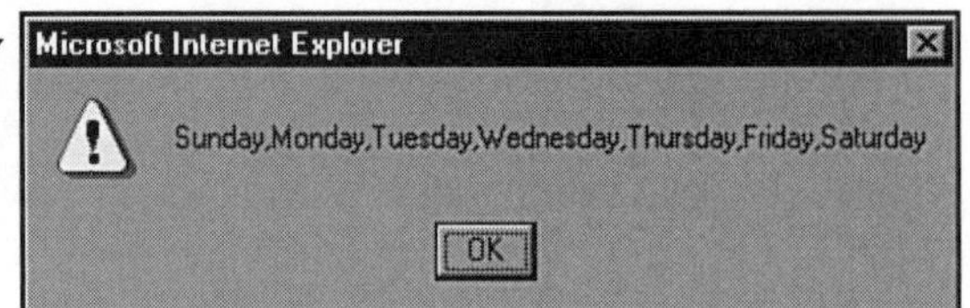

Figure 5.6: *Alert box displaying the values for all the elements in the array* `days_of_week`*.*

EXERCISE

Experiment with using arrays to hold simple values. Practice adding the values of the elements in the arrays. Practice retrieving all the values, as well as retrieving individual values.

Use the `length` property to tell you the number of elements in each array.

Exercise—Interactive Story

EXAMPLE

Let's work through an example that uses arrays to create an interactive story. You might be familiar with this type of "adlib" game in which the user is asked for a series of words—for example, adjectives, nouns, and so on. The user's answers are then inserted into a well-known piece of text to make a totally unique and hopefully amusing story. Here's how to create your own game:

1. Choose the story/rhyme/lyrics you want to use, pick out the words you want to replace, and give them each a unique variable name:

```
Once upon a entry1 dreary,
while I pondered, entry2 and weary,
Over many a entry3 and curious volume
of entry4 lore--
While I entry5, nearly napping,
entry6 there came a tapping,
As of some one entry7 rapping, rapping
at my entry8 door.
"'Tis some entry9," I muttered,
"tapping at my entry8 door--
Only this and nothing more."
```

Notice that the variable `entry8` has been used twice—this is so that whatever word the user types in will be used in both lines of the story.

Save this text—we will be returning to it shortly.

2. Now make a list of suitable descriptions for each of the replaced words:

    - "A time of day"
    - "A feeling"
    - "An adjective—eg. sunny"
    - "An adjective—eg. sunny"
    - "A verb—past tense, eg. walked"
    - "An adverb—eg. quickly or monstrously"
    - "An adverb—eg. quickly or monstrously"
    - "A room in a house"
    - "A profession"
    - "An exclamation!"

    These will be the prompt messages that tell the user which kind of word to type in. In a moment, you will create an array out of these descriptions.

    Meanwhile, make a list of default words that will appear in the story. These can be funny suggestions of your own if you want. They will be used in the final story if the user just hits OK and doesn't type anything:

    ```
    "lunchtime"
    "wet"
    "plump"
    "malodorous"
    "wriggled"
    "hungrily"
    "fiercely"
    "bathroom"
    "Web developer"
    "Yipes"
    ```

    Now you're ready to start JavaScripting!

3. Start with your template file and create a new array to hold the messages you want to appear in the prompt box, adding the prompt strings to the elements directly:

    ```
    <script language="JavaScript">
    <!-- Cloaking device on!
    ```

```
// create array for prompts
var promptmsg = new Array("A time of day","A feeling","An adjective - eg
➥sunny", "An adjective - eg sunny","A verb - past tense eg walked","An
➥adverb - eg quickly or monstrously","An adverb  - eg quickly or
➥monstrously","A room in a house",
"A profession","An exclamation!");

// Cloaking device off -->
</script>
```

4. Next, create an array to hold the default words you want to appear in the story:

```
<script language="JavaScript">
<!-- Cloaking device on!
// create array for prompts
var promptmsg = new Array("A time of day","A feeling","An adjective - eg
➥sunny", "An adjective - eg sunny","A verb - past tense eg walked","An
➥adverb - eg quickly or monstrously","An adverb  - eg quickly or
➥monstrously","A room in a house", "A profession","An exclamation!");

// create array for default text
var defaulttxt = new Array("lunchtime","wet","plump","malodorous"
➥,"wriggled","hungrily","fiercely","bathroom","Web developer","Yipes");

// Cloaking device off -->
</script>
```

5. Now create variables for the inputted prompts:

```
<script language="JavaScript">
<!-- Cloaking device on!
// create array for prompts
var promptmsg = new Array("A time of day","A feeling","An adjective - eg
➥sunny", "An adjective - eg sunny","A verb - past tense eg walked","An
➥adverb - eg quickly or monstrously","An adverb  - eg quickly or
➥monstrously","A room in a house", "A profession","An exclamation!");

// create array for default text
var defaulttxt = new Array("lunchtime","wet","plump","malodorous"
➥,"wriggled","hungrily","fiercely","bathroom","Web developer","Yipes");
```

```
// variables for prompt inputs
var entry1, entry2, entry3, entry4, entry5, entry6, entry7, entry8, entry9,
➥entry10;

// Cloaking device off -->
</script>
```

6. Next, write the JavaScript to bring up the prompt boxes, adding the prompt message and default text by using array element values:

```
<script language="JavaScript">
<!-- Cloaking device on!
// create array for prompts
var promptmsg = new Array("A time of day","A feeling","An adjective - eg
➥sunny", "An adjective - eg sunny","A verb - past tense eg walked","An
➥adverb - eg quickly or monstrously","An adverb  - eg quickly or
mon➥strously","A room in a house", "A profession","An exclamation!");

// create array for default text
var defaulttxt = new Array("lunchtime","wet","plump","malodorous"
➥,"wriggled","hungrily","fiercely","bathroom","Web developer","Yipes");

// variables for prompt inputs
var entry1, entry2, entry3, entry4, entry5, entry6, entry7, entry8, entry9,
➥entry10;

// bring on the prompts!
entry1  = prompt(promptmsg[0], defaulttxt[0]);
entry2  = prompt(promptmsg[1], defaulttxt[1]);
entry3  = prompt(promptmsg[2], defaulttxt[2]);
entry4  = prompt(promptmsg[3], defaulttxt[3]);
entry5  = prompt(promptmsg[4], defaulttxt[4]);
entry6  = prompt(promptmsg[5], defaulttxt[5]);
entry7  = prompt(promptmsg[6], defaulttxt[6]);
entry8  = prompt(promptmsg[7], defaulttxt[7]);
entry9  = prompt(promptmsg[8], defaulttxt[8]);
entry10 = prompt(promptmsg[9], defaulttxt[9]);

// Cloaking device off -->
</script>
```

7. Now that you have all the pieces in place, you can return to the story/rhyme/lyrics text you saved earlier. You need to turn each line into an alert that contains the story text.

   Inside the parentheses, the text should appear in double quotes ("). Remember that you can include single quotes (') inside double quotes and vice versa. In the ninth line of the story, notice that both single and double quotes are used in the text. Enclose the text in double quotes, and to display the double quote, you can use the escape character for the double quote (\"). This enables the double quote to be displayed without causing an error.

The strings of text and the variable values the user typed in are concatenated together using the + operator.

CAUTION

Those of you familiar with Microsoft Visual Basic or VBScript might find yourselves using the ampersand (&) character to concatenate by mistake; this is a common error!

```
<script language="JavaScript">
<!-- Cloaking device on!
// create array for prompts
var promptmsg = new Array("An adjective - eg sunny","A verb - past tense
➥eg walked","An adverb - eg quickly or monstrously","An adverb  - eg
➥quickly or monstrously","A room in a house","A profession","An
➥exclamation!");


// create array for default text
var defaulttxt = new Array("lunchtime","wet","plump","malodorous"
➥,"wriggled","hungrily","fiercely","bathroom","Web developer","Yipes");

// variables for prompt inputs
var entry1, entry2, entry3, entry4, entry5, entry6, entry7, entry8, entry9,
➥entry10;

// bring on the prompts!
entry1  = prompt(promptmsg[0], defaulttxt[0]);
entry2  = prompt(promptmsg[1], defaulttxt[1]);
entry3  = prompt(promptmsg[2], defaulttxt[2]);
entry4  = prompt(promptmsg[3], defaulttxt[3]);
entry5  = prompt(promptmsg[4], defaulttxt[4]);
entry6  = prompt(promptmsg[5], defaulttxt[5]);
entry7  = prompt(promptmsg[6], defaulttxt[6]);
entry8  = prompt(promptmsg[7], defaulttxt[7]);
entry9  = prompt(promptmsg[8], defaulttxt[8]);
entry10 = prompt(promptmsg[9], defaulttxt[9]);

// bring on the alert boxes!
alert("Once upon a " + entry1 + " dreary,")
alert("while I pondered, " + entry2 + " and weary,")
alert("Over many a " + entry3 + " and curious volume")
alert("of " + entry4 + " lore")
```

```
alert("While I " + entry5 + ", nearly napping,")
alert(entry6 + " there came a tapping,")
alert("As of someone " + entry7 + " rapping,")
alert("rapping at my " + entry8 + " door.")
alert("\"'Tis some " + entry9 + ",\" I muttered,")
alert("tapping at my " + entry8 + " door")
alert("Only " + entry10 + "! and nothing more.")
// Cloaking device off -->
</script>
```

8. Save the file you are working on and load it into the browser to create your own interactive story! Go through the various prompt boxes and watch your hopefully hilarious story outputted into alert boxes.

Optimizations

One possible optimization relates to the prompt boxes. Instead of declaring the variables first and then calling the prompt boxes, a shorthand way of doing this is to perform the declaring of the variable and displaying of the prompt box all on one line:

```
var entry1  = prompt(promptmsg[0], defaulttxt[0]);
var entry2  = prompt(promptmsg[1], defaulttxt[1]);
var entry3  = prompt(promptmsg[2], defaulttxt[2]);
var entry4  = prompt(promptmsg[3], defaulttxt[3]);
var entry5  = prompt(promptmsg[4], defaulttxt[4]);
var entry6  = prompt(promptmsg[5], defaulttxt[5]);
var entry7  = prompt(promptmsg[6], defaulttxt[6]);
var entry8  = prompt(promptmsg[7], defaulttxt[7]);
var entry9  = prompt(promptmsg[8], defaulttxt[8]);
var entry10 = prompt(promptmsg[9], defaulttxt[9]);
```

EXERCISE

Can you see any other possible optimizations?

Use an array instead of variables to hold the values inputted from the prompt boxes (`entry1` to `entry10`).

Use an alert box to add some instructions for the user at the beginning to let him know what to expect and comment your code well!

Escape Characters

In the interactive story example, you saw a JavaScript escape character in action—the `\"`, which in a string represents a double quote. Escape characters are used in strings to do the following:

- Prevent certain characters from causing errors
- Add formatting (such as carriage returns) to strings

Table 5.1 lists the available escape characters.

Table 5.1: Escape Characters

Sequence	Name
`\b`	Backspace
`\t`	Horizontal tab
`\f`	Form feed
`\n`	New line (line feed)
`\r`	Carriage return
`\"`	Double quote
`\'`	Single quote
`\\`	Backslash

These can be placed anywhere in the string and need no whitespace before or after them.

Here are some examples of escape characters in action:

- Carriage return

```
<script language="JavaScript">
<!-- Cloaking device on!
alert("A carriage return lies right\rin the middle of this line!");
// Cloaking device off -->
</script>
```

Figure 5.7 shows the result of placing the carriage return in the string.

Figure 5.7: *Alert box showing the carriage return.*

- Single and double quotes

```
<script language="JavaScript">
<!-- Cloaking device on!
alert("\"That wasn\'t how it was at all!\" she said.");
// Cloaking device off -->
</script>
```

Figure 5.8 shows the result of placing the quote in the string.

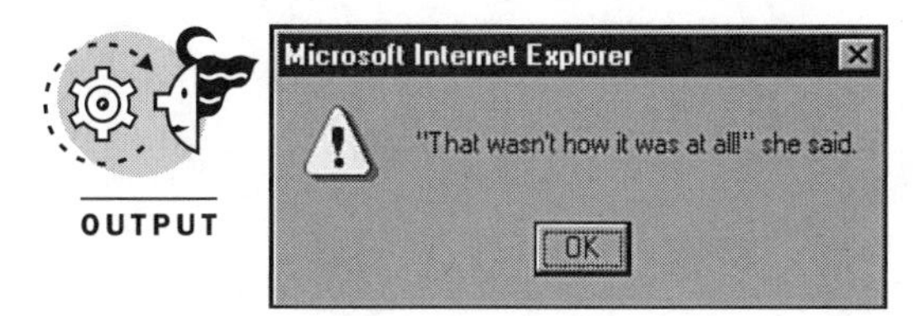

Figure 5.8: *Alert box showing the single and double quotes.*

- Tabs

```
<script language="JavaScript">
<!-- Cloaking device on!
alert("This line has a tab\there");
// Cloaking device off -->
</script>
```

Figure 5.9 shows the effect of the tab on the string.

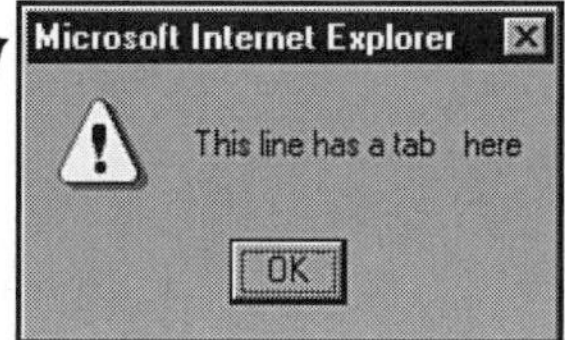

Figure 5.9: *Alert box showing the insertion of a tab.*

EXERCISE

Modify the interactive story example so that you use one alert box to display the whole text. (Tip: You will need to use the escape character `\r` to create a carriage return between each line.)

What's Next

Now that you are comfortable with variables and arrays, the next chapter moves on to look at expressions, conditions, and operators.

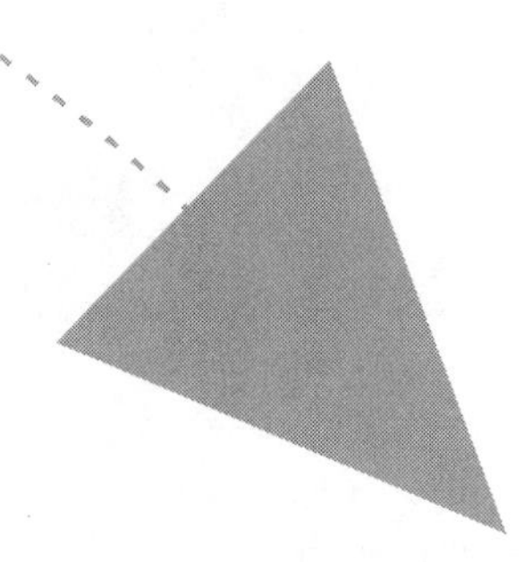

6

Expressions, Conditions, Operators, and More Strings and Numbers

In the previous chapter, you saw how variables and arrays can be used within JavaScript code to hold information in the form of values. In this chapter, you build on this and look at how to work with that information.

This chapter teaches you about the following:

- Expressions
- Conditions
- Various types of operators and how to use them
- Converting string types to numbers—and vice versa!

More on Terminology—What Are Expressions and Conditions?

It's hard to learn any kind of computer language without having to step outside it every so often and look in, and JavaScript is no different. Let us take you aside for a moment and look at some of the new terminology you need to be familiar with before you can continue on your JavaScript journey.

Expressions and Conditions

With variables and arrays, you are free to store pretty much all the data you want in a variety of types. However, eventually you will want to do more with that information than just perform a plain output of it onto the screen or into an alert box. You'll want to change it, manipulate it, or verify it. Expressions and conditions are used for just those purposes.

Expressions are used to combine two or more values and give you a third, new, value. So, as a quick example, a sum such as the following is an expression:

- 1 + 2 = 3

You combine two values (1 and 2) to give you a third (3).

Another example is

- 3 + 3 - 1 = 5

Here, three values (3, 3, and 1) are combined to produce another value (5).

Conditions, on the other hand, compare values and return a Boolean truth value—true or false. An example of a condition is

- Are lemons yellow? Yes

Or, another example is

- Does 3 + 3 = 6? Yes

Note how both these conditions are questions with yes or no answers (okay, maybe the lemon question could have a maybe). For the purposes of JavaScript (and other computer languages), conditions result in yes or no values.

NOTE

Learning JavaScript is beneficial because it gives you an insight into other programming languages. Plus, it is true that, after you learn one computer language, the rest seem easier to learn!

Introducing Operators

Expressions and conditions combine data using operators. *Operators* must work on something to be able to operate. They can work on one piece of data, which makes them *unary* operators. They can work on two pieces of data, which makes them *binary* operators, or they can work on three pieces of data, which makes them *ternary* operators.

Let's look at some of the more common operators.

Arithmetic Operators

These operators are the familiar mathematical ones. They are

- Plus (+)

  ```
  1 + 3 = 4
  ```

- Minus (-)

  ```
  2 - 1 = 1
  ```

- Division (/)

  ```
  4 / 2 = 2
  ```

- Multiplication (*)

  ```
  2 * 2 = 4
  ```

- Modulus (%)

  ```
  9 % 5 = 4
  ```

NOTE

All these operators are binary.

The only arithmetic operator that might need further explanation is the modulus operator. This operator, also called the *remainder* operator, looks at what is left over after a division. Therefore, 5 goes into 9 once with 4 left over. When using integers, the result also is an integer. However, with real numbers (floating-point numbers, not integers), the result is a real number. For example

```
5.5 % 2.2 = 1.1
```

CAUTION

JScript 1.0 truncates real numbers to integers before applying the modulus operator, so 5.3 % 2.2 = 1.

Be careful when using these operators because they can, if used improperly, result in `NaN` or `Infinity`. Dividing by 0 is one such operation that can cause problems.

JavaScript Examples

Here are some examples of arithmetic operators in action.

NOTE

The contents outside the script block have been omitted. All these examples were created using the blank template file.

- Plus operator: + (see Figure 6.1)

```
<script language="JavaScript">
<!-- Cloaking device on!
var a = 6, b = 4;
alert(a + b);
// Cloaking device off -->
</script>
```

***Figure 6.1:** The plus operator in action.*

- Minus operator: - (see Figure 6.2)

```
<script language="JavaScript">
<!-- Cloaking device on!
var a = 6, b = 4;
alert(a - b);
// Cloaking device off -->
</script>
```

***Figure 6.2:** The minus operator in action.*

- Division operator: / (see Figure 6.3)

```
<script language="JavaScript">
<!-- Cloaking device on!
var a = 6, b = 3;
alert(a / b);
// Cloaking device off -->
</script>
```

Figure 6.3: The division operator in action.

- Multiplication operator: `*` (see Figure 6.4)

```
<script language="JavaScript">
<!-- Cloaking device on!
var a = 6, b = 3;
alert(a * b);
// Cloaking device off -->
</script>
```

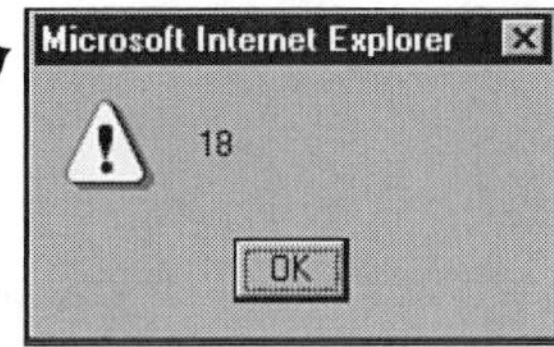

Figure 6.4: The multiplication operator in action.

- Modulus operator: `%` (see Figure 6.5)

```
<script language="JavaScript">
<!-- Cloaking device on!
var a = 6, b = 4;
alert(a % b);
// Cloaking device off -->
</script>
```

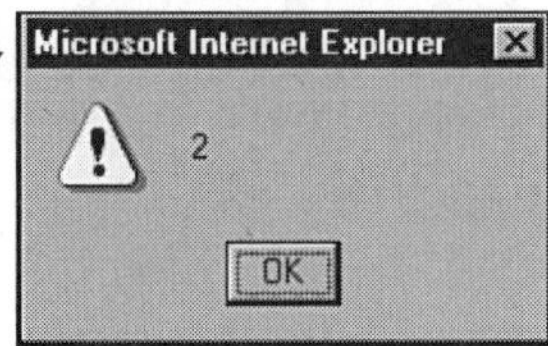

Figure 6.5: The modulus operator in action.

EXERCISE

Practice using the arithmetic operators as shown in the previous examples.

Relational Operators

Relational operators are used for comparisons. These operators are as follows:

- Less than: <

  `5 < 6`

- Less than or equal to: <=

  `6 <= 6` or `6 <= 7`

- Greater than: >

  `7 > 4`

- Greater than or equal to: >=

  `5 >= 5` or `5 >= 4`

- Equal to: ==

  `5 == 5`

- Not equal to: `!=`

  `5 != 3`

NOTE

These are all binary operators.

Here, you see examples of numbers being compared, but you can also use them on strings. (More on this later.) One thing that is best obeyed is that the two things compared must be of the same type. If they are not, JavaScript attempts to convert the data from one type to another, but this isn't always a success. To be on the safe side, keep things being compared the same type.

Logical Operators

How *logical* operators work isn't so clear. Their function will become clearer when you start to use them in statements, such as `If` statements.

The three logical operators are as follows:

- Logical and

  `&&`

- Logical or

  `||`

- Logical not

  `!`

NOTE

Logical and and logical or are binary, whereas logical not is unary.

These operators let you combine the results of several variable tests into one easy-to-use result.

Logical and (`&&`) means that both sides must be true. A simple real-world example of `&&` in action might be the thought process that a driver goes through before hitting the brakes on his car: Car going too fast `&&` driver wants to slow down.

Logical or (`||`) means that at least one side must be true. Using the car analogy again, a driver's thought process before turning on the headlights might be Getting dark `||` visibility poor.

Logical not (`!`) returns the opposite of a true/false. So, to turn on the car's headlights, it has to be `!` light (therefore dark).

NOTE

Don't worry if some of these seem a little vague right now. You'll get plenty of opportunity to use them later, and by the time you have created a few real JavaScript examples, you'll definitely have the gist of it!

Miscellaneous Unary Operators

As the name suggests, these are unary operators that act on one value. These operators are

- Prefix and postfix increment

  `++`

- Prefix and postfix decrement

  `--`

- Unary plus

  `+`

- Unary minus

  `-`

Unary minus simply changes the sign of the value from negative to positive and vice versa. Of the four, this is the simplest to understand. Unary plus, on the other hand, doesn't do this; it is used to change the operand to the number type (say, from a string).

The prefix/postfix increment/decrement operators provide you a fast, easy way to say x = x + 1 and x = x - 1. However, the prefix and postfix parts have an overall effect on the outcome of the use of these operators.

Prefix operators are easy and work as expected.

If a = 5, then

```
++a + 2 = 8
```

because a was incremented to 6 before 2 was added, whereas

```
--a + 2 = 6
```

because a was decremented by 1 to 4 before 2 was added.

Postfix operators act differently because the increment or decrement is not carried out until after the old value is used in the expression. So, if a = 5 then

```
a++ + 2 = 7
```

because only after the expression is the increment carried out.

The same is true for the following:

```
a-- + 2 = 7
```

This is because the decrement of a is not carried out until after the old value is used in the expression.

TIP

The best way to remember this is that if the operators are in front (prefix) then the operation is carried out first. However, if they come after (postfix) then the operation is carried out after the expression.

JavaScript Examples

- Prefix increment (see Figure 6.6)

```
<script language="JavaScript">
<!-- Cloaking device on!
var a = 6, b = 2;
alert(++a + b);
// Cloaking device off -->
</script>
```

***Figure 6.6:** The prefix increment operator in action.*

- Prefix decrement (see Figure 6.7)

```
<script language="JavaScript">
<!-- Cloaking device on!
var a = 6, b = 2;
alert(--a + b);
// Cloaking device off -->
</script>
```

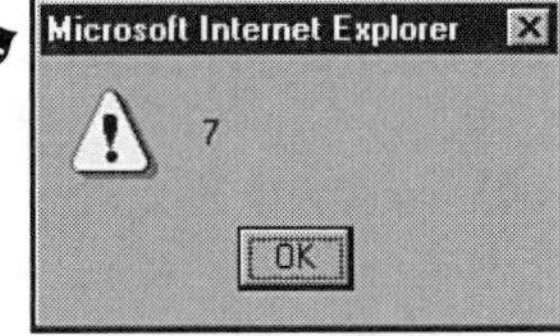

Figure 6.7: *The prefix decrement operator in action.*

- Postfix increment (see Figure 6.8)

```
<script language="JavaScript">
<!-- Cloaking device on!
var a = 6, b = 2;
alert(a++ + b);
alert(a);
// Cloaking device off -->
</script>
```

Here, you see a second alert box (seen in Figure 6.9) used to show that the value of a has been incremented by 1 *after* the expression.

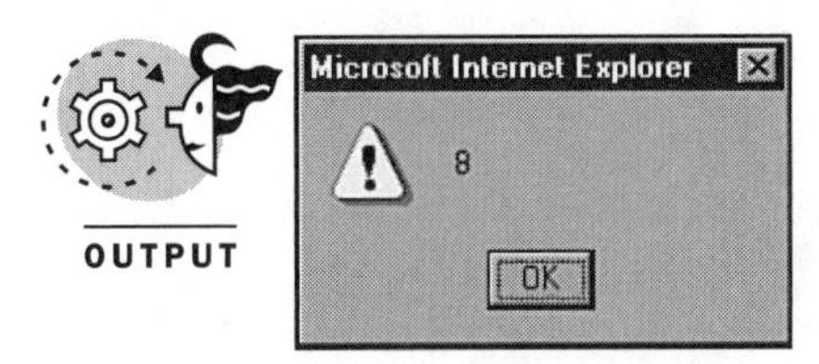

Figure 6.8: *The postfix increment operator in action.*

Figure 6.9: *The second alert box confirms an increment of* a *by 1.*

- Postfix decrement (see Figure 6.10)

```
<script language="JavaScript">
<!-- Cloaking device on!
var a = 6, b = 2;
alert(a-- + b);
alert(a);
// Cloaking device off -->
</script>
```

Here, you see a second alert box (seen in Figure 6.11) used to show that the value of a has been decremented by 1 *after* the expression.

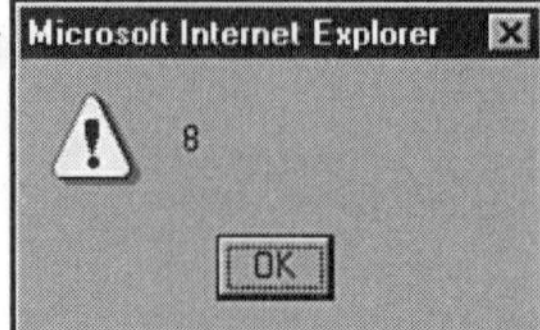

Figure 6.10: *The postfix decrement operator in action.*

Figure 6.11: *Second alert box confirms decrement of* a *by 1.*

Assignment Operators

The most obvious assignment operator is the plain assignment (=). It is used to copy a value into a variable. You've already used this one, but just to hammer in the point here is an example where the variable a is given the value 3:

```
a = 3
```

It can also be used to set multiple variables to the same values. In the following example, all the variables (a, b, c, and d) are set to 5:

```
a = b = c = d = 5
```

The other operators in this group are called *compound* and work very similarly to ++ and --.

Here are a few examples:

`x += 3` is the same as `x = x + 3`

`x -= 3` is the same as `x = x - 3`

`x *= 3` is the same as `x = x * 3`

`x /= 3` is the same as `x = x / 3`

JavaScript Examples

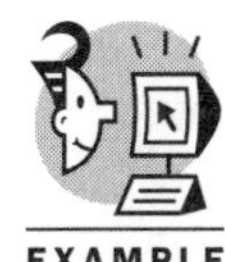

- Compound operator: += (see Figure 6.12)

```
<script language="JavaScript">
<!-- Cloaking device on!
var x = 6;
alert(x += 2);
// Cloaking device off -->
</script>
```

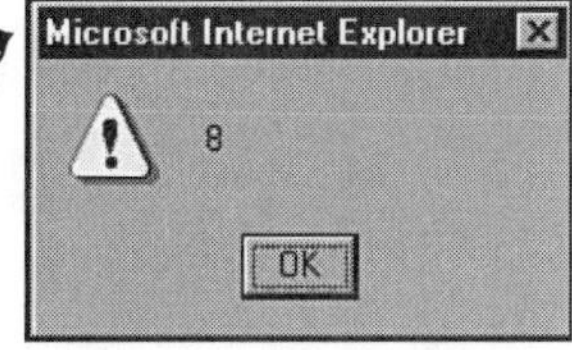

Figure 6.12: *The alert box confirms that the value of* x *has been increased by 2.*

- Compound operator: -= (see Figure 6.13)

```
<script language="JavaScript">
<!-- Cloaking device on!
var x = 6;
alert(x -= 2);
// Cloaking device off -->
</script>
```

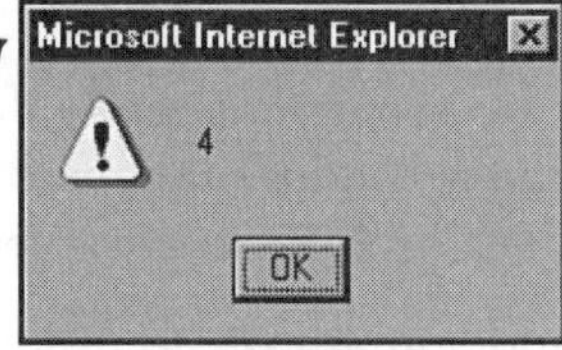

Figure 6.13: *The alert box confirms that the value of* x *has been decreased by 2.*

- Compound operator: *= (see Figure 6.14)

```
<script language="JavaScript">
<!-- Cloaking device on!
var x = 6;
```

```
alert(x *= 2);
// Cloaking device off -->
</script>
```

Figure 6.14: *The alert box confirms that the value of* `x` *has been multiplied by 2.*

- Compound operator: `/=` (see Figure 6.15)

```
<script language="JavaScript">
<!-- Cloaking device on!
var x = 6;
alert(x /= 2);
// Cloaking device off -->
</script>
```

Figure 6.15: *The alert box confirms that the value of* `x` *has been divided by 2.*

Miscellaneous Operators

Three more operators you need to know about that really don't fit into any of the previous categories are the ternary conditional operator (`?:`), the binary string concatenation operator (`+`), and the unary `typeof` operator.

The conditional operator is a quick and simple way to assign one of two possible values to a variable, depending on the outcome of a condition. Consider the following example:

```
W = 1, X = 2, Y = 3, Z = 4
Ans = (W < X) ? Y : Z
```

`Ans` is equal to `4`.

This looks complicated, but it isn't really. Here's how it works: If the expression before the ? (which is a condition) is `true` then the value of the expression on the left side of the colon (`:`) is assigned to the variable `Ans`. Otherwise, the expression on the left side is used (as is the case with this example).

The string concatenation operator is used to create a new string out of two separate strings by joining them together (concatenation):

```
A = "JavaScript "
B = "by Example!"
C = A + B
```

NOTE

Notice how this operator is the same as the arithmetic plus operator. This different meaning for the same operator is one of the areas of JavaScript that causes beginners confusion. To avoid that, you must use the correct term for each operator. Avoid terms such as "plus" and "minus" because they are vague!

The final operator is the `typeof` operator. This operator is used to tell you the type of data held in a variable or returned by a condition.

CAUTION

The `typeof` operator is not present in Netscape Navigator 2.02.

Table 6.1 show the seven commonly encountered outputs, depending on the type on which it is operating.

Table 6.1: **`typeof`** *Strings*

Type	Result
Undefined	`"undefined"`
Null	`"object"`
Boolean	`"boolean"`
Number	`"number"`
String	`"string"`
Object (not a function)	`"object"`
Object (a function)	`"function"`

NOTE

Another operator you have already used in Chapter 5, "JavaScript Arrays and Escape Characters," is the `new` operator. This one enables you to create new objects (such as `Array`).

Time for some examples!

Examples of Miscellaneous Operators

- Conditional operator: `?:`

Example 1 (see Figure 6.16)

```
<script language="JavaScript">
<!-- Cloaking device on!
Var w = 1, x = 2, y = 3, z = 4, ans;
ans = (w > x) ? y : z
alert(ans);
// Cloaking device off -->
</script>
```

Figure 6.16: *The alert box confirms that the value of* `ans` *is* `4`.

Example 2 (see Figure 6.17)

```
<script language="JavaScript">
<!-- Cloaking device on!
var w = 1, x = 2, y = 3, z = 4, ans;
ans = (w < x) ? y : z
alert(ans);
// Cloaking device off -->
</script>
```

Figure 6.17: *The alert box confirms that the value of* `ans` *is* `3`.

- String concatenation operator: `+`

Example 1 (see Figure 6.18)

```
<script language="JavaScript">
<!-- Cloaking device on!
Var A = "JavaScript ", B = "by Example!";
```

```
C = A + B;
alert;
// Cloaking device off -->
</script>
```

Figure 6.18: *The alert box displaying* `JavaScript by Example!`.

Example 2 (see Figure 6.19)

NOTE

This example demonstrates what happens if you try to concatenate a string digit with a number. No error is generated because the number is converted to a string automatically, but the result might not be what you expect.

```
<script language="JavaScript">
<!-- Cloaking device on!
var A = "10", B = 5;
C = A + B;
alert;
// Cloaking device off -->
</script>
```

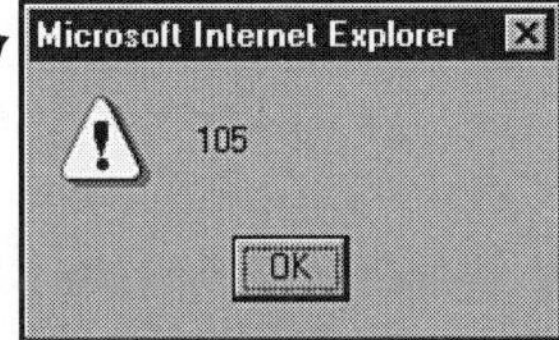

Figure 6.19: *The alert box displays the string* `105`.

- `typeof` operator: `typeof` (see Figures 6.20, 6.21, and 6.22)

Example 1

```
<script language="JavaScript">
<!-- Cloaking device on!
var x = "Hello", y;
alert("Variable x value is " + typeof(x));
alert("Variable y value is " + typeof(y));
```

```
alert("Variable z value is " + typeof(z));
// Cloaking device off -->
</script>
```

Figure 6.20: *The alert box displays the* `typeof` *of variable* `x`.

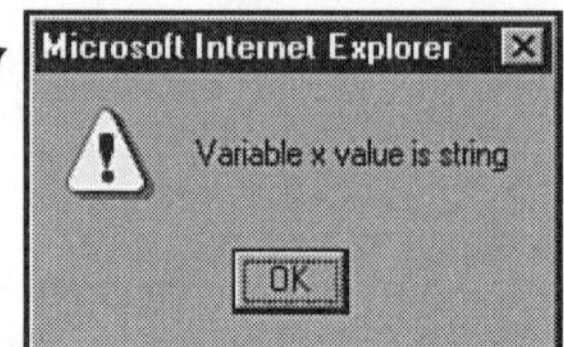

Figure 6.21: *The alert box displays the* `typeof` *of variable* `y`.

Figure 6.22: *The alert box displays the* `typeof` *of variable* `z`.

EXERCISE

This chapter has been a busy one so far, but it has not only given you a good grounding in operators but also a chance to practice writing JavaScript, adding comments, and using variables and methods. As an exercise, try to create some simple JavaScript examples using the operators covered here. Not only will this be good practice (practice makes perfect!) but also, by using your own examples, you will get a better feel for the operators; after a short while they will become second nature.

Revisiting Strings and Numbers

Let's quickly revisit strings and numbers with an example of a very simple JavaScript calculator! In this example, you'll not only look at a way to use operators but you will also find out how you can change string digits to numbers through a process called *type conversion*.

The JavaScript Calculator

1. Start off with the bare HTML template:

```
<html>
<head>
<title>A Simple Page</title>
<script language="JavaScript">
<!-- Cloaking device on!

// Cloaking device off -->
</script>
</head>
<body>

</body>
</html>
```

2. Declare the variables you will use here. You should have two variables for each of the numbers the user will input—one for the operator the user wants to use and a final one to hold the answer:

```
<html>
<head>
<title>A Simple Page</title>
<script language="JavaScript">
<!-- Cloaking device on!
var num1, op, num2, ans;
// Cloaking device off -->
</script>
</head>
<body>

</body>
</html>
```

3. Next, use the `prompt()` method to prompt the user for the first number to enter, and assign this to the variable `num1`:

```
<html>
<head>
<title>A Simple Page</title>
<script language="JavaScript">
<!-- Cloaking device on!
var num1, op, num2, ans;
num1 = prompt("Enter a number:","a number");
// Cloaking device off -->
</script>
</head>
<body>

</body>
</html>
```

4. Add another prompt, this time to ask for the operator to use. Assign this value to the variable op:

```
<html>
<head>
<title>A Simple Page</title>
<script language="JavaScript">
<!-- Cloaking device on!
var num1, op, num2, ans;
num1 = prompt("Enter a number:","a number");
op = prompt("Enter an operator (+, -, *, / and %)", "operator");
// Cloaking device off -->
</script>
</head>
<body>

</body>
</html>
```

5. Next, add another prompt for the second number. This is assigned to num2:

```
<html>
<head>
<title>A Simple Page</title>
<script language="JavaScript">
<!-- Cloaking device on!
var num1, op, num2, ans;
num1 = prompt("Enter a number:","a number");
op = prompt("Enter an operator (+, -, *, / and %)", "operator");
num2 = prompt("Enter another number:", "a number");
// Cloaking device off -->
</script>
</head>
<body>

</body>
</html>
```

6. Now, perform the sum. Here you must evaluate the sum using the method `eval()`. This method does the math for you. However, before you can do the math, you need to change the string variables num1 and num2 into numbers. You can do this by declaring them as numbers. The result of the evaluation is passed to the variable ans:

NOTE

The `eval()` method is covered in more detail in later chapters.

```
<html>
<head>
<title>A Simple Page</title>
<script language="JavaScript">
<!-- Cloaking device on!
var num1, op, num2, ans;
num1 = prompt("Enter a number:","a number");
op = prompt("Enter an operator (+, -, *, / and %)", "operator");
num2 = prompt("Enter another number:", "a number");
ans = eval(Number(num1)+ op + Number(num2));
// Cloaking device off -->
</script>
</head>
<body>

</body>
</html>
```

7. Finally, use the `alert()` method to display the value of `ans`. In the alert box, you will see that the sum is rebuilt and displayed by concatenating the values for the variables with spaces and the equal sign (=), making the output clear and unambiguous:

```
<html>
<head>
<title>A Simple Page</title>
<script language="JavaScript">
<!-- Cloaking device on!
var num1, op, num2, ans;
num1 = prompt("Enter a number:","a number");
op = prompt("Enter an operator (+, -, *, / and %)", "operator");
num2 = prompt("Enter another number:", "a number");
ans = eval(Number(num1)+ op + Number(num2));
alert(num1 + " " + op + " " + num2 + " = " + ans);
// Cloaking device off -->
</script>
</head>
<body>

</body>
</html>
```

8. Save the file and load the page into the browser. At the prompt boxes, type in numbers or operators and watch it do the math for you! (See Figure 6.23.)

Figure 6.23: *Alert box displays the answer to the sum you posed JavaScript!*

NOTE

You might have guessed that the way to convert numbers to strings is to declare them as strings.

The following is an example:

String(varname)

What's Next

Now that you have a firm grasp of variables, arrays, and operators, you are ready to venture into JavaScript statements.

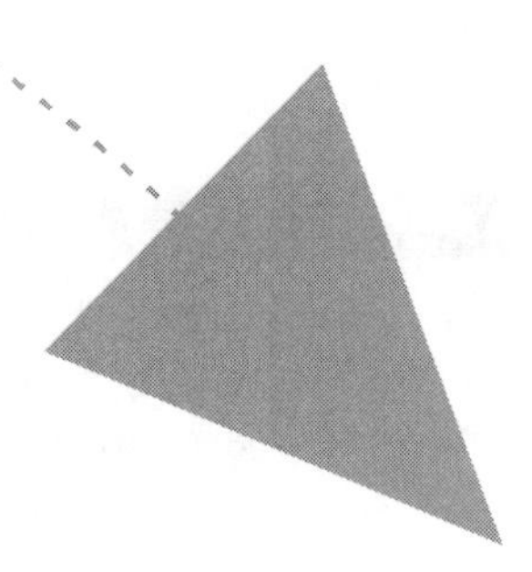

7

Using Statements in JavaScript

Statements are the stuff of great JavaScript! By learning how to use statements in your JavaScript, you will see your scripts move to a whole new level, allowing you to do much more complex things with ease.

This chapter teaches you about the following:

- What statements are
- The `variable` statement
- The `if` statement
- Iteration statements
- The `continue` statement
- The `break` statement
- The `switch` statement

What Are Statements?

All JavaScript that is written, whether it be a single line or a monster mini-program, consists of a sequence of *statements*. You've already seen such statements. The following alert box being generated is a result of a statement:

```
<script language="JavaScript">
<!-- Cloaking device on!
alert("This is a statement!");
// Cloaking device off -->
</script>
```

So is this:

```
<script language="JavaScript">
<!-- Cloaking device on!
var ournames = "Adrian and Kathie";
// Cloaking device off -->
</script>
```

And here are several more statements:

```
<script language="JavaScript">
<!-- Cloaking device on!
var ournames = "Adrian and Kathie", ans;
alert("Welcome from " + ournames);
ans = prompt("Do you like JavaScript?", "Yes or No");
alert(ans);
// Cloaking device off -->
</script>
```

All the statements you write are processed top to bottom (unless, as you'll see later, you organize it otherwise). But notice something else that each statement has. Yes, there, at the end of each line is a semicolon (;). In JavaScript, semicolons are the proper way of showing that a statement has finished (similar to a full stop in a sentence). You don't *need* to add them because JavaScript will just assume you were lazy and will add them for you—but you should add them for two reasons:

- They help make your JavaScript more readable.
- Not using them can cause problems under some circumstances because JavaScript will place them in the incorrect locations.

Let's take a look at some different types of statements available to the JavaScripter.

The variable Statement

EXAMPLE

variable is a statement you already know how to use, and it is included here only to reinforce the idea of a statement being similar to a complete sentence in English. Therefore, a variable statement such as

```
var this_year = 2001
```

says to create a variable called this_year and assign it the value 2001. That's a complete sentence.

The if Statement

The if statement is an example of a flow control statement that has many uses.

The if statement enables your JavaScript script to choose between one of two alternative groups of statements to run (or *execute*). The choosing is done with a Boolean (true of false) condition.

Let's revisit the confirm box in this example and look at how you can make this type of message box work by using an if statement.

EXAMPLE

The first thing you must do is create a simple confirm box using the confirm() method:

```
<script language="JavaScript">
<!-- Cloaking device on!
confirm("Do you want to proceed with this book?  Click OK to proceed otherwise
➥click Cancel.");
// Cloaking device off -->
</script>
```

This now presents the user with two options: OK and Cancel (see Figure 7.1). Next, let's write code to deal with those who click OK (no one would even think of clicking Cancel, would they?).

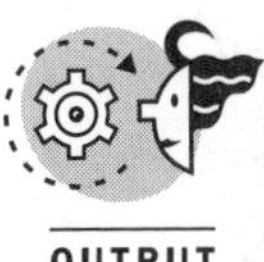

OUTPUT

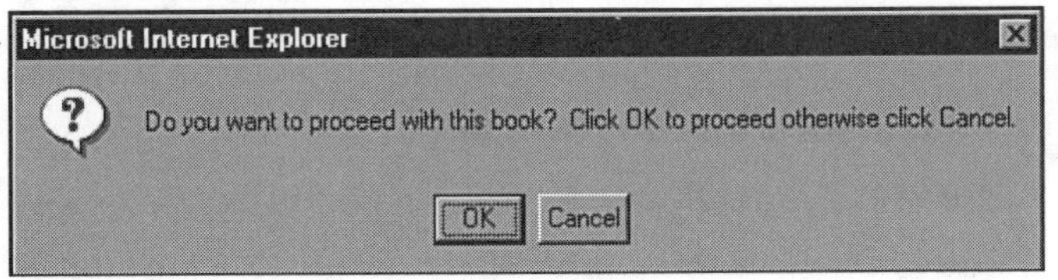

Figure 7.1: *The confirm box displayed.*

When the user clicks OK, she is creating a Boolean value of `true`, which you can use to detect what she has clicked. To do this, you must assign a variable to the `confirm()` method, as follows:

```
<script language="JavaScript">
<!-- Cloaking device on!
var response = confirm("Do you want to proceed with this book?
➥Click OK to proceed otherwise click Cancel.");
// Cloaking device off -->
</script>
```

This variable, `response`, holds the answer that the user gives to the question (in much the same way as for the `prompt()` method, the variable holds the string the user types in). So, if (or when!) she clicks OK, the value `true` is assigned to the variable `response` (see Figure 7.2). You can use an `if` statement to look for this.

EXAMPLE

Here is the JavaScript to do this:

```
<script language="JavaScript">
<!-- Cloaking device on!
var response = confirm("Do you want to proceed with this book?
➥Click OK to proceed otherwise click Cancel.");
if ( response == true )
{
alert("A fine choice!");
}
// Cloaking device off -->
</script>
```

OUTPUT

***Figure 7.2:** The alert box that's displayed when OK is clicked.*

Let's step through this line by line:

```
if ( response == true )
```

This line is the beginning of the `if` statement (note that it doesn't end with a semicolon), and it contains the condition that asks whether `response` has the value set to `true`. If it does, you move on to the next line.

The next line contains the opening curly brace (`{`), a character that many beginners new to JavaScript find difficult to understand. However, the function of curly braces is quite straightforward. Curly braces ({ and }) are used to enclose the statements for clarity.

TIP

Think of curly braces as defining paragraphs within the statement—so if something is true then do

```
{
this;
that;
and the other;
}
```

NOTE

There are a few schools of thought on the placement of curly braces. However, the convention used here is that they are placed on separate lines for the best JavaScript clarity.

Moving on to the next line, this is used to display the alert box congratulating the user on making a fine choice. Finally, you see the closing curly brace (}).

If you save this file and load it into the browser, you can take a look at how it works.

First, you are greeted by the confirm box (see Figure 7.3).

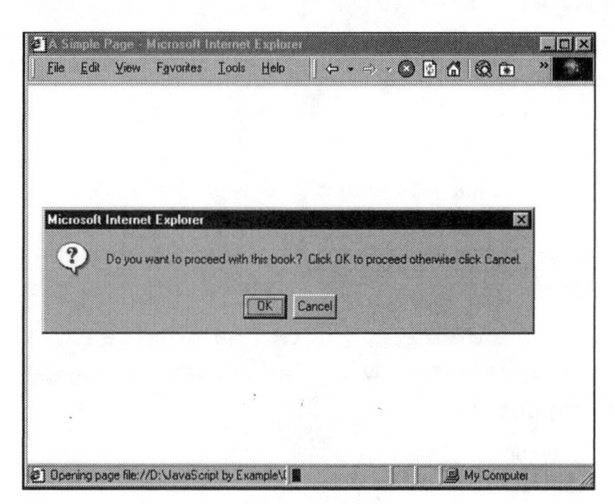

Figure 7.3: *The confirm box greets you.*

Then, when you click OK, it is replaced by the alert box (see Figure 7.4).

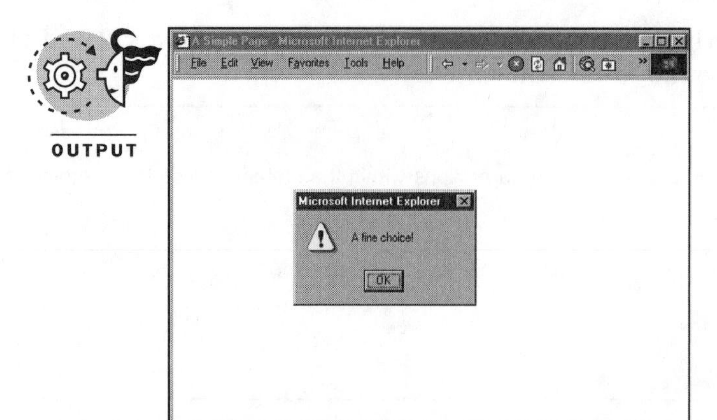

***Figure 7.4:** The alert box.*

So, the bare skeleton for the `if` statement is as follows:

```
if (condition)
{
statement1
}
```

The condition is always required and is a Boolean expression.

`statement1` is optional. (You don't have to put anything here; although it does defeat the object of the JavaScript you've written because you can do nothing without adding an `if` statement!) However, if there are any statements here, they are executed if the condition is `true`.

NOTE

If the condition is `null` or `undefined` then it is treated as false.

OK, so the JavaScript can handle someone clicking OK, but what about Cancel? This is where the next part of the `if` statement comes in—`else`. By adding an `else` to the statement, you can handle the exceptions to the condition (in this case, responding with Cancel, which assigns the value `false` to the variable `response`):

```
<script language="JavaScript">
<!-- Cloaking device on!
var response = confirm("Do you want to proceed with this book?
➥Click OK to proceed otherwise click Cancel.");
if ( response == true )
{
alert("A fine choice!");
}
else
```

```
{
alert("Are you sure?  JavaScript is fun!");
}
// Cloaking device off -->
</script>
```

The `else` part is tacked on at the end after the closing curly brace. In addition, the statements here are enclosed in a new set of curly braces. Make this addition and save the file; then try the Cancel button again (see Figure 7.5).

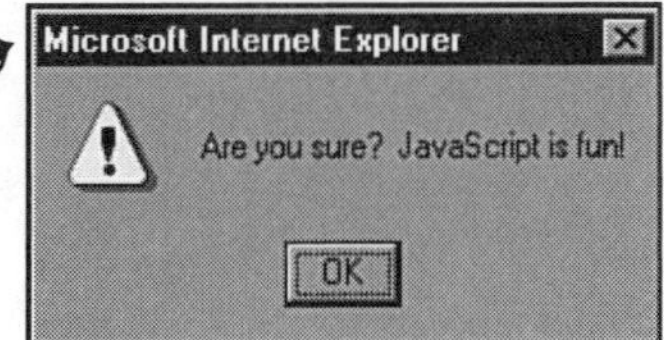

Figure 7.5: *The alert box shown when Cancel is clicked.*

So, the skeleton structure of the `if ... else` statement is as follows:

```
if (condition)
{
statement1
}
else
{
statement2
}
```

EXERCISE

Rewrite the previous JavaScript so that the condition for which the `if` statement is testing is `response == false`.

Iteration Statements

An iteration is the repetition of a sequence of statements either

- A specified number of times
- Until a condition is met

Four iteration statements are available:

- The `do ... while` statement
- The `while` statement
- The `for` statement
- The `for ... in` statement

Each of these statements performs a slightly different task, but each is a useful statement to learn how to use.

The do ... while Statement

EXAMPLE

The `do ... while` statement runs a statement or a block of statements and then repeats the whole process until the condition expression is false. An example will clarify this:

```
<script language="JavaScript">
<!-- Cloaking device on!
var x = 1
do
{
++x;
alert(x);
}
while (x < 10);
// Cloaking device off -->
</script>
```

The previous code has a variable, `x`, the initial value of which is `1`. Next, the `do` section of the script specifies that `1` should be added to `x` and the value then displayed in an alert box. The `while` part of the script specifies that this needs to be done while `x` is less than `10`.

EXAMPLE

It doesn't have to be numbers that the `do ... while` statement works on. In the following example, the prompt box continues to reappear until a text string is typed in. After some text is typed in, the `while` part of the script becomes `false`, and the next part of the script is run, displaying the alert box:

```
<script language="JavaScript">
<!-- Cloaking device on!
do
{
sometext = prompt("Enter some text","");
}
while (sometext == "");
alert(sometext);
// Cloaking device off -->
</script>
```

EXAMPLE

Note that for the previous example to work, no default text can be in the input box. However, a quick modification gets around that:

```
<script language="JavaScript">
<!-- Cloaking device on!
do
{
```

```
sometext = prompt("Enter some text","Type some text");
}
while (sometext == "Type some text" || sometext == "" || sometext == null);
alert(sometext);
// Cloaking device off -->
</script>
```

This example gets around three issues:

- The user leaving in the default text
- The user leaving the input box blank
- The user clicking Cancel

This functionality is accomplished by using the logical or operator (`||`). The `do` part is run while `sometext` is equal to `"Type some text"`, or is empty or `null` (the user has clicked Cancel).

NOTE

This kind of example shouldn't be overused in the real world. Reserve it for when it is vitally important that the user type in a value, such as an email address to which some information should be sent. Overuse can irritate visitors, especially if they can't even cancel out of the message box!

EXAMPLE

Caution must be exercised when using any kind of iteration statement because it is easy to make a mistake and loop the code forever! Here is an example of just that (but it's probably best you don't try running this example!):

```
<script language="JavaScript">
<!-- Cloaking device on!
var x = 1
do
{
++x;
alert(x);
}
while (x > 0);
// Cloaking device off -->
</script>
```

This example will have you clicking the OK button of the alert box forever because there is no way for `x` to become less than or equal to zero by continually adding 1 to the previous value!

CAUTION

Be very careful with this kind of error because it can very easily lock up or even crash your visitor's browser!

EXERCISE

How could the previous example be corrected so that it works properly?

The `while` Statement

EXAMPLE

The `while` statement is similar to the `do ... while` statement and works in much the same way:

```
<script language="JavaScript">
<!-- Cloaking device on!
var x = 1
while (x < 10)
{
++x;
alert(x);
}
// Cloaking device off -->
</script>
```

NOTE

Beginners normally find the `do ... while` statement easier to understand. This usually has to do with how they work. A `do ... while` statement is always run at least once in the course of the script, whereas a `while` statement need not be run at all (depending on the circumstances). This can sometimes confuse those new to JavaScript.

EXERCISE

Create a prompt box example (similar to the `do ... while` example) using the `while` statement.

The `for` Statement

EXAMPLE

The `for` statement is also similar to the previous statements, but it is a bit more complex. The difference is in the fact that built-in is a method of keeping count so that the whole thing can't go on forever:

```
<script language="JavaScript">
<!-- Cloaking device on!
for (x = 1; x < 10; ++x)
{
alert(x);
}
// Cloaking device off -->
</script>
```

CAUTION

However, if set up incorrectly, such as

```
for (x=1;x>0;x++)
```

it could indeed go on forever!

Take a look at the line that does most of the work:

```
for (x = 1; x < 10; ++x)
```

What this line says, in a compact form, is the following: For `x = 1` to `x < 10`, increment the value of `x` by `1`. The statement that follows is then run until the condition is met.

A shorthand way of thinking of the `for` statement is

```
for (initialization; test; increment)
```

`initialization` is the value of the variable at the beginning; `test` is the Boolean condition; and `increment` (or `decrement`) is what is carried out on the `initialization` variable until the test is `false`.

Here is an example in which, for each step, the variable is decreased by 2:

```
<script language="JavaScript">
<!-- Cloaking device on!
for (x = 10; x >= 0; x = x - 2)
{
alert(x);
}
// Cloaking device off -->
</script>
```

The following is another example in which the `for` statement is used to create 10 elements of an array and assign each a value corresponding to its position. Finally, when this is done, the contents of the array are outputted to an alert box. Here's the example (see the output in Figure 7.6):

```
<script language="JavaScript">
<!-- Cloaking device on!
var myarray = new Array();
for (i = 0; i < 10; i++)
{
myarray[i] = i;
}
alert(myarray);
// Cloaking device off -->
</script>
```

Figure 7.6: *The contents of* `myarray`.

EXERCISE

Modify the previous example so that an array containing 100 elements is created.

The `for ... in` Statement

The final iteration statement you will look at here is the `for ... in` statement. This statement is used to execute one or more statements for elements of an array.

This enables you to use a single statement to work on all the elements of an array without having to write separate statements for each.

In this example, you see the `for ... in` statement used to add 1 to the value of each of the five elements in the array `myarray`:

```
<script language="JavaScript">
<!-- Cloaking device on!
var myarray = new Array(5);
myarray[0] = 5
myarray[1] = 8
myarray[2] = 10
myarray[3] = 18
myarray[4] = 180
for (x in myarray)
{
myarray[x] = ++myarray[x];
}
alert(myarray);
// Cloaking device off -->
</script>
```

The line `for (x in myarray)` enables `x` to sequentially take on the number specifying an element of an array and causes each iteration's value to be incremented by 1 (as demonstrated in Figure 7.7).

Figure 7.7: The final value of the elements in `myarray`.

Another example of when the `for ... in` loop is useful is in populating elements of an array with strings such as image filenames (you'll see how this might be used later). Say, for example, you need to populate the elements for an array with 10 filenames for images (`img0.gif`, `img1.gif`, `img2.gif`, ... `img9.gif`). Using the `for ... in` statement for this is easy:

```
<script language="JavaScript">
<!-- Cloaking device on!
var myarray = new Array("","","","","","","","","","");
for (x in myarray)
{
myarray[x] = "img" + x + ".gif";
}
alert(myarray);
// Cloaking device off -->
</script>
```

The final alert box (presented in Figure 7.8) shows the contents of the 10 elements.

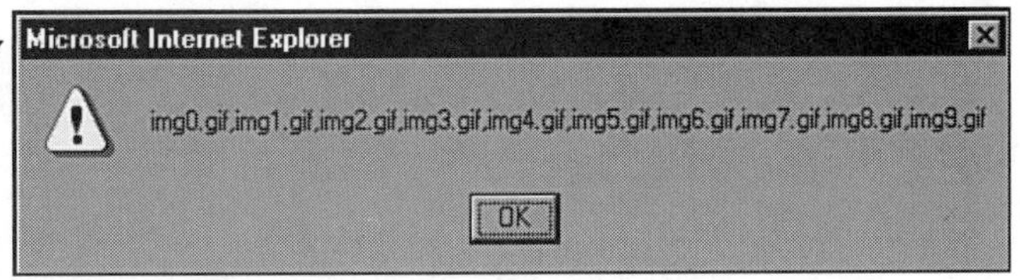

Figure 7.8: The final values of the 10 elements in `myarray`.

NOTE

Don't worry if you feel that the overall concept of the `for ... in` statement doesn't seem too clear. You will get plenty of opportunity later in the book to use it.

EXERCISE

Modify the previous example so that an array containing five hyperlinks is created.

The `continue` Statement

The `continue` statement is used in conjunction with the `while`, `do...while`, `for`, and `for...in` statements. The `continue` statement enables you to force the computer to perform another iteration.

Therefore, if the `continue` statement is placed directly in the body of a statement, all statements that follow are ignored. Here's an example:

```
<script language="JavaScript">
<!-- Cloaking device on!
var x = 0;
while (x < 10)
{
x++;
alert(x);
continue;
alert("You never see this!");
}
// Cloaking device off -->
</script>
```

This effect is generally undesirable, and it is far better to use the `continue` statement inside `if` statements. In this example, the alert box is bypassed when `x = 5`:

```
<script language="JavaScript">
<!-- Cloaking device on!
var x = 0;
while (x < 10)
{
x++;
if (x == 5)
{
continue;
}
alert(x);
}
// Cloaking device off -->
</script>
```

You can modify this example so that only odd numbers are displayed by using the condition `if (x % 2 == 0)`, which is true when `x` is even (the results are shown in Figure 7.9):

```
<script language="JavaScript">
<!-- Cloaking device on!
var x = 0;
while (x < 10)
{
```

```
x++;
if (x % 2 == 0)
{
continue;
}
alert(x);
}
// Cloaking device off -->
</script>
```

Figure 7.9: *Only odd numbers are displayed.*

Or, by changing the condition, it can be made to display even numbers only (with the new output shown in Figure 7.10):

```
<script language="JavaScript">
<!-- Cloaking device on!
var x = 0;
while (x < 10)
{
x++;
if (x % 2 != 0)
{
continue;
}
alert(x);
}
// Cloaking device off -->
</script>
```

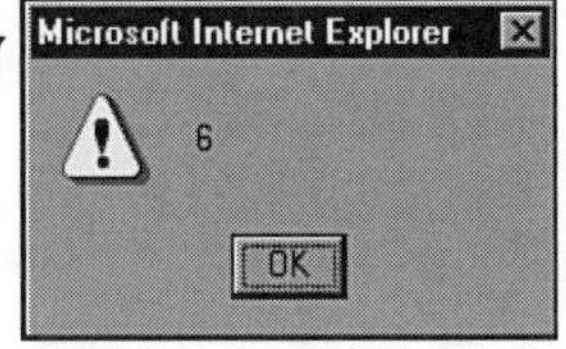

Figure 7.10: *By changing the condition, now only even numbers are displayed.*

EXERCISE

Experiment with the `continue` statement in a few sample scripts. Experiment with various conditions to really get a feel for how it works.

The break Statement

Going hand-in-hand with the `continue` statement is the `break` statement. Whereas the `continue` statement forces another iteration, the `break` statement jumps you out of the loop completely!

You typically use the `break` statement in `while`, `for`, `for ... in`, and `do ... while` statements (and `switch` statements, which we've not covered yet).

In the following example, the first alert box (displaying a 1) is shown, after which the `break` statement comes into force and kicks you out of the loop:

```
<script language="JavaScript">
<!-- Cloaking device on!
var x = 0;
while (x < 10)
{
x++;
alert(x);
break;
alert("Never seen!");
}
// Cloaking device off -->
</script>
```

Again, the best way to use the `break` statement is in conjunction with an `if` statement. This example enables you to type in the number at which you want the `while` statement exited:

```
<script language="JavaScript">
<!-- Cloaking device on!
var x = 0, breakat;
breakat = prompt("Pick a number between 1 and 10 to break at", "");
while (x < 10)
{
{
if (x == breakat)
break;
}
alert(x);
x++;
}
// Cloaking device off -->
</script>
```

The `while` iteration statement is executed until the value of `x` equals the value of `breakat`, at which point the loop is exited. So, if you type a `5` into the prompt box, alert boxes for 1–4 are displayed.

EXERCISE

Experiment with the `break` statement in a few sample scripts. Also, again, experiment with various conditions to really get a feel for how it works.

The switch Statement

The `switch` statement enables you to execute one or more statements when a specified expression's value matches a label.

The script takes on the following layout:

```
switch (expression)
{
case label1:
statementlist
case label2:
statementlist
}
```

In the following example, the value inputted into the prompt box determines which statements are run (the before and after are shown in Figures 7.11 and 7.12):

```
<script language="JavaScript">
<!-- Cloaking device on!
var yourchoice;
yourchoice = prompt("Choose a number between 1 and 4", "1, 2, 3 or 4")
switch (yourchoice)
{
case "1":
alert("You typed in a 1");
break;
case "2":
alert("You typed in a 2");
break;
case "3":
alert("You typed in a 3");
break;
case "4":
alert("You typed in a 4");
break;
}
// Cloaking device off -->
</script>
```

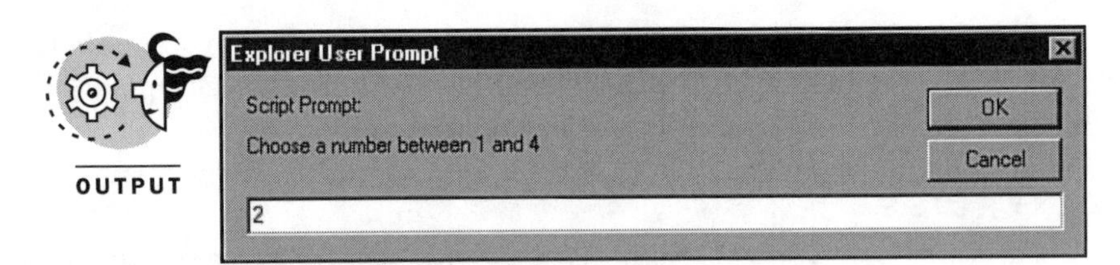

Figure 7.11: *A value inputted into the prompt box.*

Figure 7.12: *The alert box shows which statement is run.*

Each block of statements needs to end with a `break` statement; otherwise, every statement below that particular case is run.

Sometimes, it is useful to include a default group of statements to run if none of the label values matches the expression. One such instance is the previous example, if the number typed wasn't between 1 and 4.

```
<script language="JavaScript">
<!-- Cloaking device on!
var yourchoice;
yourchoice = prompt("Choose a number between 1 and 4", "1, 2, 3 or 4")
switch (yourchoice)
{
case "1":
alert("You typed in a 1");
break;
case "2":
alert("You typed in a 2");
break;
case "3":
alert("You typed in a 3");
break;
case "4":
alert("You typed in a 4");
break;
default:
alert("You didn't type in a number between 1 and 4");
break;
}
// Cloaking device off -->
</script>
```

Another way to use the `switch` statement is with the confirm box you looked at earlier. In the following, you are looking for the Boolean values `true` and `false`. Because no other possible outcomes exist here (only two options are available to click—OK and Cancel), there is no need for default statements:

```
<script language="JavaScript">
<!-- Cloaking device on!
var yourchoice;
yourchoice = confirm("Are you at your computer now?")
switch (yourchoice)
{
case true:
alert("See, I'm psychic!");
break;
case false:
alert("Eh?  How can you be doing this then?");
break;
}
// Cloaking device off -->
</script>
```

When you load this page into the browser, you are faced with the confirm box shown in Figure 7.13.

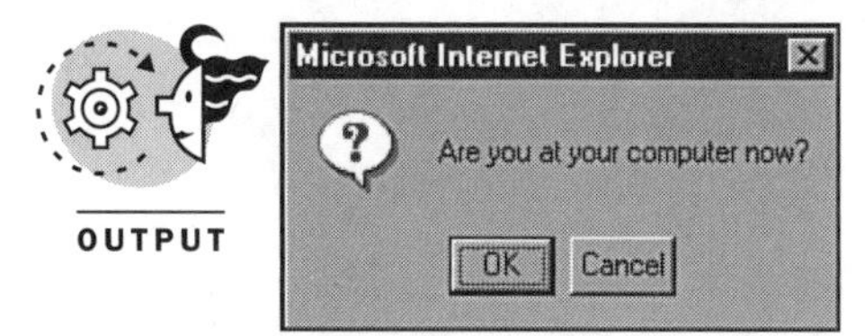

Figure 7.13: The initial confirm box.

Click Cancel, and you see the alert box shown in Figure 7.14.

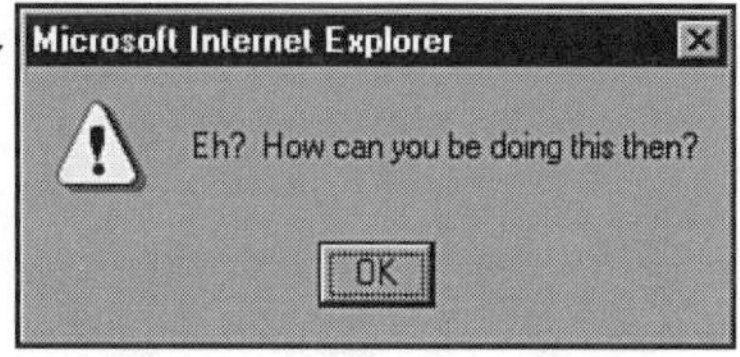

Figure 7.14: The alert box shows which statement is run.

EXERCISE

Use the `switch` statement to write a script that will run different statements when the letters a, b, c, d, and e are entered into a prompt box. Remember to include a default statement for entries that aren't expected.

What's Next

Your JavaScript knowledge is increasing exponentially now! The final fundamental step you need to take is to change your code from being sequential (running top to bottom) to being compartmentalized using functions, which is the topic of the next chapter!

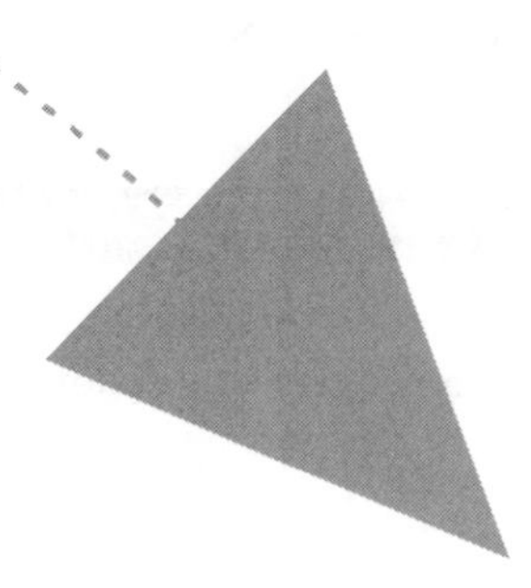

Write Better JavaScript Scripts by Using Functions and Events

So far, your JavaScript code has consisted of a statement or a group of statements that are all run sequentially from top to bottom. This is great for simple scripts, but in most cases you don't want all your JavaScript to run when the page loads. You might want only a few statements to run at the beginning and then a few more at some other point in time. This is where functions come into their own.

This chapter teaches you about the following:

- What functions are
- How to use functions
- Using events to trigger functions
- Passing information to and from functions
- The `return` statement

What Are Functions?

In their simplest form, *functions* are a group of statements that do something and that are placed under one name. A function takes the following form:

```
function functionname()
{
statements go here!;
}
```

A function consists of the word `function` followed by the name you give the function, such as `yourMessage`. Then, parentheses are placed after the function name—for example, `yourMessage()`. These are required, and an error is generated if they are omitted.

NOTE

For the moment, these parentheses will remain empty. Later in this chapter, you'll see what they are used for.

After the parentheses are the opening and closing curly braces, in between which are the statements.

Each function you use must be given a name, and no two functions on a page can have the same name. The function can then be run (or *invoked* or *called*) from the Web page—we'll look at how later.

Your First Function

EXAMPLE

Things might seem a little complex until you do it the first time, so let's get you writing your first function. Follow these steps:

1. Open your HTML template page in your favorite text editor.
2. Start off the function by writing (in the script block) the word `function` and giving it a name (this one will be called `yourMessage`). Remember to include the parentheses at the end of the line:

```
<script language="JavaScript">
<!-- Cloaking device on!
function yourMessage()

// Cloaking device off -->
</script>
```

3. Next, add the pair of curly braces:

```
<script language="JavaScript">
<!-- Cloaking device on!
function yourMessage()
```

```
{

}
// Cloaking device off -->
</script>
```

CAUTION

Remember to start with the opening curly brace ({) and end with the closing curly brace (}). A common error among those new to JavaScript is to mix up the order of the braces, which results in the JavaScript not working.

4. Next, add a simple statement:

```
<script language="JavaScript">
<!-- Cloaking device on!
function yourMessage()
{
alert("Your first function!");
}
// Cloaking device off -->
</script>
```

5. Save your work and load it into the browser to see what happens.

   Nothing happens! Hmm. Don't worry! This doesn't mean that something is wrong with your JavaScript. The reason for this is that you haven't *called* the function yet. You must do this because, unlike just typing straight statements into the script block—which are run as soon as the browser encounters them—functions aren't automatically run, so you must do some more scripting to make it work!

   You can call a JavaScript function in several ways. The simplest but least effective way is to call it directly in the script block. This is done by simply placing the function name in the script block:

```
<!-- Cloaking device on!

yourMessage();

function yourMessage()
{
alert("Your first function!");
}
// Cloaking device off -->
</script>
```

6. Save the page again and load it into the browser to see your work in action! (See Figure 8.1.)

OUTPUT

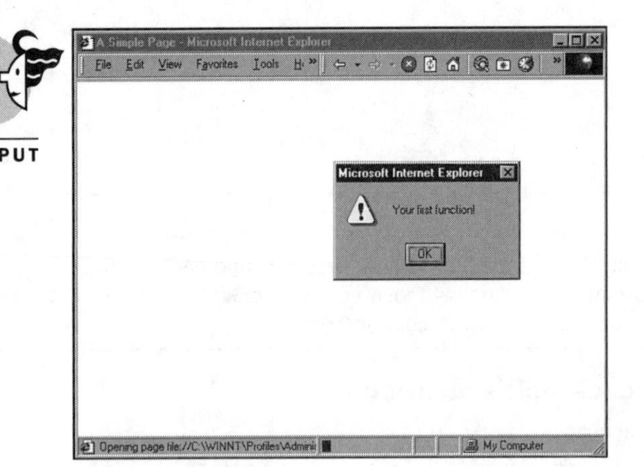

Figure 8.1: *An alert box is displayed, showing that the function has been called and run.*

The way we called the function in the previous example is probably one of the most useless ways of doing it. Even though it works, it really is no different from typing straight statements directly into the script block as you did before.

As you will see later, this is useful for calling one function from another function. But before you can do that, you need to know how to run functions, and to do that, you first need to learn about events. *Events* enable you to have better control over how and when your functions are run.

Events

The trick to calling functions is to use events to do the work for you. JavaScript is *event-driven*, which means everything that happens is the result of an event or causes some event to occur. Opening a new page in the browser window is an event. Moving the mouse pointer is an event. Clicking is an event. The four events you will use the most in this book are

- `onLoad`
- `onClick`
- `onMouseover`
- `onMouseout`

Let's run through each of these quickly so that you're familiar with them before we continue.

The `onLoad` Event

The `onLoad` event is the event that occurs when something has loaded—for example, the browser has finished loading a page into the browser window. This event occurs only when all of the page (including images if they are set to load) has finished downloading.

NOTE

You may be interested to note that the event that occurs when the page is *unloaded* (by moving on to another page or closing the browser window) is called `onUnload`.

The `onLoad` event is a great event to use when you want functions to be triggered after the page has loaded and is ready for use.

The `onClick` Event

The `onClick` event occurs when the user clicks somewhere on the page. As you will see later, various elements on the page (such as hyperlinks, images, buttons, and text) can respond separately to the `onClick` event.

This event is useful when you want to create JavaScripts that interact with the user.

The `onMouseover` Event

This event is similar to the `onClick` event but happens not when the user clicks an element on the page, but when the user moves the mouse pointer over it. This event again can be assigned to almost any object on a Web page (text, images, buttons, hyperlinks, and so on).

Again, this is great for interactivity between script and user.

The `onMouseout` Event

Again, this event is similar to the `onMouseover` event, but it occurs when the mouse pointer is moved off an object.

Using Events

Okay, so you know about four events, but how do you use them? Well, let's start with the `onLoad` event.

Using the `onLoad` Event

To use the `onLoad` event to trigger a JavaScript function, you must place the following event handler in the `<body>` tag of the Web page:

```
<body onLoad="functionname()">
```

NOTE

An *event handler* is a piece of code that handles the event and does something as a result of it occurring, such as running a JavaScript function.

All you now must do to trigger the `yourMessage()` function is type its name between the double quotes of the event handler—for example, `<body onLoad="yourMessage()">`. Now, save the page and load it into the browser window:

```
<html>
<head>
<title>A Simple Page</title>
<script language="JavaScript">
<!-- Cloaking device on!
function yourMessage()
{
alert("Your first function!");
}
// Cloaking device off -->
</script>
</head>
<body onLoad="yourMessage()">

</body>
</html>
```

Using the `onClick` Event

What about some of the other events? What if you want to use the `onClick` event instead? Simple, just change `onLoad` to `onClick`:

```
<html>
<head>
<title>A Simple Page</title>
<script language="JavaScript">
<!-- Cloaking device on!
function yourMessage()
{
alert("Your first function!");
}
// Cloaking device off -->
</script>
</head>
<body onClick="yourMessage()">

</body>
</html>
```

If you save this and load it into the browser, you see that nothing happens until you click anywhere on the page, and then the function is run!

However, just clicking anywhere in the page isn't the best way possible to do this. A far better way would be if you could control things in a more specific way—for example, clicking a hyperlink. This is easy! Instead of adding the event handler to the `<body>` tag, you just add the `onClick` event handler directly to the hyperlink:

```
<html>
<head>
<title>A Simple Page</title>
<script language="JavaScript">
<!-- Cloaking device on!
function yourMessage()
{
alert("You clicked on a link!");
}
// Cloaking device off -->
</script>
</head>
<body>
<a href="http://www.kingsley-hughes.com" onClick="yourMessage()">My Web site!
➥</a>
</body>
</html>
```

If you load this example into your Web browser and click the link, you see the message box appear before the page pointed to in the URL is retrieved (see Figure 8.2).

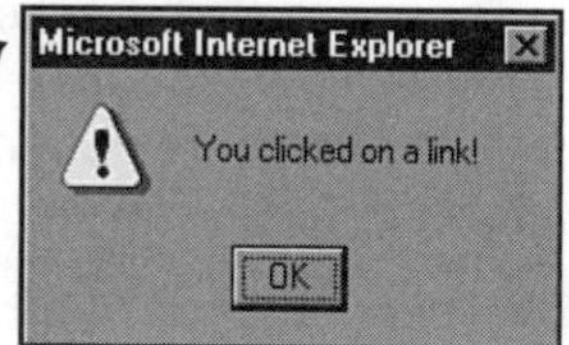

Figure 8.2: *An alert box is displayed when the hyperlink is clicked.*

Using the onMouseover Event

Hyperlinks also lend themselves well to being used for `onMouseover` events. Here is a simple example in which the `overMessage()` function is triggered when the user moves the mouse pointer over the hyperlink:

```
<html>
<head>
<title>A Simple Page</title>
```

```
<script language="JavaScript">
<!-- Cloaking device on!
function overMessage()
{
alert("This is a great link - click on it!");
}
// Cloaking device off -->
</script>
</head>
<body>
<a href="http://www.kingsley-hughes.com" onMouseover="overMessage()">My Web
➥site!</a>
</body>
</html>
```

EXERCISE

Create a page containing a hyperlink that has a function that will be triggered when the user moves the mouse pointer off it.

CHALLENGE

Can you create another page that brings up a farewell message when the user leaves the Web page? Hint: Remember the `onUnload` event?

Creating Effective Functions!

Now that you've had a chance to write your first function and have practiced how to use events to trigger functions, you're ready to delve a little deeper.

The best way to think of functions is as a group of statements that perform a particular job. This can be a simple job requiring no more than one statement (as we saw previously) or a more complex function requiring many statements. Either way, functions perform a particular job.

So, if you return to the interactive story example, you can tidy this up and make it more user friendly by putting all the script into a function and using the `onClick` event on a button to trigger it off (see Figure 8.3):

```
<html>
<head>
<title>A Simple Page</title>
<script language="JavaScript">
<!-- Cloaking device on!
function story()
{
// create array for prompts
var promptmsg = new Array("A time of day","A feeling","An adjective - eg sunny",
```

```
➥"An adjective - eg sunny","A verb - past tense eg walked","An adverb - eg
➥quickly or monstrously","An adverb  - eg quickly or monstrously","A room in
➥a house", "A profession","An exclamation!");

// create array for default text
var defaulttxt = new Array("lunchtime","wet","plump","malodorous","wriggled",
➥"hungrily","fiercely","bathroom","Web developer","Yipes");

// variables for prompt inputs
var entry1, entry2, entry3, entry4, entry5, entry6, entry7, entry8, entry9,
➥entry10;

// bring on the prompts!
entry1  = prompt(promptmsg[0], defaulttxt[0]);
entry2  = prompt(promptmsg[1], defaulttxt[1]);
entry3  = prompt(promptmsg[2], defaulttxt[2]);
entry4  = prompt(promptmsg[3], defaulttxt[3]);
entry5  = prompt(promptmsg[4], defaulttxt[4]);
entry6  = prompt(promptmsg[5], defaulttxt[5]);
entry7  = prompt(promptmsg[6], defaulttxt[6]);
entry8  = prompt(promptmsg[7], defaulttxt[7]);
entry9  = prompt(promptmsg[8], defaulttxt[8]);
entry10 = prompt(promptmsg[9], defaulttxt[9]);

// bring on the alert boxes!
alert("Once upon a " + entry1 + " dreary,")
alert("while I pondered, " + entry2 + " and weary,")
alert("Over many a " + entry3 + " and curious volume")
alert("of " + entry4 + " lore")
alert("While I " + entry5 + ", nearly napping,")
alert(entry6 + " there came a tapping,")
alert("As of someone " + entry7 + " rapping,")
alert("rapping at my " + entry8 + " door.")
alert("\"'Tis some " + entry9 + ",\" I muttered,")
alert("tapping at my " + entry8 + " door")
alert("Only " + entry10 + "! and nothing more.")
}
// Cloaking device off -->
</script>
</head>
<body>
<h1>Interactive Story!</h1>
<p>Click <input type="button" value="HERE" onClick="story()"> to start the
➥story!</p>
</body>
</html>
```

OUTPUT

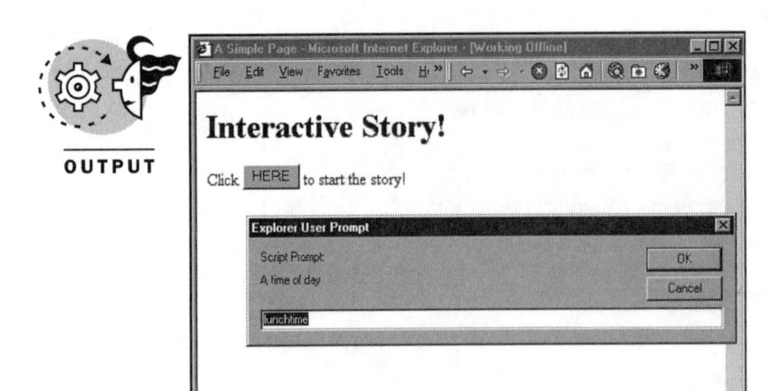

Figure 8.3: *The interactive story with a few additions to the page—now it's much friendlier.*

This is a very quick and simple way a function can be used to tidy up a page.

Functions Running Functions!

EXAMPLE

You've seen how events can be used to trigger functions, but what about one function triggering another? That's simple! Here is an example of a function that contains an alert box triggered by the `onLoad` event and that triggered another function itself:

```
<html>
<head>
<title>A Simple Page</title>
<script language="JavaScript">
<!-- Cloaking device on!
function firstMessage()
{
alert("Here is the first message!");
secondMessage();
}

function secondMessage()
{
alert("And here is the second!");
}
// Cloaking device off -->
</script>
</head>
<body onLoad="firstMessage()">

</body>
</html>
```

When you load this page into the browser, the `onLoad` event triggers the function `firstMessage()`, which displays the first alert box (see Figure 8.4).

Figure 8.4: *The first alert box displayed by the `onLoad` event running `firstMessage()`.*

However, the second alert box is generated by the function `secondMessage()`, which is called from the function `firstMessage()` (see Figure 8.5). Figure 8.6 shows a schematic of the order in which the functions are run.

Figure 8.5: *The second alert box displayed by the function `firstMessage()` calling `secondMessage()`.*

```
<html>
<head>
<title>A Simple Page</title>
<script language="JavaScript">
<!-- Cloaking device on!
function firstMessage()
{
alert("Here is the first message!");
secondMessage();
}

function secondMessage()
{
alert("And here is the second!");
}
// Cloaking device off -->
</script>
</head>
<body onLoad="firstMessage()">

</body>
</html>
```

Figure 8.6: *The order in which the JavaScript functions are run.*

If you don't call the next function at the end of the current function, the order in which things happen won't be quite as straightforward. Consider the following example:

```
<html>
<head>
<title>A Simple Page</title>
<script language="JavaScript">
<!-- Cloaking device on!
function firstMessage()
{
alert("Here is the first message!");
secondMessage();
alert("And here is the third!");
}

function secondMessage()
{
alert("And here is the second!");
}
// Cloaking device off -->
</script>
</head>
<body onLoad="firstMessage()">

</body>
</html>
```

What happens here is that the function `firstMessage()` is triggered by the `onLoad` event and the first alert box is displayed (see Figure 8.7 for a schematic and Figure 8.8 for the result as seen in the browser).

When the call for the function `secondMessage()` is reached, a jump from `firstMessage()` to `secondMessage()` occurs and that function is run, which means the next alert box displayed is the one in this function (see Figure 8.9).

When the function `secondMessage()` has completed, the code skips back to the point at which it left `firstMessage()` and continues with the remaining statements (see Figures 8.10 and 8.11).

NOTE

This effect, called *branching*, is a useful technique to understand and use; however, it does mean you should comment your code well so that it is all clear and unambiguous.

EXERCISE

Practice using this kind of branching in a few of your own JavaScript examples. Try putting multiple branches in functions and see what happens.

Comment your code well so that all the steps and branches are clear to you!

```
<html>
<head>
<title>A Simple Page</title>
<script language="JavaScript">
<!-- Cloaking device on!
function firstMessage()
{
alert("Here is the first message!");
secondMessage();
alert("And here is the third!");
}

function secondMessage()
{
alert("And here is the second!");
}
// Cloaking device off -->
</script>
</head>
<body onLoad="firstMessage()">

</body>
</html>
```

Figure 8.7: *The* `onLoad` *event triggers the* `firstMessage()` *function and the first alert box is displayed.*

Figure 8.8: *The first alert box is displayed.*

Figure 8.9: *The second alert box is displayed.*

```
<html>
<head>
<title>A Simple Page</title>
<script language="JavaScript">
<!-- Cloaking device on!
function firstMessage()
{
alert("Here is the first message!");
secondMessage();
alert("And here is the third!");
}

function secondMessage()
{
alert("And here is the second!");
}
// Cloaking device off -->
</script>
</head>
<body onLoad="firstMessage()">

</body>
</html>
```

***Figure 8.10:** After `secondMessage()` has finished, the remaining statements in `firstMessage()` are run.*

***Figure 8.11:** The final alert box is displayed.*

What Are Those Parentheses For?

Now let's talk about those parentheses at the end of the function name—they've got to be there for some reason, right?

These parentheses are actually used to hold a *parameter*. Parameters act just like variables and can hold just about any data you want—text strings, numbers, Boolean values, and so on.

Let's look at an example of a function that uses parameters:

```
<html>
<head>
<title>A Simple Page</title>
<script language="JavaScript">
<!-- Cloaking device on!
function yourMessage(quote)
{
```

```
alert(quote);
}
// Cloaking device off -->
</script>
</head>
<body>
<p>Click <input type="button" value="HERE" onClick="yourMessage('How come dumb
➥stuff seems so smart while you\'re doing it!')"> for a message!</p>
<br>
<p>Click <input type="button" value="HERE" onClick="yourMessage('How do you tell
➥when you run out of invisible ink?')"> for another message!</p>
</body>
</html>
```

NOTE

Notice the use of the escape character (\') for the single quote in the message for the first button—if it is omitted, an error occurs!

This is a page that contains two buttons. If you click a button, an alert box containing a message is displayed. The message displayed is passed from the `onClick` event handler to the function parameter. This parameter has the name `quote`. It acts just like a variable, and its value is passed to the alert box to be displayed.

If that seems a bit complicated, take a look at Figure 8.12.

```
<html>
<head>
<title>A Simple Page</title>
<script language="JavaScript">
<!-- Cloaking device on!
function yourMessage(quote)
{
alert(quote);
}
// Cloaking device off -->
</script>
</head>
<body>
<p>Click <input type="button" value="HERE"
onClick="yourMessage('How come dumb stuff seems so
smart while you\'re doing it!')"> for a message!</p>
<br>
<p>Click <input type="button" value="HERE"
onClick="yourMessage('How do you tell when you run
out of invisible ink?')"> for another message!</p>
</body>
</html>
```

Figure 8.12: *How the script is processed and the parameter handled.*

NOTE

Just like variables, try to give your parameters names that remind you of their purposes.

The nice thing about using functions and parameters for this kind of example is that you can easily add more buttons and quotes without having to alter or add to your JavaScript:

```
<html>
<head>
<title>A Simple Page</title>
<script language="JavaScript">
<!-- Cloaking device on!
function yourMessage(quote)
{
alert(quote);
}
// Cloaking device off -->
</script>
</head>
<body>
<p>Click <input type="button" value="HERE" onClick="yourMessage('How come dumb
➥stuff seems so smart while you\'re doing it!')"> for a message!</p>
<br>
<p>Click <input type="button" value="HERE" onClick="yourMessage('How do you tell
➥when you run out of invisible ink?')"> for another message!</p>
<br>
<p>Click <input type="button" value="HERE" onClick="yourMessage('Do run with
scissors ... sorry, I mean DON\'T run with scissors!')"> for another
➥message!</p>
<br>
<p>Click <input type="button" value="HERE" onClick="yourMessage('If it isn\'t
➥broken, fix it till it is.')"> for a final message!</p>

</body>
</html>
```

TIP

This Web page would be a lot more complicated if the parameters weren't used and each button needed a separate function.

EXERCISE

Create a few similar examples that use functions and parameters. Notice how using parameters makes the code easier to write and understand than if separate functions are used.

Keep practicing your JavaScript comments!

Using Parameters Between Functions

You can use parameters to pass data from one function (the *referring* function) to another (the *receiving* function).

Here is a simple example of this in action:

```
<html>
<head>
<title>A Simple Page</title>
<script language="JavaScript">
<!-- Cloaking device on!
function first()
{
var x = 3, y = 5;
doAdd(x, y);
}

function doAdd(x, y)
{
alert(x + y);
}
// Cloaking device off -->
</script>
</head>
<body onLoad="first()">

</body>
</html>
```

In this example, the referring function (`first()`) is passing `x` and `y` to the parameters in the receiving function (`doAdd()`), which performs the math and outputs the answer.

This might seem of dubious value to you now (why not do the math in the first function and not have the second function?), but in a moment you'll see how sharing the workload between functions can be useful.

The return Statement

One statement you didn't look at in the previous chapter is the `return` statement. (Well, in fact there is one other—the `with` statement—but you'll come across that in the next chapter!)

The `return` statement was omitted from the previous chapter because it deals specifically with *functions* and at that time, you hadn't discovered functions. So, let's take a look at it now.

You've seen how parameters can be used to pass data from a referring function to a receiving function so that it can work on the data; well, there is a way to pass the result back. This is done with the `return` statement:

```
<html>
<head>
<title>A Simple Page</title>
<script language="JavaScript">
<!-- Cloaking device on!
function calcAvg()
{
var inpNum1 = prompt("Enter a number","Number here");
var inpNum2 = prompt("Enter a number","Number here");
var inpNum3 = prompt("Enter a number","Number here");
var inpNum4 = prompt("Enter a number","Number here");
numAvg = doCalcAvg(inpNum1, inpNum2, inpNum3, inpNum4);
alert("The average of the four numbers you entered is: " + numAvg);
}

function doCalcAvg(inpNum1, inpNum2, inpNum3, inpNum4)
{
var ans;
ans = (Number(inpNum1) + Number(inpNum2) + Number(inpNum3) + Number(inpNum4)) /
➥4;
return (ans);
}
// Cloaking device off -->
</script>
</head>
<body onLoad="calcAvg();">
</body>
</html>
```

Here is an example using the `return` statement whereby the user can enter four numbers via a series of prompt boxes and the JavaScript then tells her the average of those four numbers. If you take a look at the code, you see two functions. The first is called `calcAvg()` and is the function run by the `onLoad` event. This function mainly deals with the input and output, handling the prompt and alert boxes. It also passes four variables to the function `doCalcAvg()`, which receives them as parameters.

CAUTION

If you call a function that uses the `return` statement without assigning a variable, such as

```
doCalcAvg(inpNum1, inpNum2, inpNum3, inpNum4);
```

it results in the script not functioning properly because the returning data has nowhere to go.

The function `doCalcAvg()` then performs the calculation on the data and uses the `return` statement to pass back the result (held in a variable called `ans`). See Figures 8.13 and 8.14 for the schematic and results.

```
<html>
<head>
<title>A Simple Page</title>
<script language="JavaScript">
<!-- Cloaking device on!
function calcAvg()
{
var inpNum1 = prompt("Enter a number","Number here");
var inpNum2 = prompt("Enter a number","Number here");
var inpNum3 = prompt("Enter a number","Number here");
var inpNum4 = prompt("Enter a number","Number here");
numAvg = doCalcAvg(inpNum1, inpNum2, inpNum3, inpNum4);
alert("The average of the four numbers you entered is: " +
numAvg);
}

function doCalcAvg(inpNum1, inpNum2, inpNum3, inpNum4)
{
var ans;
ans = (Number(inpNum1) + Number(inpNum2) + Number(inpNum3)
+ Number(inpNum4)) / 4;
return (ans);
}
// Cloaking device off -->
</script>
</head>
<body onLoad="calcAvg();">
</body>
</html>
```

Figure 8.13: *The order that the statements are run in the two functions.*

NOTE

Note how the receiving (`numAvg`) and returning (`ans`) variables have different names. This is the best way to avoid any problems—you just need to remember which variable goes where.

OUTPUT

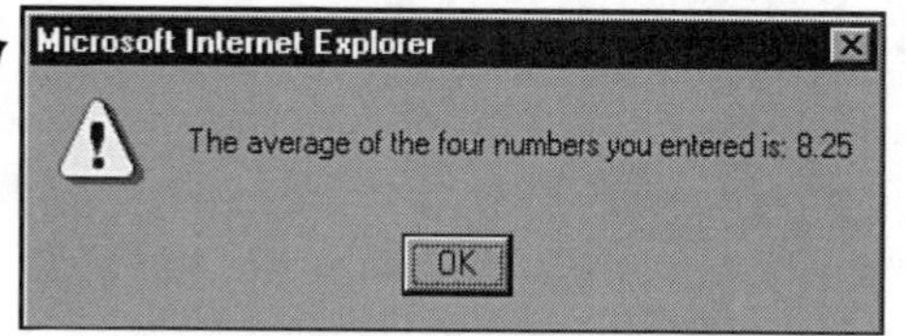

Figure 8.14: *The result of the calculation is displayed in an alert box.*

An important point to note about the `return` statement is that, although a function can receive more than one parameter, it can return only a single value back to the calling function.

This leads you to the design strategy of creating functions that receive data and work on it to output a single value. Mathematical calculations are a good example of how this is useful, but other uses might include an online form process in which you want a function to calculate postage costs. An added benefit is that, if your postage costs change, they are all in one function and not spread out in many different functions!

Exercise—Temperature Conversion JavaScript

1. Consider the following example. This example is closely based on the example you looked at previously:

```
<html>
<head>
<title>A Simple Page</title>
<script language="JavaScript">
<!-- Cloaking device on!
function inputCels()
{
var cels = prompt("Enter a temperature in Degrees Celsius","Enter a
➥temperature");
ansFah = doFahCalc(cels);
alert(cels + " Degrees Celsius is " + ansFah + " Degrees Fahrenheit");
}

function inputFah()
{
var fah = prompt("Enter a temperature in Degrees Fahrenheit","Enter a
➥temperature");
ansCel = doCelCalc(fah);
alert(fah + " Degrees Fahrenheit is " + ansCel + " Degrees Celsius");
}

function doCelCalc(fah)
{
var ans = ((Number(fah) - 32) / 1.8);
return (ans);
}

function doFahCalc(cels)
{
var ans = ((1.8 * Number(cels)) + 32);
return (ans);
}
// Cloaking device off -->
</script>
</head>
```

```
<body>
<input type="button" value="Convert Celsius to Fahrenheit"
➥onClick="inputCels();">
<br>
<br>
<input type="button" value="Convert Fahrenheit to Celsius"
➥onClick="inputFah();">
</body>
</html>
```

2. Take a look at this code (type it in and run it or download the examples and try it out). Try to work out what each statement does and how they interact through parameters and the `return` statement.
3. Add comments to the script to help you understand how it works.
4. Try modifying the example to use different mathematical equations (sales tax, gas mileage, and so on).
5. Most important of all, have fun! Take it easy; look at the previous examples and use them as a guide to help you to understand the interactions in this JavaScript example. It will take a little time, and it isn't necessarily easy, but it's definitely worth it! By going through this example for yourself, and perhaps even creating an example of your own, you are consolidating your JavaScript knowledge, which will help you on your way to JavaScript success!

EXERCISE

Try your hand at creating functions that pass data back and forth using parameters and the `return` statement. Follow the previous example if you find it difficult to begin, and simply change the variable names. After a while, you'll find that it comes easily to you.

What's Next

You now know how to write functions, use parameters to simplify your JavaScript, and use the `return` statement to pass data. In the next chapter, you get more practice with functions when you move on to looking at an area of JavaScript that beginners are normally daunted by—objects!

See you there!

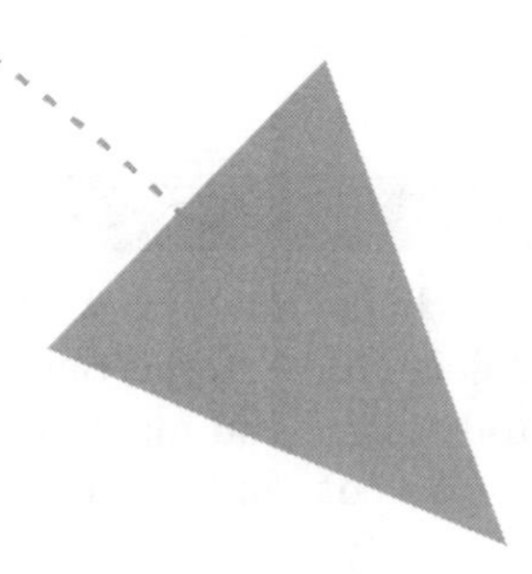

Getting the Most Out of Objects

You've covered the script block; you've covered statements; and you've covered operators, functions, and events. It's now time to look at JavaScript objects!

This chapter teaches you about the following:

- What objects are
- Objects and browsers—different objects for different browsers
- The `Math` object and how to use it
- The `Date` object and how to use it
- The `String` object and how to use it
- Using the `with` statement with objects

Objects—What Are They?

In their simplest terms, *objects* are collections of methods and properties. Remember the analogy that objects are things. Objects have properties (such as computers have monitors, cars have wheels, and so on), and methods are things that objects can do (cars can move, scissors can cut, and so on).

If you put objects, properties, and methods together, you start to get a better idea of what objects are. In JavaScript, objects and their respective properties and methods are put together by separating them with periods (`.`), which is called *dot syntax*. So, if the real world was controlled by JavaScript, you might have the following:

```
computers.monitors
cars.wheels
scissors.cut()
```

Notice how this enables you to better describe an object (`computer.monitor` is specific) or describe a process (`scissors.cut`). This dot syntax enables you to drill deeper into objects and become more specific:

```
cars.wheels.rear.right
```

NOTE

This drilling down will become more obvious later when we look at browser objects, as opposed to JavaScript objects.

Objects and Browsers

One thing that always seems to come as a surprise to the budding JavaScripter is that not all browsers support the same objects. Mostly this is because the various browser manufacturers each want to add their own proprietary things to the JavaScript standard they include with their browsers. However, thanks mainly to the ECMAScript standard and partially to the common origin of both Microsoft's JScript and Netscape Navigator's JavaScript, most of the objects are available in both browsers.

As an example, take a look at the following. The ECMAScript standard contains the following objects:

- `Array`—Enables the creation of a new array
- `Boolean`—Creates a new Boolean value
- `Date`—Enables basic storage and retrieval of dates and times
- `Function`—Creates a new function

- `Global`—An object whose purpose is to collect global methods (such as `eval`) into one object
- `Math`—An object that provides basic mathematics functionality and constants
- `Number`—An object representing the number data
- `Object`—Provides functionality common to all JavaScript objects
- `RegExp`—A global object that stores information about the results of regular expression pattern matches (in text string searches)
- `String`—Enables manipulation and formatting of text strings and the location of substrings within strings

But the JScript 5.5 engine included with Internet Explorer 5.5 also has the following objects:

- `Enumerator`
- `Regular Expression`
- `VBArray`
- `ActiveXObject`
- `GetObject`

To keep things simple here, only ECMAScript standard objects are covered in this book.

The JavaScript Objects—A Closer Look

Several of the objects present in JavaScript are there for advanced users and as such don't need to be covered here (although the end of this chapter has a complete listing of all the properties and methods available for all the ECMAScript objects). In this chapter, you look at three of the most interesting and useful objects present in JavaScript. These are

- The `Math` object
- The `Date` object
- The `String` object

The `Math` Object

The `Math` object brings to JavaScript all the basic mathematical functionality and constants you are likely to need.

Let's look at some examples of the `Math` object in action.

Using the PI Property

The π constant is one constant (equal to about 3.1415, although the numbers go on forever with the millionth number being a 1!) you might want to use, especially if you deal with circles. π returns the ratio of the circumference of a circle to its diameter. The following shows it in action as a simple circle area calculator using the mathematical formula `Pi x r^2` or `Pi x r x r` (see Figure 9.1):

```
<script language="JavaScript">
<!-- Cloaking device on!
inpRadius = prompt("Enter the radius for your circle","Radius - digits only!");
alert(Math.PI * ((inpRadius)*(inpRadius)));
// Cloaking device off -->
</script>
```

Figure 9.1: *The circle area calculator in action.*

All this property does is hold a value for the mathematical constant π; the same thing could be achieved by using variables. However, the `PI` property of the `Math` object does it without you having to look up the value for π!

Here is another example, this time using three functions—one to calculate the area of a circle, another to calculate the circumference, and a final one to calculate the volume of a sphere (see Figure 9.2):

```
<html>
<head>
<title>A Simple Page</title>
<script language="JavaScript">
<!-- Cloaking device on!
function calcArea()
{
inpRadius = prompt("Enter the radius for your circle","Radius - digits only!");
alert(Math.PI * ((inpRadius)*(inpRadius)));
}

function calcPeri()
{
inpRadius = prompt("Enter the radius for your circle","Radius - digits only!");
alert(2 * Math.PI * (inpRadius));
}
```

```
function calcVol()
{
inpRadius = prompt("Enter the radius for your sphere","Radius - digits only!");
alert(Math.PI * ((inpRadius)*(inpRadius)*(inpRadius)) * (4/3));
}
// Cloaking device off -->
</script>
</head>
<body>
<h1>All about Circles and Spheres!</h1>
<p>Click <input type="button" value="HERE" onclick="calcArea();"> to calculate
➥circle area!</p>
<br>
<p>Click <input type="button" value="HERE" onclick="calcPeri();"> to calculate
➥circle perimeter!</p>
<br>
<p>Click <input type="button" value="HERE" onclick="calcVol();"> to calculate
➥sphere volume!</p>
</body>
</html>
```

OUTPUT

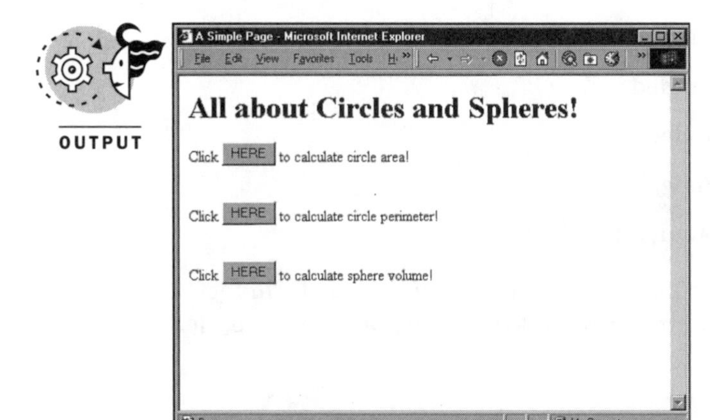

Figure 9.2: *The new, improved circle area calculator in action!*

Using the max and min Methods

Two interesting methods of the `Math` object are the `max` and `min` methods. These enable you to find the greater or lesser of supplied numerical expressions.

EXAMPLE

Here is a simple example:

```
<script language="JavaScript">
<!-- Cloaking device on!
inp1 = prompt("Enter a number","Number goes here");
inp2 = prompt("Enter a number","Number goes here");
```

```
inp3 = prompt("Enter a number","Number goes here");
alert("The largest number entered was " + Math.max(inp1, inp2, inp3));
alert("The smallest number entered was " + Math.min(inp1, inp2, inp3));
// Cloaking device off -->
</script>
```

The first alert box uses the `max` method to show the highest number entered, while the second alert box uses the `min` method to display the lowest. This is a simple example that shows the power of these methods. A more complex example might involve the display of highest and lowest prices in a price list or the highest and lowest test scores for students.

Using the `round` Method

This is a handy method when dealing with awkward numbers (real numbers of the type you are looking at here are one kind of awkward number) because it enables you to round them off to the nearest integer.

If the decimal portion of a positive number is 0.5 or greater, the value returned is equal to the smallest integer greater than the number. Otherwise, `round` returns the largest integer less than or equal to the number. So

- 1.45 is rounded to 1.
- 6.93 is rounded to 7.
- 7.5 is rounded to 8.
- 0.5 is rounded to 1.
- 0.49 is rounded to 0.

Here is an example using the `round` method. It is, in fact, a modification of the circle calculator—this time returning answers rounded to the nearest integer (see Figure 9.3):

```
<html>
<head>
<title>A Simple Page</title>
<script language="JavaScript">
<!-- Cloaking device on!
function calcArea()
{
inpRadius = prompt("Enter the radius for your circle","Radius - digits only!");
alert(Math.round(Math.PI * ((inpRadius)*(inpRadius))));
}

function calcPeri()
{
inpRadius = prompt("Enter the radius for your circle","Radius - digits only!");
```

```
alert(Math.round(2 * Math.PI * (inpRadius)));
}

function calcVol()
{
inpRadius = prompt("Enter the radius for your sphere","Radius - digits only!");
alert(Math.round(Math.PI * ((inpRadius)*(inpRadius)*(inpRadius)) * (4/3)));
}
// Cloaking device off -->
</script>
</head>
<body>
<h1>All about Circles and Spheres!</h1>
<p>Click <input type="button" value="HERE" onclick="calcArea();"> to calculate
➥circle area!</p>
<br>
<p>Click <input type="button" value="HERE" onclick="calcPeri();"> to calculate
➥circle perimeter!</p>
<br>
<p>Click <input type="button" value="HERE" onclick="calcVol();"> to calculate
➥sphere volume!</p>
</body>
</html>
```

OUTPUT

Figure 9.3: The new, improved circle area calculator in action—now with rounding!

NOTE

The equations used previously contain a lot of parentheses. The trick with parentheses is to make sure you have the same number of opening (() as closing ()) brackets. Otherwise, you will get an error.

If you want to retain some of the decimal places, a quick and simple way to do this is to first multiply the original number by 10 if you want one decimal place, by 100 if you want two, by 1000 if you want three, and so on. Then, you perform the rounding and finally divide by the number you multiplied the original number by. So, if you wanted the circle calculator to have an accuracy of two decimal places, you would do the following (see Figure 9.4):

```
<html>
<head>
<title>A Simple Page</title>
```

```
<script language="JavaScript">
<!-- Cloaking device on!
function calcArea()
{
inpRadius = prompt("Enter the radius for your circle","Radius - digits only!");
ans = ((Math.PI * ((inpRadius)*(inpRadius))) * 100);
alert((Math.round(ans)) / 100);
}

function calcPeri()
{
inpRadius = prompt("Enter the radius for your circle","Radius - digits only!");
ans = ((2 * Math.PI * (inpRadius)) * 100);
alert((Math.round(ans)) / 100);
}

function calcVol()
{
inpRadius = prompt("Enter the radius for your sphere","Radius - digits only!");
ans = ((Math.PI * ((inpRadius)*(inpRadius)*(inpRadius)) * (4/3)) * 100);
alert((Math.round(ans)) / 100);
}
// Cloaking device off -->
</script>
</head>
<body>
<h1>All about Circles and Spheres!</h1>
<p>Click <input type="button" value="HERE" onclick="calcArea();"> to calculate
➥circle area!</p>
<br>
<p>Click <input type="button" value="HERE" onclick="calcPeri();"> to calculate
➥circle perimeter!</p>
<br>
<p>Click <input type="button" value="HERE" onclick="calcVol();"> to calculate
➥sphere volume!</p>
</body>
</html>
```

Figure 9.4: *Further improvements to the circle calculator!*

Using the `random` Method

The `random` method is used to generate a pseudorandom between 0 (inclusive) and 1 (exclusive)—in other words, the number returned can be zero, but it will always be less than one (see Figure 9.5).

NOTE

The numbers generated aren't truly random (a Roulette wheel or throwing dice would give you a truly random number), hence the name *pseudorandom*. Pseudorandom numbers are generated using a specific algorithms, but they satisfy standard tests for statistical randomness.

Bottom line: They are about as random as you can get!

Using the `random` method is easy:

```
<script language="JavaScript">
<!-- Cloaking device on!
alert(Math.random());
// Cloaking device off -->
</script>
```

OUTPUT

Figure 9.5: Pseudorandom number generated by the random method.

EXAMPLE

If you want a random number integer between 0 and 10, you must multiply the random by 10 and then round it off using the `round` method (see Figure 9.6):

```
<script language="JavaScript">
<!-- Cloaking device on!
rndNum = Math.random();
rndNum = rndNum * 10;
alert(Math.round(rndNum));
// Cloaking device off -->
</script>
```

OUTPUT

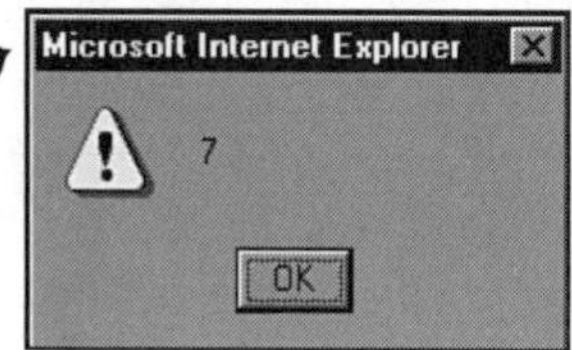

Figure 9.6: A pseudorandom number between 0 and 10.

Similarly, for a pseudorandom number between 0 and 100, you'd use the following code (see Figure 9.7):

```
<script language="JavaScript">
<!-- Cloaking device on!
rndNum = Math.random();
rndNum = rndNum * 100;
alert(Math.round(rndNum));
// Cloaking device off -->
</script>
```

Figure 9.7: *A pseudorandom number between 0 and 100.*

EXERCISE

Practice using the `Math` object in a few examples of your own. Expand on the examples given here and try out your own mathematical calculations, remembering to practice rounding off and perhaps using a few random numbers in your calculations.

The `Date` Object

The `Date` object offers you a wealth of date-related properties and methods.

To use the `Date` object, the first thing you must do is to assign it a variable name (similar to how you use the `Array` object):

```
<script language="JavaScript">
<!-- Cloaking device on!
dateVar = new Date();
// Cloaking device off -->
</script>
```

Now that you have done this, you can start to use the `Date` object.

NOTE

Using new `Date()` with no arguments returns the current date and time to which the system is set.

NOTE

The range of dates that can be represented in a `Date` object is approximately 285,616 years on either side of January 1, 1970!

Using the getFullYear Method

The first thing you can try out is retrieving the full year using the getFullYear method as follows (see Figure 9.8):

```
<script language="JavaScript">
<!-- Cloaking device on!
dateVar = new Date();
alert(dateVar.getFullYear());
// Cloaking device off -->
</script>
```

Figure 9.8: *The full year displayed in an alert box.*

Using this method returns a four-digit year irrespective of what year it is, getting around any Y2K issues. The getYear method, on the other hand, returns a two-digit year for the years 1900–1999. For dates outside that period, the four-digit year is returned. So, for example, 1995 is returned as 95, but 1825 and 2025 are returned as just that.

Using the getMonth Method

Using the getMonth method makes getting the month just as easy as getting the year. Using this method returns a number between 0 and 11 for January through December. Figure 9.9 shows the code in action.

CAUTION

Remember that the months start at 0 and not 1!

```
<script language="JavaScript">
<!-- Cloaking device on!
dateVar = new Date();
alert(dateVar.getMonth());
// Cloaking device off -->
</script>
```

Figure 9.9: *A digit representing the month displayed in an alert box.*

Using this number to display the actual month requires the use of `if` statements to test the result and assign the month name to a variable based on this condition. Here is a simple example (see Figure 9.10):

```
<script language="JavaScript">
<!-- Cloaking device on!
dateVar = new Date();
monthNow = dateVar.getMonth();
if (monthNow == 0)
{
txtMonth = "January";
}
if (monthNow == 1)
{
txtMonth = "February";
}
if (monthNow == 2)
{
txtMonth = "March";
}
if (monthNow == 3)
{
txtMonth = "April";
}
if (monthNow == 4)
{
txtMonth = "May";
}
if (monthNow == 5)
{
txtMonth = "June";
}
if (monthNow == 6)
{
txtMonth = "July";
}
if (monthNow == 7)
{
```

```
txtMonth = "August";
}
if (monthNow == 8)
{
txtMonth = "September";
}
if (monthNow == 9)
{
txtMonth = "October";
}
if (monthNow == 10)
{
txtMonth = "November";
}
if (monthNow == 11)
{
txtMonth = "December";
}
alert("The month now is: " + txtMonth);
// Cloaking device off -->
</script>
```

Figure 9.10: *The real month displayed.*

Using the getDay Method

Again, getDay method is similar to getMonth and getYear. This method returns a digit between 0 and 6, Sunday to Saturday (see Figure 9.11):

```
<script language="JavaScript">
<!-- Cloaking device on!
dateVar = new Date();
alert(dateVar.getDay());
// Cloaking device off -->
</script>
```

Figure 9.11: *A digit representing the day is displayed in an alert box.*

WARNING

It is vitally important to remember that Sunday is represented by a 0 in this example.

Hours, Minutes, Seconds... and Even Milliseconds!

Getting the current time using the `Date` object is another easy task!

The methods you use for this are `getHours`, `getMinutes`, `getSeconds`, and `getMilliseconds`. Here's an example:

```
<script language="JavaScript">
<!-- Cloaking device on!
dateVar = new Date();
alert("The time on your PC - accurate to the millisecond :-) is: " +
➥dateVar.getHours() + ":" + dateVar.getMinutes() + ":" + dateVar.getSeconds() +
➥":" + dateVar.getMilliseconds());
// Cloaking device off -->
</script>
```

Running this JavaScript gives you a very accurate time (well, as accurate as your PC clock is, anyway). See Figure 9.12 for an example.

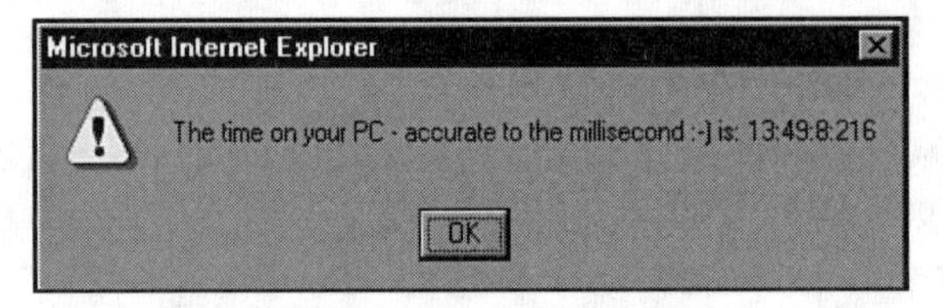

Figure 9.12: *A digit representing the hours, minutes, seconds, and milliseconds is displayed in an alert box.*

EXERCISE

Experiment with the various methods of the `Date` object in JavaScript examples of your own.

The String Object

The String object enables manipulation and formatting of text strings and also enables substrings within strings to be found.

The toUpperCase and toLowerCase Methods

Two of the simplest methods of the String objects are toUpperCase and toLowerCase. Here is a simple example in which the text inputted into a prompt box is converted to uppercase (shown in Figure 9.13):

```
<script language="JavaScript">
<!-- Cloaking device on!
inpTxt = prompt("Enter some text","HERE!");
alert(inpTxt.toUpperCase());
// Cloaking device off -->
</script>
```

Figure 9.13: *A string is converted to uppercase.*

And here is an example in which the text is converted to lowercase:

```
<script language="JavaScript">
<!-- Cloaking device on!
inpTxt = prompt("Enter some text","HERE!");
alert(inpTxt.toLowerCase());
// Cloaking device off -->
</script>
```

Figure 9.14 shows the code in action.

Figure 9.14: *A string is converted to lowercase.*

The `substring` Method

This method is used to return the substring at the specified location within a `String` object.

Here is the `substring` method in action, shown in Figure 9.15, retrieving a substring from an existing string:

```
<script language="JavaScript">
<!-- Cloaking device on!
inpTxt = "Hello there";
alert(inpTxt.substring(0, 5));
// Cloaking device off -->
</script>
```

Figure 9.15: *A substring extracted from a string.*

The `substring` method uses the two numbers in parentheses to locate the substring to withdraw from the string (see Figure 9.16). The first number is the starting location (counted from 0), starting at the beginning of the string. The second number is the ending location.

```
Hello there
012345678910

Hello
```

Figure 9.16: *A diagram showing how the substring is extracted from the string.*

NOTE

Later, you will see a much more visually exciting application of the `substring` method when we look at status bar scrollers!

NOTE

It is interesting to note that the `substring` method always uses the lower value to start from and proceeds to the larger value. This means that `inpTxt.substring(0, 4)` and `inpTxt.substring(4, 0)` return the same substring.

EXERCISE

Practice experimenting with the String object and especially pulling out substrings from strings. Try your hand at manipulating those strings with more code!

The with Statement

Turning back to statements for a short time, the with statement makes using objects in JavaScript easier by reducing the amount of code you have to write.

The with statement enables you to create a default object for a statement, thus simplifying the code and reducing the amount you have to type in.

The following is an example:

```
<script language="JavaScript">
<!-- Cloaking device on!
inp1 = prompt("Enter a number","Number goes here");
inp2 = prompt("Enter a number","Number goes here");
inp3 = prompt("Enter a number","Number goes here");
alert("The largest number entered was " + Math.max(inp1, inp2, inp3));
alert("The smallest number entered was " + Math.min(inp1, inp2, inp3));
// Cloaking device off -->
</script>
```

Using the with statement, the use of the Math object can be simplified as follows:

```
<script language="JavaScript">
<!-- Cloaking device on!
inp1 = prompt("Enter a number","Number goes here");
inp2 = prompt("Enter a number","Number goes here");
inp3 = prompt("Enter a number","Number goes here");
with (Math)
{
alert("The largest number entered was " + max(inp1, inp2, inp3));
alert("The smallest number entered was " + min(inp1, inp2, inp3));
}
// Cloaking device off -->
</script>
```

This might not seem like a substantial improvement, but if you intend to use JavaScript to work with multiple properties or methods then you will find using the with statement to be very beneficial!

Object Methods and Properties

Array Object

Properties

constructor Property | length Property | prototype Property

Methods

concat Method | join Method | pop Method | push Method | reverse Method | shift Method | slice Method | sort Method | splice Method | toLocaleString Method | toString Method | unshift Method | valueOf Method

Boolean Object

Properties

constructor Property | prototype Property

Methods

toString Method | valueOf Method

Date Object

Properties

constructor Property | prototype Property

Methods

getDate Method | getDay Method | getFullYear Method | getHours Method | getMilliseconds Method | getMinutes Method | getMonth Method | getSeconds Method | getTime Method | getTimezoneOffset Method | getUTCDate Method | getUTCDay Method | getUTCFullYear Method | getUTCHours Method | getUTCMilliseconds Method | getUTCMinutes Method | getUTCMonth Method | getUTCSeconds Method | getVarDate Method | getYear Method | setDate Method | setFullYear Method | setHours Method | setMilliseconds Method | setMinutes Method | setMonth Method | setSeconds Method | setTime Method | setUTCDate Method | setUTCFullYear Method | setUTCHours Method | setUTCMilliseconds Method | setUTCMinutes Method | setUTCMonth Method | setUTCSeconds Method | setYear Method | toGMTString Method | toLocaleString Method | toUTCString Method | toString Method | valueOf Method | parse Method | UTC Method

`Function` Object

Properties

`arguments` Property | `caller` Property | `constructor` Property | `prototype` Property

Methods

`toString` Method | `valueOf` Method

`Global` Object

Properties

`Infinity` Property | `NaN` Property

Methods

`escape` Method | `eval` Method | `isFinite` Method | `isNaN` Method | `parseFloat` Method | `parseInt` Method | `unescape` Method

`Math` Object

Properties

`E` Property | `LN2` Property | `LN10` Property | `LOG2E` Property | `LOG10E` Property | `PI` Property | `SQRT1_2` Property | `SQRT2` Property

Methods

`abs` Method | `acos` Method | `asin` Method | `atan` Method | `atan2` Method | `ceil` Method | `cos` Method | `exp` Method | `floor` Method | `log` Method | `max` Method | `min` Method | `pow` Method | `random` Method | `round` Method | `sin` Method | `sqrt` Method | `tan` Method

`Number` Object

Properties

`MAX_VALUE` Property | `MIN_VALUE` Property | `NaN` Property | `NEGATIVE_INFINITY` Property | `POSITIVE_INFINITY` Property | `constructor` Property | `prototype` Property

Methods

`toLocaleString` Method | `toString` Method | `valueOf` Method

Object Object

Properties

prototype Property | constructor Property

Methods

toLocaleString Method | toString Method | valueOf Method

RegExp Object

Properties

$1–$9 Properties | index Property | input Property | lastIndex Property | lastMatch Property | lastParen Property | leftContext Property | rightContext Property

Methods

The RegExp object has no methods.

String Object

Properties

constructor Property | length Property | prototype Property

Methods

anchor Method | big Method | blink Method | bold Method | charAt Method | charCodeAt Method | concat Method | fixed Method | fontcolor Method | fontsize Method | fromCharCode Method | indexOf Method | italics Method | lastIndexOf Method | link Method | match Method | replace Method | search Method | slice Method | small Method | split Method | strike Method | sub Method | substr Method | substring Method | sup Method | toLowerCase Method | toUpperCase Method | toString Method | valueOf Method

What's Next

With so much JavaScript in your Web pages, you'll undoubtedly encounter problems. Therefore, in the next chapter, you look at JavaScript bugs and see how to find them, as well as how to kill them!

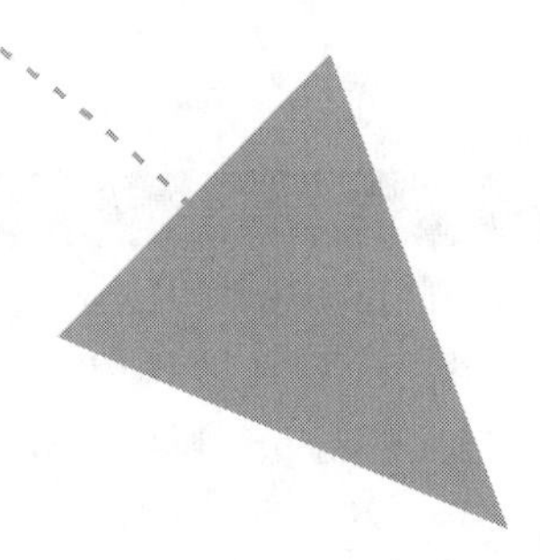

10

Bugs—How to Find Them and Kill Them

Now that you have had plenty of opportunity to work with JavaScript code, you probably have come across problems with your code. These bugs can be irritating, and they might seem hard to find, but by the end of this chapter you will be a world-class JavaScript bug buster!

This chapter teaches you about the following:

- What bugs are
- Debugging with Internet Explorer and Netscape Navigator
- Using the Microsoft Script Debugger
- Common JavaScript errors

What Are Bugs?

Bugs are problems with code, and the process of tracking down these bugs and destroying them is called *debugging*. But why such a strange analogy?

Well, in reality, no one really knows, but the term's origin has been wrongly attributed to the mid-40s pioneer programmer Grace Hopper. In 1944, Grace Hopper, a young Naval Reserve officer (she later became Admiral Hopper), was working on the Mark I computer at Harvard as one of the first people to write computer programs for it. While she was working with the later Mark II, a technician is said to have pulled a moth from between two electrical relays in the computer, the "bug" that was keeping the program from running. This moth was apparently kept on display by the Navy for many years and is now the property of the Smithsonian.

Debugging is the name given to the process of finding and fixing (or sometimes bypassing) these computer bugs.

NOTE

Don't be put off by bugs in your JavaScript. It's easy to get disheartened in the beginning, but rest assured, you'll soon develop an eye for them and be able to spot them early on before they become a problem.

Types of Bugs

Just like the real world, which has many species of creepy-crawlies, the computer world has many types of computer bugs. There are, in fact, a few different "species" of computer bugs. Some of the most common are

- Syntax errors
- Runtime errors
- Logic errors
- Incorrect use of operator precedence

Let's take a look at what each of these means.

Introducing Syntax Errors

Syntax errors are the most common type of error programmers come across. *Syntax* is the rules of grammar and spelling for a computer language, and, because computers are more picky about language than we humans, you need to be very careful when communicating with them. You have to learn to obey their rules. This means, for instance, that when you use a string, you must enclose it in quotes. And there is no point thinking you can leave out one of the quotes—the computer will catch you!

JavaScript code is examined for syntax errors as it is being loaded into the browser, so any errors show up quickly.

The following is an example of such an error:

```
txtString = "Hello there
```

Another example of a syntax error is poor spelling:

```
fnction callMe()
{
alert("This script has a syntax error in the spelling of function");
}
```

Runtime Errors

Runtime errors occur as the JavaScript script tries to perform something the system cannot do. They are called runtime errors because they can occur at any time during the lifetime of the script.

A common example of a runtime error is trying to call a function that doesn't exist (such as when you misspell the function name):

```
<html>
<head>
<title>A Simple Page</title>
<script language="JavaScript">
<!-- Cloaking device on!
function myFuncion()
{
alert("Hello there");
}
// Cloaking device off -->
</script>
</head>
<body onLoad="myFunction()">

</body>
</html>
```

Logic Errors

Logic errors aren't really JavaScript errors but errors in the way the script works. You might have a script that calculates sales tax, but instead of adding it to the total, the script subtracts it. This is a logic error.

Operator Precedence

Operator precedence is similar to a logic error but relates to how operators are dealt with in mathematics.

The following is an example:

```
ans = num1 - num2 * num3;
```

If you assign arbitrary numbers to num1, num2, and num3—say 3, 1, and 6—what will the answer be? Will it be 12 (3 minus 1 equals 2, multiplied by 6) or -3 (6 multiplied by -1 equals -6, plus 3)? In fact, the answer will be -3 because of the order in which operators are processed. Multiplication is carried out before subtraction.

The order of operator *importance* is as follows:

- ()—Grouping
- -- and ++—Unary operators
- *, /, and %—Multiplication, division, and modulo division
- + and -—Addition and subtraction
- <, <=, >, and >=—Less than, less than or equal to, greater than, and greater than or equal to
- == and !=—Equality and inequality
- &&—Logical AND
- ||—Logical OR
- ?:—Conditional

NOTE

Those of you familiar with algebraic precedence will find this list familiar because they are the same.

Parentheses are used to alter the order of evaluation determined by operator precedence. This means an expression within parentheses is evaluated before its value is used in the remainder of the expression. So, if you wanted the previous example to equal 12, you would write it as follows:

```
ans = (num1 - num2) * num3;
```

The following example proves this point (see Figures 10.1 and 10.2):

```
<script language="JavaScript">
<!-- Cloaking device on!
alert(3 - 1 * 6);
alert((3 - 1) * 6);
// Cloaking device off -->
</script>
```

*Figure 10.1: An alert box showing 3 - 1 * 6 equals -3.*

*Figure 10.2: An alert box showing (3 - 1) * 6 equals 12.*

Finding Errors

Let's take a look at how Netscape Navigator 4, Netscape Navigator 6, and Internet Explorer 5.5 handle the following error:

```
<script language="JavaScript">
<!-- Cloaking device on!
alrtt("This will not work!");
// Cloaking device off -->
</script>
```

Here, notice a simple syntax error—the spelling of "alert."

Figure 10.3 shows this error as handled by Netscape Navigator 4.

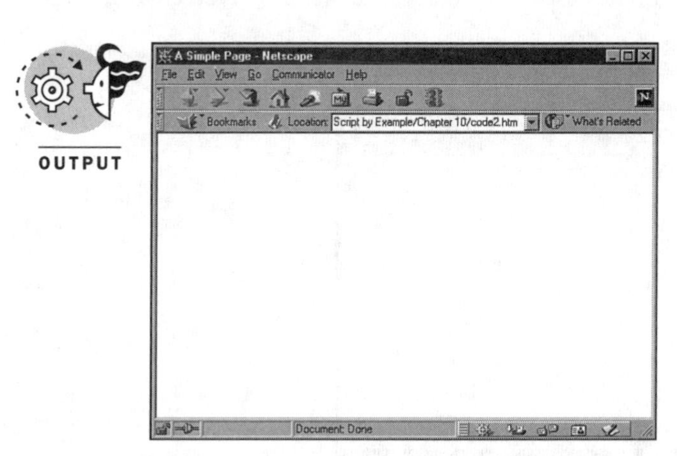

Figure 10.3: A Web page with a syntax error in Netscape Navigator 4.

As you can see from Figure 10.3, there are no visible signs of the error. Well, that isn't really true. To begin with, the alert box hasn't appeared and there was a brief flash of text in the status bar of the browser (where you now see the text "Document: Done") saying "Javascript error. Type 'javascript:' into Location for details" (you need fast eyes to see this). If you type **`javascript`** into the location bar (where you type in URLs), you get the message shown in Figure 10.4.

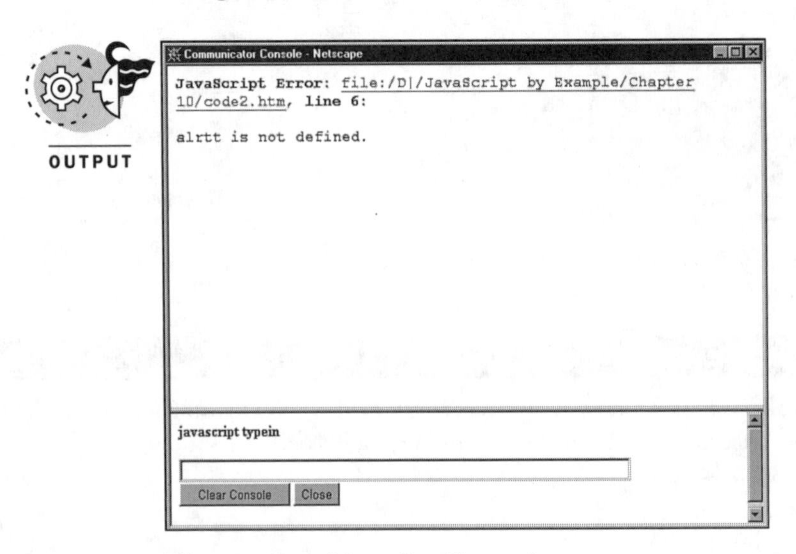

Figure 10.4: *More details on the error.*

The Communicator console shown in Figure 10.4 tells you a bit more about the error—but you've got to know where to go to get this information!

Next, Figure 10.5 shows the same error as seen by Netscape Navigator 6.

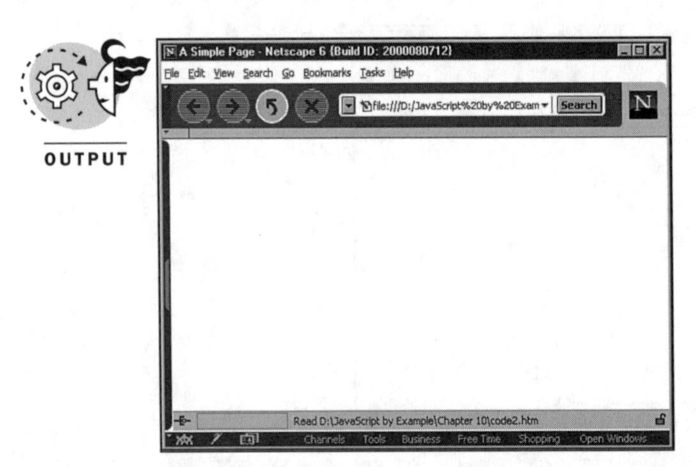

Figure 10.5: *Again, no obvious error appears on the page.*

This time, no alert box appears, nor does anything else from Netscape Navigator 6. But if you type **`javascript:`** into the location bar, a console appears (see Figure 10.6).

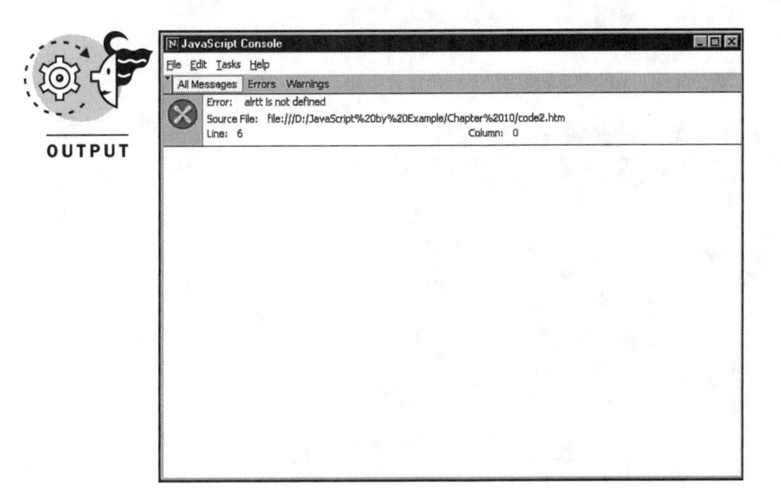

Figure 10.6: *Again, nothing obvious is shown.*

NOTE

At the time of this writing, Netscape Navigator is in a preview release and the final release might behave differently, although typing `javascript:` into the location bar probably will not change.

Finally, Figure 10.7 shows the error handled in Internet Explorer 5.5. Loading the same page into this browser flashes the text "Done, but with errors on the page" in the status bar. This is replaced by the word "Done" but with an exclamation mark icon next to it.

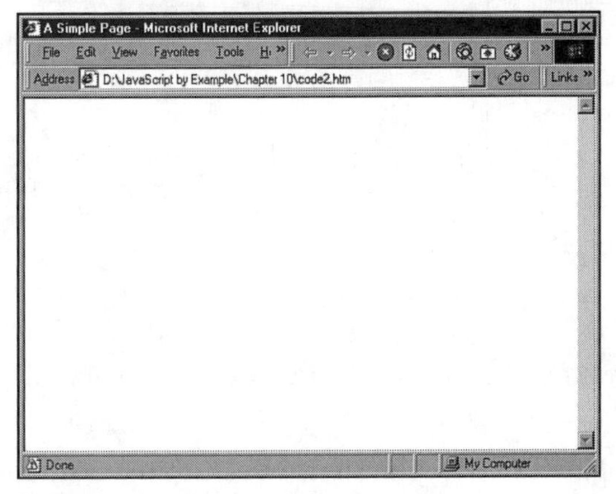

Figure 10.7: *Internet Explorer 5.5 has a status bar error message icon.*

Double-clicking this icon brings up a dialog box giving you details about the error (see Figure 10.8).

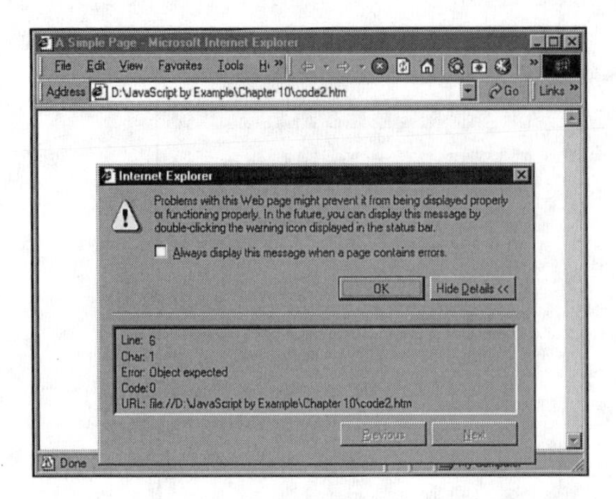

Figure 10.8: *A dialog box gives details of errors.*

Narrowing Down Errors

Have you noticed how all three browsers point to the same line as the one containing the error—line 6? This is, in fact, where the error actually occurs (see Figure 10.9).

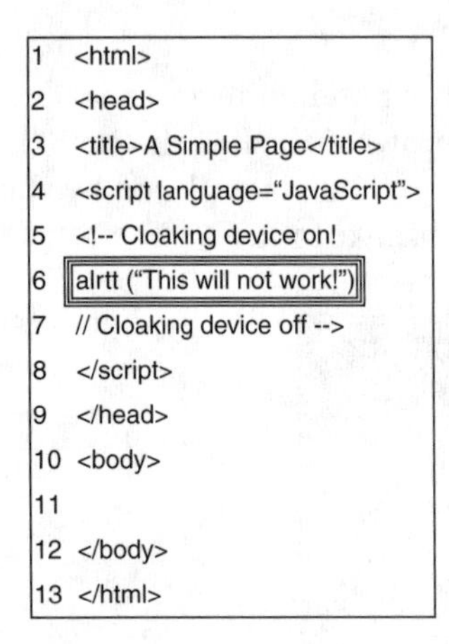

```
1  <html>
2  <head>
3  <title>A Simple Page</title>
4  <script language="JavaScript">
5  <!-- Cloaking device on!
6  alrtt ("This will not work!")
7  // Cloaking device off -->
8  </script>
9  </head>
10 <body>
11
12 </body>
13 </html>
```

Figure 10.9: *Line 6 contains the error.*

This is good news for the JavaScripter. However, every silver lining has a cloud or two:

- You must open the file and count lines until you find the error.

- The information it provides isn't clear.
- It isn't always accurate.

However, Internet Explorer users can take advantage of a program developed by Microsoft to help programmers debug Web pages. This program is called the Microsoft Script Debugger.

TIP

Download the Microsoft Script Debugger from `http://www.Microsoft.com/scripting` —it's free!

The Microsoft Script Debugger

It's suggested that you download and install the Microsoft Script Debugger before continuing further with this chapter. The installation is a simple process: Run the executable file that you downloaded and follow the onscreen wizard that guides you through the installation process.

A final step you might have to take is to check your browser setting with regards to script debugging. Click Tools and choose Internet Options (see Figure 10.10).

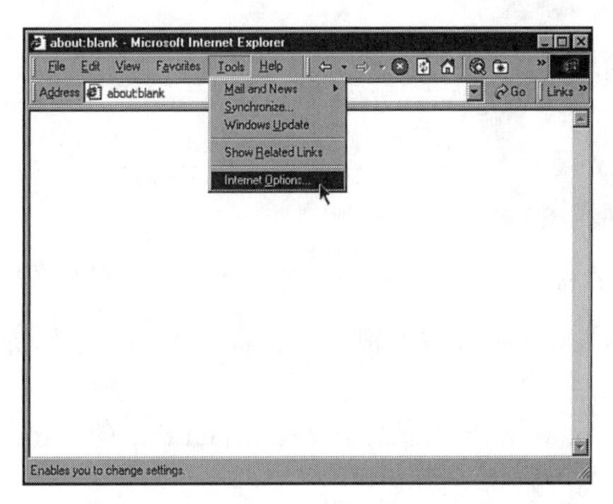

Figure 10.10: *Choose Tools and go to Internet Options.*

Click the Advanced tab and make sure that Disable Script Debugging is unchecked (see Figure 10.11).

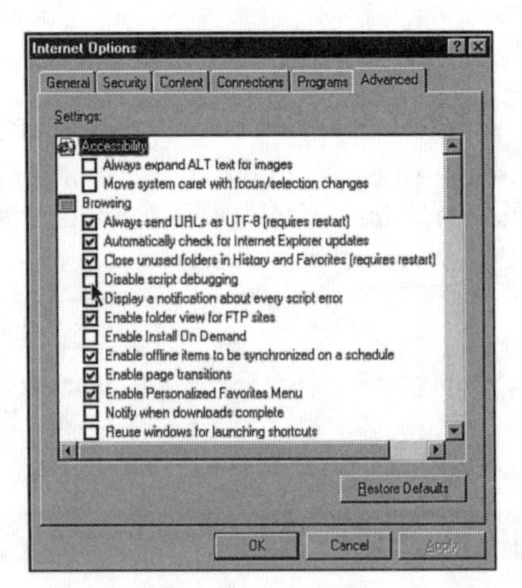

Figure 10.11: *Make sure that Disable Script Debugging is unchecked.*

Now you're ready to start using the Microsoft Script Debugger! Take the simple syntax error example you used earlier and load it into Internet Explorer again. When you load this page into Internet Explorer now, you see a dialog box giving you the option to debug the page, as shown in Figure 10.12.

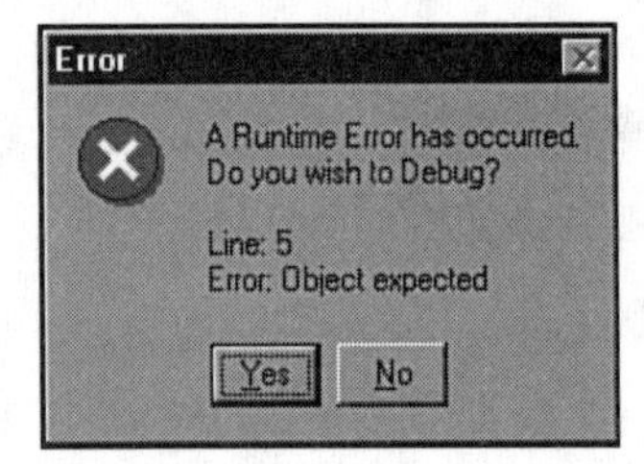

Figure 10.12: *A dialog box gives you the option to debug the page.*

If you click OK, the Script Debugger opens and the error on the page is highlighted (see Figure 10.13).

After you have spotted the error, you can open the relevant file and make the changes to the JavaScript.

NOTE

Pages are opened as read-only in the Script Debugger and therefore cannot be edited in the window. You must return to the actual file and make any necessary changes there.

Although the Microsoft Script Debugger is a tool with many uses (which include debugging server-side ASP pages), it is also useful to client-side JavaScripters. This is because it dramatically reduces the time it takes to debug JavaScript projects.

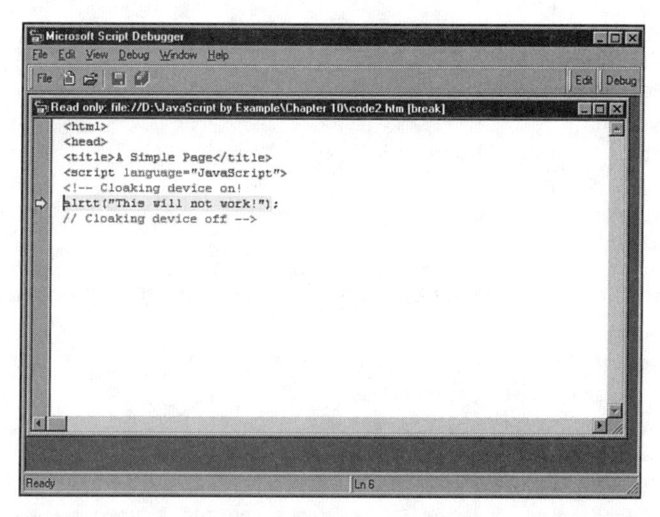

Figure 10.13: *A page with errors opened in the Microsoft Script Debugger.*

Common Errors

What follows are examples of the most common errors that newcomers to JavaScript make. They are presented to you so you will be aware of these kinds of errors and can avoid them as you write your code. They aren't presented in any sort of technical order and aren't a complete list by far, but if you can learn to identify these, your JavaScript projects will have a much better chance of working the first time.

Typos and Spellos!

Most of the errors you'll encounter when writing JavaScript (if you follow the examples laid down here) will probably fall into these categories. Typos occur when you accidentally hit the wrong key or combination of keys while typing. Examples of typos are such things as

- Pressing the wrong key:

```
<html>
<head>
<title>A Simple Page</title>
<script language="JavaScript">
<!-- Cloaking device on!
function myFunction()
{
//Hitting the wrong key when closing the parentheses below
alert("Hello there"_;
```

```
}
// Cloaking device off -->
</script>
</head>
<body onLoad="myFunction()">

</body>
</html>
```

- Forgetting to press Shift, such as before the curly bracket:

```
<html>
<head>
<title>A Simple Page</title>
<script language="JavaScript">
<!-- Cloaking device on!
function myFunction()
//Forgetting to press Shift before the curly bracket
 [
alert("Hello there");
}
// Cloaking device off -->
</script>
</head>
<body onLoad="myFunction()">

</body>
</html>
```

- hAVING cAPS lOCK oN:

```
<html>
<head>
<title>A Simple Page</title>
<script language="JavaScript">
<!-- Cloaking device on!
//Having Caps Lock on!
FUNCTION MYFUNCTION()
{
alert("Hello there");
}
// Cloaking device off -->
</script>
</head>
<body onLoad="myFunction()">

</body>
</html>
```

- Typing in the wrong mathematical operator (especially when using the numeric keypad):

```
<html>
<head>
<title>A Simple Page</title>
<script language="JavaScript">
<!-- Cloaking device on!
function myFunction()
{
//Concatenation operator wrong!
alert("Hello" - " there");
}
// Cloaking device off -->
</script>
</head>
<body onLoad="myFunction()">

</body>
</html>
```

Spellos are different from typos because spellos occur when you have spelled something incorrectly that perhaps you typed in correctly earlier. Examples include the following:

- Built-in methods and functions:

```
<html>
<head>
<title>A Simple Page</title>
<script language="JavaScript">
<!-- Cloaking device on!
function myFunction()
{
//That's not how alert is supposed to be spelled
alerg("Hello there");
}
// Cloaking device off -->
</script>
</head>
<body onLoad="myFunction()">

</body>
</html>
```

- Variables:

```
<html>
<head>
<title>A Simple Page</title>
```

```
<script language="JavaScript">
<!-- Cloaking device on!
function myFunction()
{
var msg = "Hello there";
//Wrong variable name
alert(mssg);
}
// Cloaking device off -->
</script>
</head>
<body onLoad="myFunction()">

</body>
</html>
```

Another that can occur is using the wrong bracket. Remember, JavaScript uses three types:

- ( )
- { }
- [ ]

And they are not interchangeable—you must use the correct one:

```
<html>
<head>
<title>A Simple Page</title>
<script language="JavaScript">
<!-- Cloaking device on!
function myFunction()
//Wrong bracket
(
var msg = "Hello there"
alert(msg);
// ... and here
)
// Cloaking device off -->
</script>
</head>
<body onLoad="myFunction()">

</body>
</html>
```

These are just a few examples of errors that beginners frequently make (as well as those who are not beginners!). Recognize them and your JavaScript will be a lot less buggy!

EXERCISE

Look over your examples from the past chapters and try to recall some of the difficulties you had. Was there something you did on a regular basis? Perhaps it was that you used the wrong bracket or continually misspelled a property or method. Maybe it was that you typed the wrong operator. If you made a mistake or an error on a consistent basis, spend a few minutes working on it—you'll be impressed by the results.

What's Next

Now that you have the basics of debugging under your belt, it's time to start thinking outside the box and look at different ways to add JavaScript to a Web page.

Where Does JavaScript Go?

Going Beyond the Box (or Should That Be Head?)

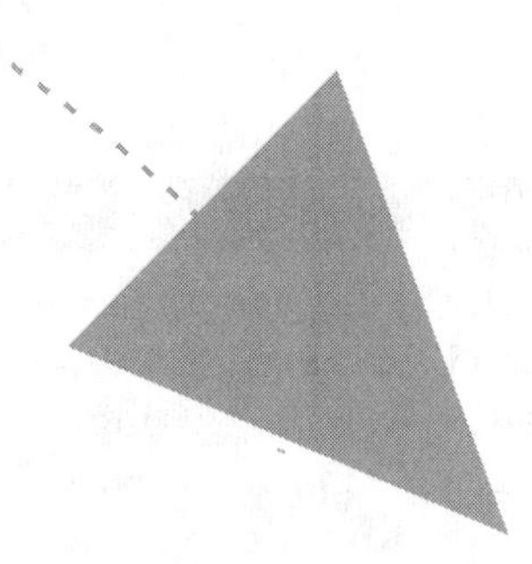

11

Going Beyond the Box (or Should That Be Head?)

Well done! You've made it this far! In this, a very short and quick chapter, you're not looking at any new JavaScript. No, what you're going to be looking at here is where you can place your JavaScript.

So far, all the JavaScript you've looked at has been confined to the header of the Web page, imprisoned in between `<script>` tags. Now it's time to look at how you can write JavaScript that can break out of these constraints.

This chapter teaches you about the following:

- What other ways you can add JavaScript to a Web page
- How to create a `.JS` file and link it to a Web page
- How to write inline JavaScript
- The advantages and disadvantages of each method

Thinking Outside the <head>!

Apart from being nestled inside `<script>` tags, JavaScript can be put in two other places to run in a Web page. It can either be in a completely separate file altogether and the JavaScript code linked to the Web page using HTML (in a similar way to how images are separate files but appear as part of the main Web page) or be inline in the `<body>` tag inside other appropriate HTML elements. Both methods have their own advantages and disadvantages, and by the end of this chapter, you'll have a pretty good idea of when and where to use each method. Both ways are easy, and you'll be using them within no time at all!

So, let's begin by looking at how to link JavaScript to the Web page.

Linking, Linking, Linking!

Linking your JavaScript to a Web page involves writing your JavaScript in a separate file and linking the Web page and this file together. Simple in concept and simple in practice!

Some conventions must be followed—well, one in fact. The file that will contain your JavaScript should have the file extension `.JS`. Those of you who like investigating how things work and why things don't will find that other file extensions will work. However, `.JS` is the recommended one to use!

WARNING

If you find that any of your linked scripts don't work, before you start to rip apart the code you've written looking for errors, check that you are referring to the correct file. A common error here is to save the file containing the JavaScript with one filename and try to link to it using another.

Whether your examples are simple or complex, the linking works in the same way. Take a look at the step-by-step creation of the following example:

1. Use your favorite text editor (we will be using faithful old Windows Notepad) and type in your JavaScript (see Figure 11.1). You don't need a `<script>` block or comment tags or anything. Type it in directly!

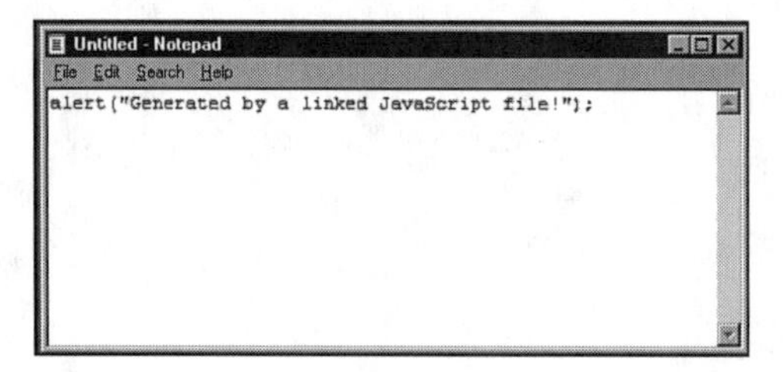

***Figure 11.1:** Some simple JavaScript typed into a text editor.*

2. Save the file as `first.js` in the same location that you will be creating your HTML page.

3. Open your standard template HTML page in the text editor. You should see the following:

```
<html>
<head>
<title>A Simple Page</title>
<script language="JavaScript">
<!-- Cloaking device on!

// Cloaking device off -->
</script>
</head>
<body>

</body>
</html>
```

4. Take out the comment tags that are in between the `<script>` block; these are not required for linking:

```
<html>
<head>
<title>A Simple Page</title>
<script language="JavaScript">
</script>
</head>
<body>

</body>
</html>
```

5. Linking a JavaScript file uses the `src` attribute of the `script` tag (in much the same way as you use the `src` attribute of the `img` tag to bring images into a page). Make the `src` attribute point to the `.JS` file.

6. Save both files and load the HTML page into the browser. As the page loads, the alert box is displayed showing that the JavaScript has been executed (see Figure 11.2).

That's it! There's nothing more to it! It really is as simple as remembering a few points:

- You type your JavaScript into a text editor.
- No `<script>` tags or HTML comment tags are required in the `.JS` file.
- You can comment your code in the same way as you normally do, using `//` or `/* */`.

- You must save the file with the `.JS` extension.
- Remember to point to the correct file using the `src` attribute of the `<script>` tag.

Simple!

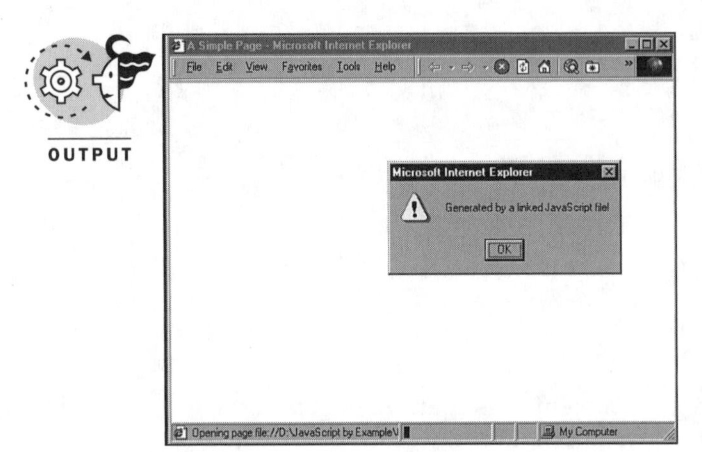

***Figure 11.2:** An alert box is displayed when a linked JavaScript file is executed.*

WARNING

Remember that word processors (such as Microsoft Word and Lotus WordPro) aren't ideal text editors for writing JavaScript because they format the contents of documents. This formatting can cause problems.

To avoid these problems, always use a simple text editor for creating HTML files and `.JS` files!

EXERCISE

Take a look at some of your previous JavaScript examples and put the JavaScript into an external `.JS` file. Go through the process of pulling the JavaScript out of the HTML page and placing it into the new document. Save the file with the `.JS` extension and link to it using the `src` attribute in the `<script>` tag.

Inline JavaScript

Inline JavaScript is JavaScript that has been typed directly into the HTML tags of a Web page. This method is again simple, but what it gains in simplicity it lacks in power. Inline JavaScript is best suited to simple examples, and any complex JavaScript is best left to one of the other methods.

Here is an example of an inline JavaScript that brings up a prompt box:

```
<html>
<head>
<title>A Simple Page</title>
<script language="JavaScript">
<!-- Cloaking device on!

// Cloaking device off -->
</script>
</head>
<body>
<p onclick="prompt('How many do you want', 'Enter quantity');">
➥Click here to specify quantity</p>
</body>
</html>
```

Clicking the text on the page brings up the prompt box, as shown in Figure 11.3.

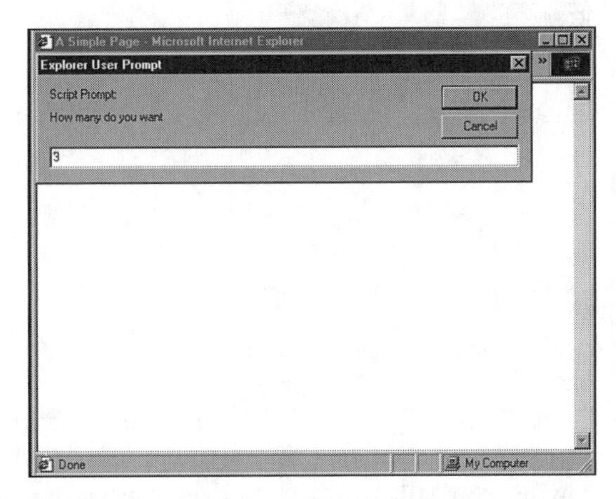

Figure 11.3: *A prompt box is displayed when text is clicked.*

Notice how all the JavaScript is in the body of the page. There is no JavaScript in the `<script>` block at all. Everything is triggered by the one `onclick` event in the `<p>` tag. Here is a more complex example in which the cost of an order is determined based on the number of units required:

```
<html>
<head>
<title>A Simple Page</title>
<script language="JavaScript">
<!-- Cloaking device on!
```

```
// Cloaking device off -->
</script>
</head>
<body>
<p onclick="units = prompt('How many do you want','Enter quantity');
➥alert('Cost per unit is $9.99, therefore total cost for ' + units +
➥' is $' + units * 9.99);">Click here to specify quantity</p>
</body>
</html>
```

Notice how the second statement in this JavaScript example comes after the semicolon on the same line, instead of being on a separate line (see Figure 11.4).

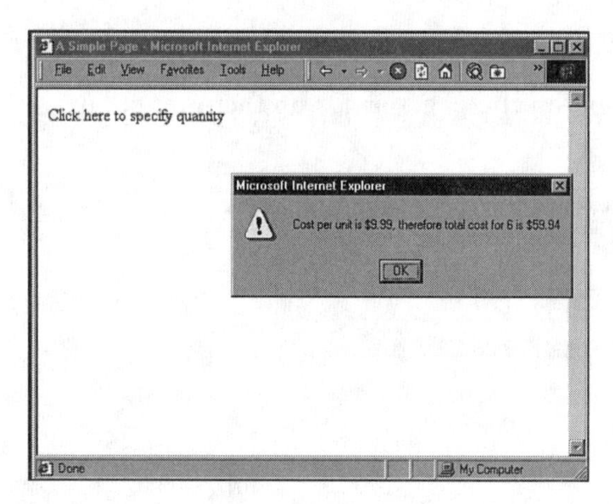

Figure 11.4: *Modified JavaScript in action.*

As you can see from the previous example, inline JavaScript enables you to add small snippets of JavaScript to a Web page quickly and easily. You can simply add them wherever you want, whenever you want.

When to Use Your <head>, When to Link, and When to Make It Inline!

The problem with having choices is knowing which one to choose! Fortunately, by following a few quick and simple rules of thumb, you can come to the right conclusion.

Rule of Thumb 1

If the JavaScript you are using is large, forget inline and go for the `<head>` or linked file.

Rule of Thumb 2

If you want to add the same JavaScript to many HTML pages, linked files will make adding and updating scripts easy.

Rule of Thumb 3

Want to add a small, one-off JavaScript to a page? Use inline code.

Rule of Thumb 4

Remember that you can mix and match the three types. Use linked files for most of JavaScript you reuse from one page to the next, put other bulky JavaScript in the `<head>`, and put one-off JavaScripts inline.

Rule of Thumb 5

If in doubt, put it in the `<head>`!

TIP

Having all three on the go in one page might seem complicated at first, but very quickly you get the hang of it; the trick is to practice, practice, practice!

EXERCISE

Here's a simple exercise. Revisit some of the examples you created in previous chapters and decide which of the three options would be the best to use (you don't need to actually do it; just go through the thought process). Which ones are best suited to inline JavaScript? Which ones are best suited to linked files? Which ones are best left in the `<head>`?

What's Next

You know JavaScript! Now you can start to really use the power JavaScript gives you by combining it with the power of Dynamic HTML!

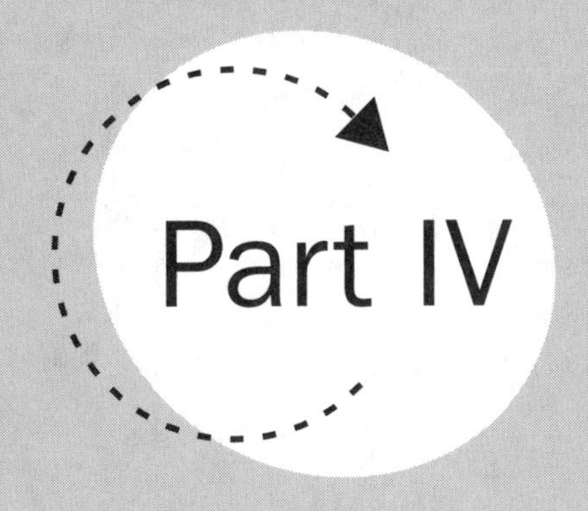

JavaScript and Dynamic HTML

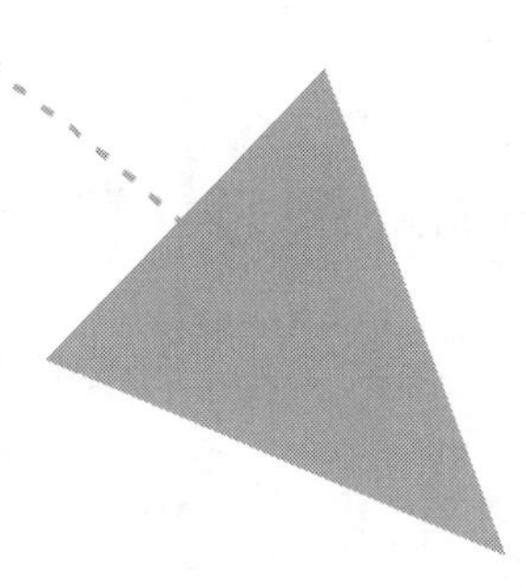

12

Dynamic HTML and JavaScript

So far, almost everything you've looked at has been pure JavaScript (okay, some aspects, such as alert, confirm, and prompt boxes aren't strictly JavaScript, but without some input and output it's hard to do anything). JavaScript is powerful and can do a lot, but have you noticed a lack of actual integration with the browser? That's because up until now, you've been looking solely at what JavaScript can do and how to do it (bear in mind that a few years ago, the kind of things we've looked at as examples so far were the limits of what you could do with JavaScript!). The next, and final, step is to combine JavaScript and HTML and the technologies provided by the browser to create the hybrid technology Dynamic HTML (DHTML)!

This chapter teaches you about the following:

- What DHTML is
- What technologies make up DHTML
- Some of the things that are possible with DHTML

The World of DHTML

Dynamic HTML is a collective term. It consists of a combination of new HTML tags and options and programming—provided by script—which lets you create Web pages that are more animated, interactive, and responsive than ever before. DHTML can even go as far as allowing Web pages to act and feel just like other applications run on the computer, blurring the divide between the hard drive and the Internet.

The features that combine to form DHTML first appeared in Netscape Navigator 4 and Microsoft Internet Explorer 4. Although the core of DHTML, having its footing in the HTML 4.0 standard, was supported by both browsers, additional technologies are supported by only one browser or the other. This is one of the problems facing developers when they use DHTML on their Web pages; the other major problem is that many Web users out there are not using the latest browser and are still using a version 3 browser or earlier.

NOTE

The issues surrounding DHTML for the various browsers (not just the differences between Internet Explorer and Navigator but also across the versions) is a book or two in its own right! What you cover here is how to write JavaScript that will interact with the various DHTML technologies. As far as is possible, examples will work on all browsers.

For an in-depth look at proprietary DHTML technologies, surf over to `http://msdn.microsoft.com/workshop` for information on Internet Explorer and `http://developer.netscape.com` for information on Netscape Navigator.

The Concepts and Features of DHTML

Microsoft and Netscape DHTML comprises the following:

- An object-oriented view of a Web page and all its elements
- Cascading style sheets (CSS) and layering of content
- Scripting that can address all (or at least most) of the page elements
- Dynamic fonts

NOTE

Dynamic fonts are not covered in this book.

TIP

Many of you might already be familiar with these technologies; if so, you're welcome to skip over this section or follow along with the rest of us.

An Object-Oriented View of Page Elements

Each element on the page (division or section, heading, paragraph, image, list, forms, and so on) is viewed as an *object*.

NOTE

Microsoft calls this the *Dynamic HTML Object Model*; Netscape calls it the *HTML Object Model*; and the W3C (the Web standards organization) calls it the *Document Object Model*. These are all different names for the same thing; go figure!

For example, each hyperlink, heading, or paragraph of text on a page can be named, given attributes of text style and color, and addressed by name in a script included on the page. This script can be written in one of many languages (for example, VBScript), but here of course you will look at using JavaScript to do this! This element on the page can then be changed as the result of a specified event, such a mouse passing over it, being clicked, a key being pressed, or a period of time elapsing.

Not only can text wording and color be changed, but everything contained within the object can be replaced with new content that includes new or additional HTML, as well as different text and images.

Style Sheets and Layering

A *style sheet* is used to describe the default style characteristics of a document or a portion of a document. This includes page layout, font type style, and size for text elements.

In as far as Web pages go, a style sheet also describes, among other things, the default background color or image that is on the page, hyperlink colors, and so on. Style sheets are a great way to ensure consistency across all or a group of pages in a document or a Web site because one style sheet can be attached to many or all of the documents making up the site.

NOTE

Just as you can have JavaScript in the page header, inline, or linked, the same is true for style sheets—which makes them very useful and versatile, indeed!

Layering is the use of style sheets to vary the content of a Web page by providing content *layers*. These layers (with each layer having its own content, such as text or images) can overlay other layers to replace them or superimpose on top of existing content. Layers can be programmed to appear as a result of user interaction with the page (such as clicking a button) or as part of a presentation.

Scripts

Scripts are the third component of DHTML and the focus of this book. Scripting has been around for some time now and in various forms (JavaScript, VBScript, Java applet, ActiveX controls, and so on), but DHTML provides an increased amount of programming power to Web pages because most elements of a page can be addressed by a simple script.

Why Do Differences Exist Between the Browsers?

A question often asked by newcomers to Web development is, "Why are there differences between Netscape Navigator and Microsoft's Internet Explorer?" The short, simple answer is that there just are differences. The longer answer involves looking at the history of the browsers and the manufacturers. Just like every other software package you use, each browser manufacturer has a different way of doing things and adds their own bells and whistles to the browser. Take two word processors, for example. The interface will be different, and so will the file formats. The buttons and hot keys will also differ, and as a result, people will have a favorite word processor they will use on a regular basis and will dislike changing brands. If all word processors were the same, the only thing that would make them unique would be their flaws.

The same thing happened with browsers, with both Netscape and Microsoft adding their own features and developing their own technologies. A race was on to create a browser that users would like, with technologies that developers wanted to use. However, what wasn't important was compatibility, and it has only been in recent years that companies have seen an advantage in following standards to make the developers' and the users' lives a little easier.

How would it be if several different TV standards existed and you could watch certain programs only if you had the right TV? Would you be expected to have three or four different TVs, just so you had all the standards and technologies covered? No, that wouldn't work, and likewise with the Web: Both users and developers were getting tired of the ever-widening gap between the browsers.

Fortunately, this gap has started to close, but it will take a few more years before the gap in technologies and standards is small enough not to make a difference.

But then, adding to the difficulty, you still have to consider all the users who don't upgrade their browsers to the latest version.

What Can You Do with DHTML?

Really, the possibilities are almost limitless. Web pages are now closer to being miniapplications than they are static documents. If you surf around the Web for a while, you'll come across all sorts of examples of DHTML put to good (and bad) use. Slide shows, Web sites with custom interfaces, image rollovers and animations, interactive presentations of text on the screen, games, form checking, and calculators are all possible, and much, much more!

In the remaining chapters of this book, you will see JavaScript put into action on some of the most common Web tasks asked of it by users while learning how and why it works.

TIP

Go on, go on an Internet safari, hunting for technology and see what you can find. Revisit some of your favorite sites and see how much interactivity and DHTML they use. What do you like? What do you want to try out for yourself?

To make DHTML work, JavaScript needs to interact with two key technologies. These are the object model of the browser and the style sheet information on the page (which is also part of the Document Object Model). The object model controls the browser and the document within it, whereas the style sheet controls the formatting and layout of elements on the page.

What's Next

In the next chapter, you discover how to use style sheets and see how JavaScript can be used to take control over them and start to make your Web pages dynamic!

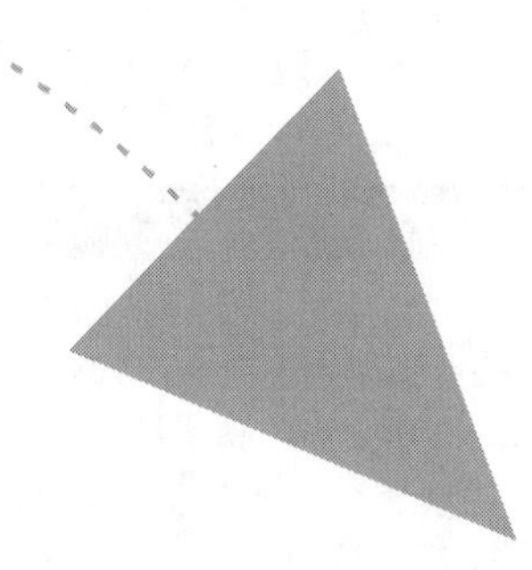

13

Cascading Style Sheets and JavaScript!

Cascading Style Sheets (also known as style sheets or CSS) are probably the best possible way to format HTML documents. Not only is CSS fast and easy to use, but it is also the best way to achieve a consistent look and feel for your entire Web site.

This chapter teaches you about the following:

- A little CSS history
- An introduction to CSS
- How CSS and JavaScript can interact together
- JavaScript/CSS examples

A Little Cascading Style Sheets History

Adopted as a standard in December 1996 by the W3C Consortium, CSS Level 1 took a major step forward by separating the content of a Web page (text, images, and so on) from the formatting of the page (layout and text enhancements, such as font information). This returned HTML back to being simply function oriented (as opposed to form oriented), but at the same time enabled users to have near-total control over how the page looked.

In May 1998, the CSS standards were changed and CSS2 was adopted, which gave the Web developer even more control over Web pages. This standard built on the existing CSS Level 1 and added functionality, such as the ability to precisely position elements and objects on a Web page and aural style sheets that allowed screen reading software to read the contents of a Web page (which is useful for visually impaired Web surfers).

NOTE

This book cannot possibly cover CSS in its entirety—CSS itself is a vast and technically rich technology. So, all we can hope to do is give you a taste of it. Fortunately, the Web has many good CSS resources that can help. Here are just a few of the good, CSS-related Web resources that Microsoft offers:

`http://msdn.microsoft.com/workshop/author/css/usingcss.asp`
`http://msdn.microsoft.com/workshop/author/css/css.asp`
`http://msdn.microsoft.com/workshop/author/css/reference/attributes.asp`

Netscape also offers a good CSS resource, which can be found at

`http://developer.netscape.com/tech/css/`

These links are correct at the time of this writing but are subject to change.

TIP

Don't worry if you don't already know CSS. This chapter doesn't assume you know anything about it. However, by the end of this chapter, you will have a few CSS tips and tricks to add to your Web development tool belt that you can use immediately in your Web projects. You can then take your time and learn how to make full use of CSS in your own time.

Introduction to CSS

On the face of it, CSS might seem complicated, but fortunately, it isn't! In its simplest form, adding CSS to a Web page is as simple as adding some new attributes to existing HTML tags.

Consider this simple Web page:

```
<html>
<head>
<title>A Simple Page</title>
<script language="JavaScript">
<!-- Cloaking device on!

// Cloaking device off -->
</script>
</head>
<body>
<h1>Welcome to this page!</h1>
<p>A lot of interesting text goes here! A lot of interesting text goes here!
➥A lot of interesting text goes here! A lot of interesting text goes here!
➥A lot of interesting text goes here!</p>
</body>
</html>
```

Say you want to give the heading an underline using CSS. To do that, you first must insert the CSS style attribute into the `<h1>` tag:

```
<html>
<head>
<title>A Simple Page</title>
<script language="JavaScript">
<!-- Cloaking device on!

// Cloaking device off -->
</script>
</head>
<body>
<h1 style="">Welcome to this page!</h1>
<p>A lot of interesting text goes here! A lot of interesting text goes here!
➥A lot of interesting text goes here! A lot of interesting text goes here!
➥A lot of interesting text goes here!</p>
</body>
</html>
```

Next, inside the quotes, you add the CSS attribute `text-decoration`:

```
<html>
<head>
<title>A Simple Page</title>
<script language="JavaScript">
<!-- Cloaking device on!

// Cloaking device off -->
</script>
</head>
```

```
<body>
<h1 style="text-decoration">Welcome to this page!</h1>
<p>A lot of interesting text goes here! A lot of interesting text goes here!
➥A lot of interesting text goes here! A lot of interesting text goes here!
➥A lot of interesting text goes here!</p>
</body>
</html>
```

Finally, you need the value for the attribute—in this case, to add an underline you need the attribute `underline`. Attributes and values are separated by a colon, so this needs to go in between the two:

```
<html>
<head>
<title>A Simple Page</title>
<script language="JavaScript">
<!-- Cloaking device on!

// Cloaking device off -->
</script>
</head>
<body>
<h1 style="text-decoration:underline">Welcome to this page!</h1>
<p>A lot of interesting text goes here! A lot of interesting text goes here!
➥A lot of interesting text goes here! A lot of interesting text goes here!
➥A lot of interesting text goes here!</p>
</body>
</html>
```

Now, save the page and view the result in the browser (see Figure 13.1)!

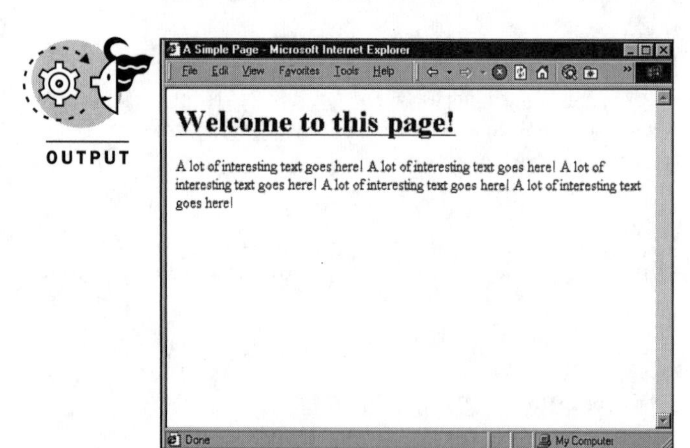

Figure 13.1: *A CSS used to add an underline to the heading.*

Take a look at some of the following simple examples, some of which you can use later when you look at how JavaScript can be used to change the values you assign to the CSS attributes.

Example 1—Changing Text Color

Here, CSS is used to make the text in the heading red (see Figure 13.2 for the output):

```
<html>
<head>
<title>A Simple Page</title>
<script language="JavaScript">
<!-- Cloaking device on!

// Cloaking device off -->
</script>
</head>
<body>
<h1 style="color:red">Welcome to this page!</h1>
<p>A lot of interesting text goes here! A lot of interesting text goes here!
➥A lot of interesting text goes here! A lot of interesting text goes here!
➥A lot of interesting text goes here!</p>
</body>
</html>
```

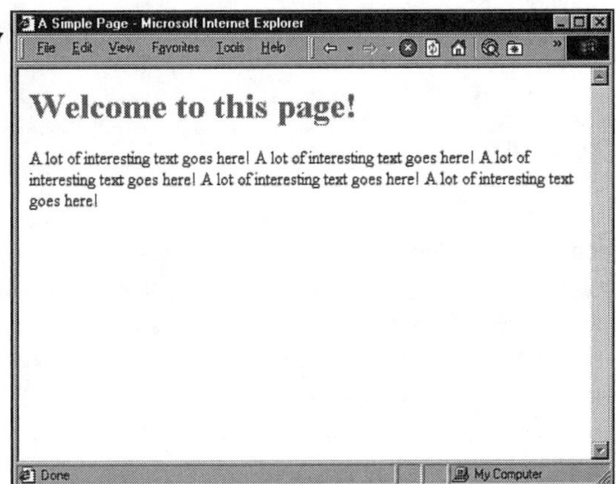

Figure 13.2: *A CSS used to change the color of the heading to red (you'll probably want to check this out for yourself!).*

Here are some of the other CSS named colors that are available:

aqua	black	blue
fuchsia	gray	green
lime	maroon	navy
olive	purple	red
silver	teal	white
yellow		

EXERCISE

Try out your own examples using some of these colors!

Example 2—Formatting Text

You've already seen how you can use CSS to add an underline or change the color of some text. But there's more you can do. To begin with, bold, italics, overline, and strikethrough are all possible using a few CSS attributes (see Figure 13.3):

```
<html>
<head>
<title>A Simple Page</title>
<script language="JavaScript">
<!-- Cloaking device on!

// Cloaking device off -->
</script>
</head>
<body>
<h1 style="text-decoration:underline">Welcome to this page!</h1>
<p>Example of <span style="font-weight:bold">bold</span> text</p>
<p>Example of <span style="font-style:italic">italics</span> text</p>
<p>Example of an <span style="text-decoration:overline">overline</span>
➥- doesn't work in Netscape Navigator 4!</p>
<p>Example of an <span style="text-decoration:line-through">line-through
➥</span></p>
<p>Example of <span style="text-transform:uppercase">uppercase</span> text</p>
<p>Example of <span style="text-transform:lowercase">LOWERCASE</span> text</p>
</body>
</html>
```

All these CSS effects work great in Internet Explorer 5.

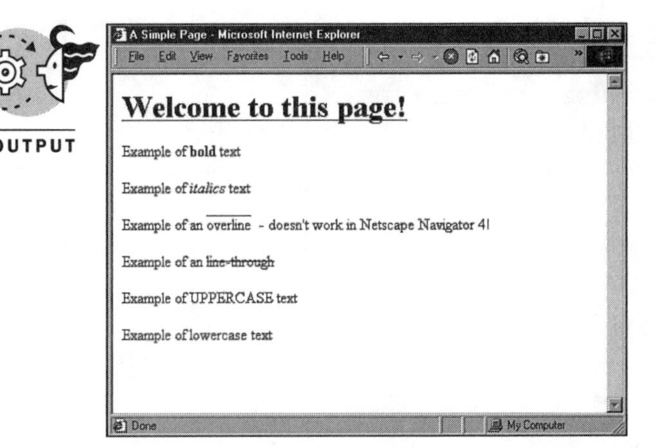

Figure 13.3: Some CSS text effects as displayed in Internet Explorer 5.

As shown in Figure 13.4, these effects also work in Netscape Navigator 6.

Figure 13.4: Some CSS text effects as displayed in Netscape Navigator 6.

However, Netscape Navigator 4 has a bit of trouble with overline (see Figure 13.5)!

Notice how all the CSS formatting is inside the HTML tag <span>. This tag is ideal for when you want to enclose text to apply CSS without otherwise affecting it. The <span> tag is a container element and passes on no formatting of its own to the text, making it ideal for this type of purpose.

EXERCISE

Experiment with these CSS attributes in some projects of your own, especially if they are new to you. Try out the <span> tag, too!

Figure 13.5: *Some CSS text effects as displayed in Netscape Navigator 4. Notice how the overline effect doesn't work.*

Example 3—Formatting Hyperlinks

Another cool thing you can do with CSS is make hyperlinks look more interesting. This technique differs from the CSS you have looked at so far because this time, you move from inline CSS (style information in the tags themselves—here inline has the same meaning as it does when referring to JavaScript) to CSS that applies to the whole page when placed in a `<style>` block in the head of the document.

Let's go through the process required to add some interesting effects to hyperlinks.

Step 1—Creating a Page with Hyperlinks

Here's a page that was created earlier:

```
<html>
<head>
<title>A Simple Page</title>
<script language="JavaScript">
<!-- Cloaking device on!

// Cloaking device off -->
</script>
</head>
<body>
<h1 style="text-decoration:underline">Welcome to this page!</h1>
<a href="http://www.mcp.com">A hyperlink</a>
<br>
<a href="http://www.kingsley-hughes.com">Another hyperlink!</a>
</body>
</html>
```

Step 2—Adding a <style> Block

A <style> block is, in many ways, similar to a <script> block. They both go inside the <head> block, and they both need HTML comment tags inside to hide the content from older browsers that aren't CSS aware. However, the similarity ends there! One thing you cannot do is put JavaScript into a <style> block (or for that matter, CSS information into a <script> block).

WARNING

Many people who use CSS on a regular basis include the <style> block in their HTML templates. The following is an example:

```
<html>
<head>
<title>A Simple Page</title>
<script language="JavaScript">
<!-- Cloaking device on!

// Cloaking device off -->
</script>
<style>
<!--

-->
</style>
</head>
<body>

</body>
</html>
```

This is a great idea, but be aware that typing your JavaScript into the wrong block will cause it to not work (the same goes for putting CSS information in the <script> block). If you choose to use a template of this kind, take care to place the technology in the appropriate block!

So, you now add the <style> block:

```
<html>
<head>
<title>A Simple Page</title>
<script language="JavaScript">
<!-- Cloaking device on!

// Cloaking device off -->
</script>
<style>
<!--
```

```
-->
</style>
</head>
<body>
<h1 style="text-decoration:underline">Welcome to this page!</h1>
<a href="http://www.mcp.com">A hyperlink</a>
<br>
<a href="http://www.kingsley-hughes.com">Another hyperlink!</a>
</body>
</html>
```

Step 3—Adding the Right CSS Attribute

Several CSS attributes can be used to add special effects to hyperlinks:

- `a:hover`—This changes the style of a hyperlink when the visitor moves her mouse pointer over the hyperlink. The link is returned to normal after the mouse pointer is moved away. It, however, does not work in Netscape 4.
- `a:active`—This changes the style of a hyperlink when the visitor clicks the hyperlink to follow it.
- `a:visited`—This changes the style of a hyperlink when the visitor has recently visited it.
- `a:link`—This sets the style of a hyperlink that the visitor hasn't yet followed.

The following example looks at using `a:hover`. To use this attribute, you first need to type it into the style block:

```
<html>
<head>
<title>A Simple Page</title>
<script language="JavaScript">
<!-- Cloaking device on!

// Cloaking device off -->
</script>
<style>
<!--
a:hover
-->
</style>
</head>
<body>
<h1 style="text-decoration:underline">Welcome to this page!</h1>
<a href="http://www.mcp.com">A hyperlink</a>
```

```
<br>
<a href="http://www.kingsley-hughes.com">Another hyperlink!</a>
</body>
</html>
```

STEP 4—CHANGING THE HYPERLINK

The final step is to add the CSS information that controls how the hyperlink is changed. This style information is placed inside curly braces after the `a:hover`. Again, note the similarities with JavaScript:

```
<html>
<head>
<title>A Simple Page</title>
<script language="JavaScript">
<!-- Cloaking device on!

// Cloaking device off -->
</script>
<style>
<!--
a:hover {}
-->
</style>
</head>
<body>
<h1 style="text-decoration:underline">Welcome to this page!</h1>
<a href="http://www.mcp.com">A hyperlink</a>
<br>
<a href="http://www.kingsley-hughes.com">Another hyperlink!</a>
</body>
</html>
```

You want the hyperlink to change to red when the mouse pointer is moved over it, so inside the curly braces you add `color:red`:

```
<html>
<head>
<title>A Simple Page</title>
<script language="JavaScript">
<!-- Cloaking device on!

// Cloaking device off -->
</script>
<style>
<!--
a:hover {color:red}
-->
</style>
</head>
```

```
<body>
<h1 style="text-decoration:underline">Welcome to this page!</h1>
<a href="http://www.mcp.com">A hyperlink</a>
<br>
<a href="http://www.kingsley-hughes.com">Another hyperlink!</a>
</body>
</html>
```

You also want to add a smart-looking overline to it. To do this, you add `text-decoration:overline` after the first attribute:value pair (`color:red`), and you use a semicolon to separate the two:

```
<html>
<head>
<title>A Simple Page</title>
<script language="JavaScript">
<!-- Cloaking device on!

// Cloaking device off -->
</script>
<style>
<!--
a:hover {color:red; text-decoration:overline}
-->
</style>
</head>
<body>
<h1 style="text-decoration:underline">Welcome to this page!</h1>
<a href="http://www.mcp.com">A hyperlink</a>
<br>
<a href="http://www.kingsley-hughes.com">Another hyperlink!</a>
</body>
</html>
```

STEP 5—SAVING THE WEB PAGE AND VIEWING IT IN THE BROWSER

Figures 13.6, 13.7, and 13.8 show the page as viewed in Internet Explorer 5, Netscape Navigator 4, and Netscape Navigator 6, respectively.

NOTE

Even though Netscape Navigator doesn't support the effects you chose here, the hyperlinks still work and no errors are displayed. This is because CSS *degrades gracefully* in browsers—when they don't support a particular effect, it is passed over and ignored. This makes using CSS easy because you don't need to be worried about errors being displayed when the user's browser isn't as up to date as you expect it to be!

Figure 13.6: *Hyperlink effects as displayed in Internet Explorer 5.*

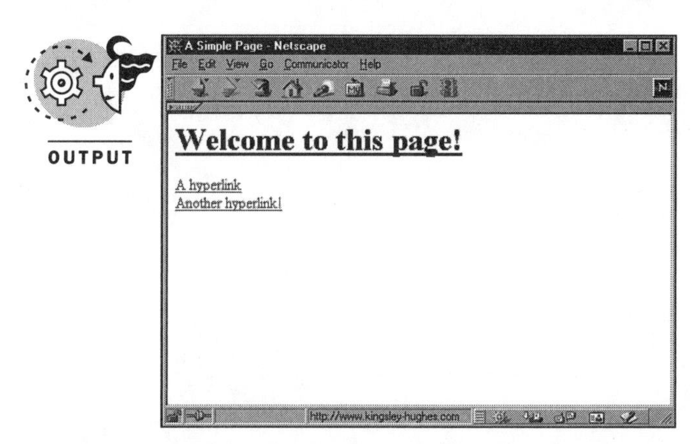

Figure 13.7: *Hyperlink effects as displayed in Netscape Navigator 4.*

Figure 13.8: *Hyperlink effects as displayed in Netscape Navigator 6.*

Example 4—Positioning

One of the most exciting developments made available in Dynamic HTML (DHTML) is the capability to take precise control over the positioning on the page of text and images. Initially, both Netscape and Microsoft had different, conflicting ways to do this. Netscape chose to have attributes added to the <layer> tag and do the positioning via HTML, whereas Microsoft chose CSS as the method of choice. Both were competing standards at the time, and eventually Microsoft's way was accepted by the W3C, making the Netscape method obsolete. Luckily, Netscape Navigator 4 supported most of the CSS positioning functions as well, which allowed developers to use this technology to create HTML pages that would work for both browsers.

Let's first look at positioning of text. Here is a simple Web page you can work on:

```
<html>
<head>
<title>A Simple Page</title>
<script language="JavaScript">
<!-- Cloaking device on!

// Cloaking device off -->
</script>
<style>
<!--

-->
</style>
</head>
<body>
<h1 style="text-decoration:underline">Welcome to this page!</h1>
<p>Some simple text for positioning</p>
</body>
</html>
```

Three of the commonly used attributes that are used to position anything are

- `position`—This attribute has two values of interest: `absolute` and `relative`. The difference between the two is subtle. The `absolute` value uses the top-left corner of the browser window as the origin point from which to work, and all measurements relating to position are calculated from this point. `relative`, on the other hand, takes the position *from which the element would have appeared on the page if no positioning information was provided*. After you see this in action, you'll understand it.

- `top`—This attribute is used to give the offset from the origin that the element needs to be moved by. The measurement can be given in a variety of forms (pixels, inches, centimeters, millimeters, and so on). For our examples here, you will look at pixels in action. Positive values for `top` move the element down the page, whereas negative values push the element up toward the top of the browser window.
- `left`—This is similar to `top`, but it works horizontally. Positive values move the elements to the right, whereas negative values move it to the left. Again, although this sounds a bit complex, after you try it, you'll understand it.

The CSS information you see can be placed either in the `<style>` block or inline. Here is a simple inline example:

```
<html>
<head>
<title>A Simple Page</title>
<script language="JavaScript">
<!-- Cloaking device on!

// Cloaking device off -->
</script>
<style>
<!--

-->
</style>
</head>
<body>
<h1 style="text-decoration:underline">Welcome to this page!</h1>
<p style="position:absolute;top:125px;left:200px">Some simple text for
➥positioning</p>
</body>
</html>
```

So, what does this CSS do? Well, to begin with, the text is positioned `absolute`, which means the positions will be relative to the top-left corner of the browser window. `top` has been set to `125px` (which stands for 125 pixels). This means the text will be 125 pixels down from the top. `left` is set to `200px`, which means the text will be 200 pixels from the left edge of the browser window.

Figures 13.9–11 show the results in each of the browsers.

Figure 13.9: *Positioned text displayed in Internet Explorer 5.*

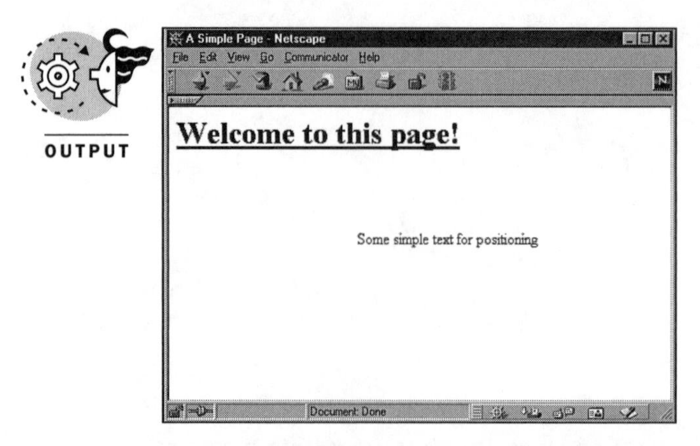

Figure 13.10: *Positioned text displayed in Netscape Navigator 4.*

Figure 13.11: *Positioned text displayed in Netscape Navigator 6.*

The same can be done with images, too:

```
<html>
<head>
<title>A Simple Page</title>
<script language="JavaScript">
<!-- Cloaking device on!

// Cloaking device off -->
</script>
<style>
<!--

-->
</style>
</head>
<body>
<h1 style="text-decoration:underline">Welcome to this page!</h1>
<img src="circle.gif" style="position:absolute;top:125px;left:200px">
</body>
</html>
```

As you can see in Figures 13.12–14, this method works for Internet Explorer 5 and Netscape Navigator 6, but fails in Netscape Navigator 4.

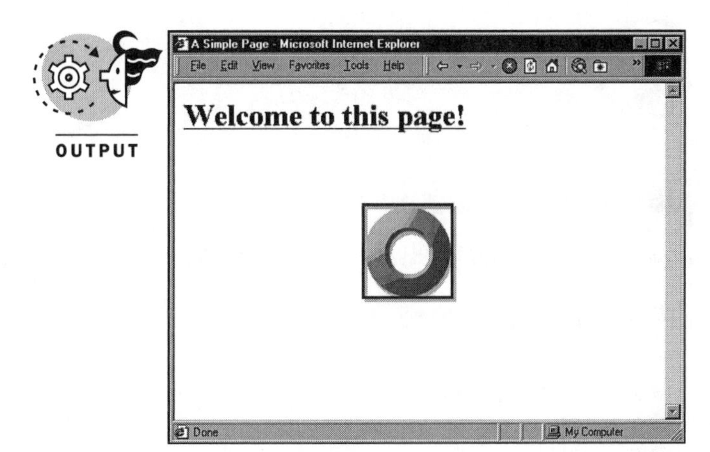

Figure 13.12: *Positioned image displayed in Internet Explorer 5.*

Figure 13.13: *Positioned image fails to display properly in Netscape Navigator 4.*

Figure 13.14: *Positioned image displayed in Netscape Navigator 6.*

However, if you try it this way, it works:

```
<html>
<head>
<title>A Simple Page</title>
<script language="JavaScript">
<!-- Cloaking device on!

// Cloaking device off -->
</script>
<style>
<!--

-->
</style>
```

```
</head>
<body>
<h1 style="text-decoration:underline">Welcome to this page!</h1>
<div style="position:absolute;top:125px;left:200px">
<img src="circle.gif">
</div>
</body>
</html>
```

In this example, another container element—the <div> tag—is used to surround the image (see Figure 13.15).

Figure 13.15: *The positioned image now displays properly in Netscape Navigator 4.*

If, instead of using absolute positioning, you try relative, you can start to see the difference (see Figure 13.16):

```
<html>
<head>
<title>A Simple Page</title>
<script language="JavaScript">
<!-- Cloaking device on!

// Cloaking device off -->
</script>
<style>
<!--

-->
</style>
</head>
<body>
<h1 style="text-decoration:underline">Welcome to this page!</h1>
<div style="position:relative;top:125px;left:200px">
```

```
<img src="circle.gif">
</div>
</body>
</html>
```

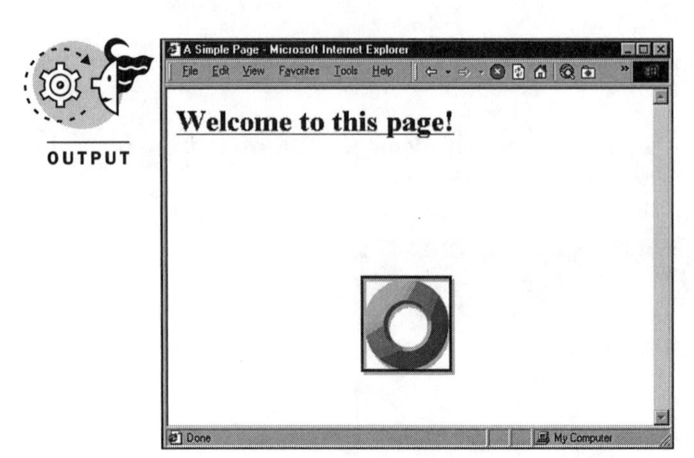

Figure 13.16: *The image positioned relatively appears lower on the page than images positioned absolutely.*

The reason for this image being placed lower on the page is that the positioning origin (that is, the point from which the browser moves the image) is the position the image would have occupied if no CSS information was present. This can be a handy method when you want to create offsets such as indenting images a few pixels to the right to make a margin.

Example 5—Three-Dimensional Work (Well, 2.5D to Be Exact!)

2.5D refers to the capability to not only control the `top` and `left` positions of images and text on the page, but also to control the *stacking order* of elements. Normally, in HTML the stacking order is determined by the object's position in the HTML code. If one thing is below another in terms of code placement, it will be on top. Here is some text with the image below it in the HTML (Figure 13.17 shows the result):

```
<html>
<head>
<title>A Simple Page</title>
<script language="JavaScript">
<!-- Cloaking device on!

// Cloaking device off -->
</script>
<style>
<!--
```

```
-->
</style>
</head>
<body>
<h1 style="position:absolute;top:15px;left:10px;text-decoration:underline">
➥Welcome to this page!</h1>
<div style="position:absolute;top:15px;left:200px">
<img src="circle.gif">
</div>
</body>
</html>
```

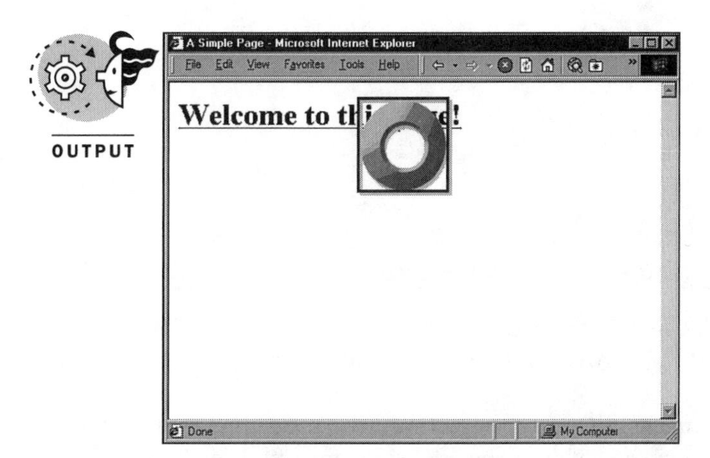

Figure 13.17: *The stacking order in HTML is dictated by the order of the elements in the HTML code.*

By simply swapping the position of the two elements in the HTML code, you can change the stacking order. Figure 13.18 shows the result:

```
<html>
<head>
<title>A Simple Page</title>
<script language="JavaScript">
<!-- Cloaking device on!

// Cloaking device off -->
</script>
<style>
<!--

-->
</style>
</head>
<body>
<div style="position:absolute;top:15px;left:200px">
```

```
<img src="circle.gif">
</div>
<h1 style="position:absolute;top:15px;left:10px;text-decoration:underline">
➥Welcome to this page!</h1>
</body>
</html>
```

Figure 13.18: *Change the order of the elements in the HTML and you change the stacking order as displayed in the browser.*

However, this method is pretty hard to control, and the last thing you want to be fiddling with is the order of the HTML elements. A far better way is to use the CSS attribute `z-index` to do the work for you. The values for `z-index` are numbers, and the element with the highest number goes on top. So, if you modify the previous example, you can change the natural order of things:

```
<html>
<head>
<title>A Simple Page</title>
<script language="JavaScript">
<!-- Cloaking device on!

// Cloaking device off -->
</script>
<style>
<!--

-->
</style>
</head>
<body>
<div style="position:absolute;top:15px;left:200px;z-index:2">
<img src="circle.gif">
</div>
```

```
<h1 style="position:absolute;top:15px;left:10px;text-decoration:underline;
➥z-index:1">Welcome to this page!</h1>
</body>
</html>
```

As far as the HTML is concerned, the text should be on top (see Figure 13.19).

Figure 13.19: *Using* `z-index` *to control the stacking order.*

However, in the browser window, it is the image that wins!

JavaScript and CSS

So, you've seen some CSS in action. Think it's cool, eh? Well, combining it with JavaScript takes it to a whole new level!

The trick with a CSS/JavaScript combination is to realize that what you are always doing is using JavaScript to change CSS attribute values. Now, do this after the page has loaded and the user sees things change on the page right in the browser—and that's Dynamic HTML!

Let's give you the opportunity to dive straight in with an example based on the text color example you saw earlier.

NOTE

This example works only in Internet Explorer 4 and higher.

```
<html>
<head>
<title>A Simple Page</title>
<script language="JavaScript">
<!-- Cloaking device on!
```

```
// Cloaking device off -->
</script>
</head>
<body>
<h1 style="color:red">Welcome to this page!</h1>
<p>A lot of interesting text goes here! A lot of interesting text goes here!
➥A lot of interesting text goes here! A lot of interesting text goes
➥here! A lot of interesting text goes here!</p>
</body>
</html>
```

Let's say you want to change this a little so that the text in the heading is red only when the user moves the mouse over it. Can this be done with CSS and JavaScript? You bet it can!

Step 1—Removing the Existing Style Information

This might seem to be a bit of a backward step, but it has to be done:

```
<html>
<head>
<title>A Simple Page</title>
<script language="JavaScript">
<!-- Cloaking device on!

// Cloaking device off -->
</script>
</head>
<body>
<h1>Welcome to this page!</h1>
<p>A lot of interesting text goes here! A lot of interesting text goes here!
➥A lot of interesting text goes here! A lot of interesting text goes here!
➥A lot of interesting text goes here!</p>
</body>
</html>
```

Step 2—Adding an ID

Because you need to have a way to refer to the element on which you need the JavaScript to act, you need to add the `id` attribute to the `<h1>` tag. This `id` is a short descriptive name that enables you to pinpoint what you want your JavaScript to work on:

```
<html>
<head>
<title>A Simple Page</title>
<script language="JavaScript">
<!-- Cloaking device on!
```

```
// Cloaking device off -->
</script>
</head>
<body>
<h1 id="head1">Welcome to this page!</h1>
<p>A lot of interesting text goes here! A lot of interesting text goes here!
➥A lot of interesting text goes here! A lot of interesting text goes here!
➥A lot of interesting text goes here!</p>
</body>
</html>
```

Step 3—Adding the Event Handler

The next step is to add an event handler to the element to detect the user moving the mouse pointer over the heading. The event that corresponds to this is the `onMouseover` event. This is also a good time to choose the function name, so the event can trigger the appropriate function:

```
<html>
<head>
<title>A Simple Page</title>
<script language="JavaScript">
<!-- Cloaking device on!

// Cloaking device off -->
</script>
</head>
<body>
<h1 id="head1" onMouseover="colorchange()">Welcome to this page!</h1>
<p>A lot of interesting text goes here! A lot of interesting text goes here!
➥A lot of interesting text goes here! A lot of interesting text goes here!
➥A lot of interesting text goes here!</p>
</body>
</html>
```

Step 4—Writing Some JavaScript

Now for the fun part—the JavaScript!

So, first things first, add the function skeleton:

```
<html>
<head>
<title>A Simple Page</title>
<script language="JavaScript">
<!-- Cloaking device on!
function colorchange()
{
```

```
}
// Cloaking device off -->
</script>
</head>
<body>
<h1 id="head1" onMouseover="colorchange()">Welcome to this page!</h1>
<p>A lot of interesting text goes here! A lot of interesting text goes here!
➥A lot of interesting text goes here! A lot of interesting text goes here!
➥A lot of interesting text goes here!</p>
</body>
</html>
```

And now you need the JavaScript that does the work. All you need is a single line to do this, and it consists of four parts:

- The pointer to the position in the page on which you want the JavaScript to act, which in this case is `head1`.
- What aspect the JavaScript is supposed to work on—in this case, the `style` of it.
- Which style attribute to change—here it's the `color`.
- Finally, the new value you want the style attribute to take on, which in this case is `red`.

Put all these together and you come up with the following:

```
head1.style.color = "red"
```

Add this to the function and save the page. Your completed page should look like this:

```
<html>
<head>
<title>A Simple Page</title>
<script language="JavaScript">
<!-- Cloaking device on!
function colorchange()
{
head1.style.color = "red";
}
// Cloaking device off -->
</script>
</head>
<body>
<h1 id="head1" onMouseover="colorchange()">Welcome to this page!</h1>
<p>A lot of interesting text goes here! A lot of interesting text goes here!
➥A lot of interesting text goes here! A lot of interesting text goes here!
➥A lot of interesting text goes here!</p>
</body>
</html>
```

Next, load your page into the browser and take a look at what happens when you move the mouse pointer over the heading. If all has gone well, it should change color!

However, notice how the text doesn't change back when you move the mouse pointer off it (see Figure 13.20). To make this happen, you need to write a new JavaScript function that is run when the mouse pointer is moved off the text. You do this by using the `onMouseout` event:

```
<html>
<head>
<title>A Simple Page</title>
<script language="JavaScript">
<!-- Cloaking device on!
function colorchange()
{
head1.style.color = "red";
}

function colorchangeback()
{
head1.style.color = "black";
}
// Cloaking device off -->
</script>
</head>
<body>
<h1 id="head1" onMouseover="colorchange()" onMouseout="colorchangeback()">
➥Welcome to this page!</h1>
<p>A lot of interesting text goes here! A lot of interesting text goes here!
➥A lot of interesting text goes here! A lot of interesting text goes here!
➥A lot of interesting text goes here!</p>
</body>
</html>
```

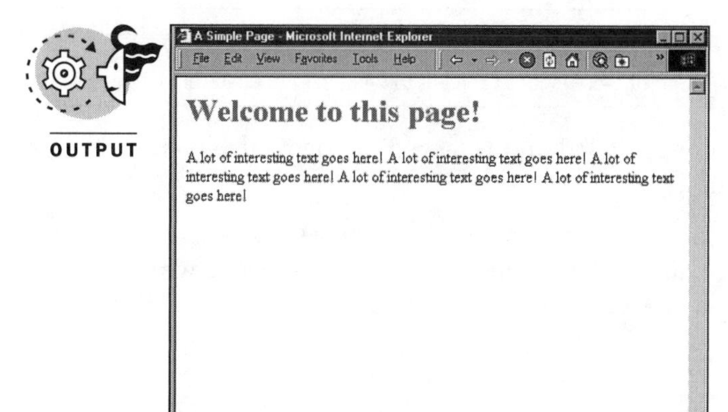

Figure 13.20: *JavaScript and CSS in action.*

Let's take a look at another example; this time using the `text-decoration` attribute.

CAUTION

When using CSS attributes that have hyphens in JavaScript, you must remove the hyphens, join the two words together, and make the first letter of the second part uppercase. Therefore, `text-decoration` becomes `textDecoration` when used in script.

```
<html>
<head>
<title>A Simple Page</title>
<script language="JavaScript">
<!-- Cloaking device on!
function addunderline()
{
head1.style.textDecoration = "underline"
}

function removeunderline()
{
head1.style.textDecoration = "none"
}
// Cloaking device off -->
</script>
</head>
<body>
<h1 id="head1" onMouseover="addunderline()" onMouseout="removeunderline()">
➥Welcome to this page!</h1>
<p>A lot of interesting text goes here! A lot of interesting text goes here!
➥A lot of interesting text goes here! A lot of interesting text goes here!
➥A lot of interesting text goes here!</p>
</body>
</html>
```

WARNING

Note the capitalization of `textDecoration`—if this is typed in all lowercase, the script fails!

Now the underline is added and removed as the mouse pointer is moved over the heading text.

You can extend this to cover a few more of the values possible for `text-decoration`, at the same time getting some practice with a few more events. Here, the `onClick` event has been used to add an `overline` (see Figure 13.21):

```
<html>
<head>
<title>A Simple Page</title>
<script language="JavaScript">
```

```
<!-- Cloaking device on!
function addunderline()
{
head1.style.textDecoration = "underline"
}

function removeunderline()
{
head1.style.textDecoration = "none"
}

function addoverline()
{
head1.style.textDecoration = "overline"
}
// Cloaking device off -->
</script>
</head>
<body>
<h1 id="head1" onMouseover="addunderline()" onMouseout="removeunderline()"
➥onClick="addoverline()">Welcome to this page!</h1>
<p>A lot of interesting text goes here! A lot of interesting text goes here!
➥A lot of interesting text goes here! A lot of interesting text goes here!
➥A lot of interesting text goes here!</p>
</body>
</html>
```

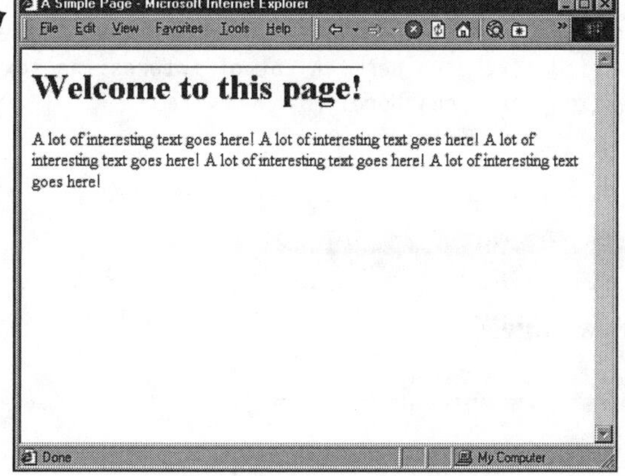

Figure 13.21: *Overline added using the* `onClick` *event.*

Finally, here is the line-through triggered by the `onDblclick` event (double-click). The result is shown in Figure 13.22:

```
<html>
<head>
<title>A Simple Page</title>
```

```
<script language="JavaScript">
<!-- Cloaking device on!
function addunderline()
{
head1.style.textDecoration = "underline"
}

function removeunderline()
{
head1.style.textDecoration = "none"
}

function addoverline()
{
head1.style.textDecoration = "overline"
}

function addlinethrough()
{
head1.style.textDecoration = "line-through"
}
// Cloaking device off -->
</script>
</head>
<body>
<h1 id="head1" onMouseover="addunderline()" onMouseout="removeunderline()"
➥onClick="addoverline()" ondblclick="addlinethrough()">Welcome to this
➥page!</h1>
<p>A lot of interesting text goes here! A lot of interesting text goes here!
➥A lot of interesting text goes here! A lot of interesting text goes here!
➥A lot of interesting text goes here!</p>
</body>
</html>
```

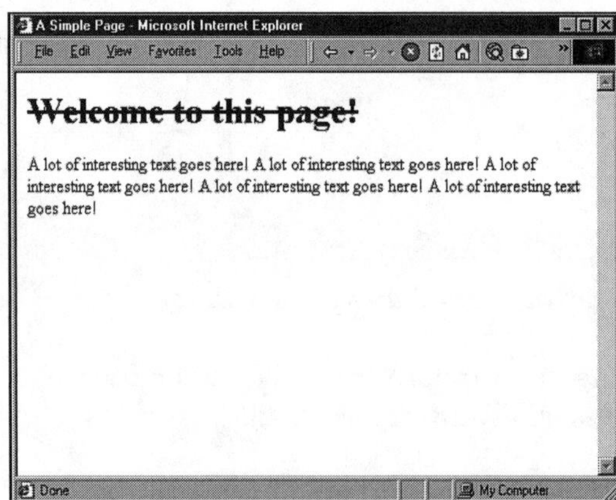

Figure 13.22: *Line-through in action.*

Creating Animation!

Now comes some of the cool stuff—using CSS and JavaScript to create animation on a Web page. And the great thing about the animation you look at here is that the user doesn't need any plug-ins or downloads because it's all built into the browser, and to top it all off, it's fast!

What Is Animation?

Animation is the process of making something move or appear to move. Because in the computer world everything manipulated onscreen is light, let's look at how to make things *appear* as though they are moving.

Animation has two components. The first is the distance that is moved between successive frames, which is called the *jump*. The second is the time interval in between each successive jump, which is called the *interval*. If you have an animation in which the jump is large and the interval is long, the animation looks slow and rough. It won't look at though something is moving in a natural way, but more as though it is blinking in and out of existence, moving with each blink. If the jump is small and the interval is also small, it looks much smoother; although, if you go too far, things again start to look strange. There is a great deal of room for experimentation, and there is no single right answer to cover all animation needs.

In the computer world, the jump can be measured in one of many units, but the best unit to use is the pixel. This is because it is the smallest unit of measurement that every computer monitor understands—so much less room for error exists! As for intervals, the best unit to use is the millisecond (1/1000 of a second, meaning that 1000 milliseconds make up a second).

NOTE

An image on a television screen is updated 24 times a second, or roughly once every 40 milliseconds! This is so fast that the eye doesn't notice the image change, which is why it looks so smooth. Although, if you take a picture of a TV with a camera or video camera, you'll see this process in action.

What's the catch? Well, the main one is that Internet Explorer and Netscape Navigator work differently. No surprise there, but what makes it worse is that Netscape 4 and Netscape 6 also work differently!

To keep things simple here, you look at just two ways—one for Internet Explorer 5 and one for Netscape Navigator 4. This way, you capture the greatest share of the browser market share and at the same time, you can keep the examples a little more manageable.

NOTE

At the time of this writing, Netscape Navigator 6 is in a preview release phase and not fully finalized. For more information on CSS for Netscape Navigator 6, visit the Netscape Developer Web site at `http://developer.netscape.com`.

Let's first look at how animation is done in Internet Explorer.

Animation and Internet Explorer 5

First things first: Let's start with the Web page that needs animating. This example animates the text so that it moves from left to right:

```
<html>
<head>
<title>A Simple Page</title>
<script language="JavaScript">
<!-- Cloaking device on!

// Cloaking device off -->
</script>
</head>
<body>
<div>
Text ... on the go!
</div>
</body>
</html>
```

The first addition to make is to add an `id` to the `<div>` tag surrounding the text to give it a meaningful name:

```
<html>
<head>
<title>A Simple Page</title>
<script language="JavaScript">
<!-- Cloaking device on!

// Cloaking device off -->
</script>
</head>
<body>
<div id="ani1">
Text ... on the go!
</div>
</body>
</html>
```

Next, use CSS to position the text in its starting position:

```
<html>
<head>
<title>A Simple Page</title>
<script language="JavaScript">
<!-- Cloaking device on!

// Cloaking device off -->
</script>
</head>
<body>
<div id="ani1" style="position:absolute;left:10;top:10">
Text ... on the go!
</div>
</body>
</html>
```

Now, you start to work on the JavaScript function. Begin by putting the skeleton of it in place. This function will be called `moveTxt()`:

```
<html>
<head>
<title>A Simple Page</title>
<script language="JavaScript">
<!-- Cloaking device on!
function moveTxt()
{

}
// Cloaking device off -->
</script>
</head>
<body>
<div id="ani1" style="position:absolute;left:10;top:10">
Text ... on the go!
</div>
</body>
</html>
```

Now start work on the actual body of the JavaScript. Because there is no point having the text continue indefinitely to the right of the page, you need some way to control this. The best way is to use an `if` statement to check for the position of the text and then run the script only if the text is less than, say, 500 pixels from the left. This is done using the `pixelLeft` CSS attribute.

TIP

Remember to add the second set of curly braces for the statements that are run when the `if` statement is true.

```
<html>
<head>
<title>A Simple Page</title>
<script language="JavaScript">
<!-- Cloaking device on!
function moveTxt()
{
if (ani1.style.pixelLeft < 500)
{

}
}
// Cloaking device off -->
</script>
</head>
<body>
<div id="ani1" style="position:absolute;left:10;top:10">
Text ... on the go!
</div>
</body>
</html>
```

Now, let's look at the final statements that control the animation. First, you must deal with the jump. With each step, the text jumps two pixels to the right. Not only do you use the `pixelLeft` attribute to read the position of the text, but you also use it to change the position by incrementing it by 2:

```
<html>
<head>
<title>A Simple Page</title>
<script language="JavaScript">
<!-- Cloaking device on!
function moveTxt()
{
if (ani1.style.pixelLeft < 500)
{
ani1.style.pixelLeft += 2;
}
}
// Cloaking device off -->
</script>
</head>
```

```
<body>
<div id="ani1" style="position:absolute;left:10;top:10">
Text ... on the go!
</div>
</body>
</html>
```

Next is the interval. This is controlled using the `setTimeout` method, which enables you to rerun a function after a specified period of time has elapsed. Here, you set the interval to 50 milliseconds before rerunning the `moveTxt()` function:

```
<html>
<head>
<title>A Simple Page</title>
<script language="JavaScript">
<!-- Cloaking device on!
function moveTxt()
{
if (ani1.style.pixelLeft < 500)
{
ani1.style.pixelLeft += 2;
setTimeout("moveTxt()", 50);
}
}
// Cloaking device off -->
</script>
</head>
<body>
<div id="ani1" style="position:absolute;left:10;top:10">
Text ... on the go!
</div>
</body>
</html>
```

This whole process now repeats until the `if` statement is false. The last thing to do is trigger the script. To do this use the `onLoad` event:

```
<html>
<head>
<title>A Simple Page</title>
<script language="JavaScript">
<!-- Cloaking device on!
function moveTxt()
{
if (ani1.style.pixelLeft < 500)
{
ani1.style.pixelLeft += 2;
setTimeout("moveTxt()", 50);
```

```
}
}
// Cloaking device off -->
</script>
</head>
<body onLoad="moveTxt()">
<div id="ani1" style="position:absolute;left:10;top:10">
Text ... on the go!
</div>
</body>
</html>
```

Save this and take a look at it in Internet Explorer (see Figure 13.23).

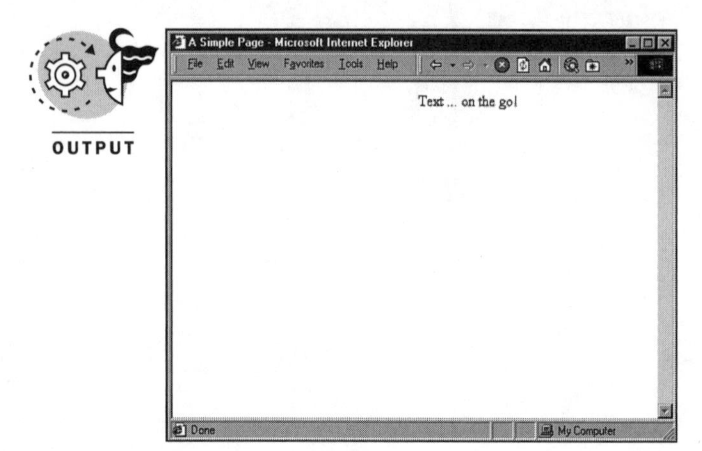

***Figure 13.23:** Moving text… on the go!*

Doing the Same Thing … Only in Netscape Navigator 4!

If you want to do the same thing in Netscape Navigator 4, you can pick up the trail at the point where you were about to add the statements to the JavaScript function in the Internet Explorer example:

```
<html>
<head>
<title>A Simple Page</title>
<script language="JavaScript">
<!-- Cloaking device on!
function moveTxt()
{
```

```
}
// Cloaking device off -->
</script>
</head>
<body>
<div id="ani1" style="position:absolute;left:10;top:10">
Text ... on the go!
</div>
</body>
</html>
```

As in the previous example, you need to add an `if` statement. However, this time, the syntax for the expression used is slightly different. This time, you need the following:

```
<html>
<head>
<title>A Simple Page</title>
<script language="JavaScript">
<!-- Cloaking device on!
function moveTxt()
{
if (document.ani1.left < 500)
{

}
}
// Cloaking device off -->
</script>
</head>
<body>
<div id="ani1" style="position:absolute;left:10;top:10">
Text ... on the go!
</div>
</body>
</html>
```

A subtle difference exists that causes the incompatibilities, but that's enough!

The next statement is again slightly different from the Internet Explorer example; however, the `setTimeout` statement is identical:

```
<html>
<head>
<title>A Simple Page</title>
<script language="JavaScript">
<!-- Cloaking device on!
```

```
function moveTxt()
{
if (document.ani1.left < 500)
{
document.ani1.left += 2;
setTimeout("moveTxt()", 50);
}
}
// Cloaking device off -->
</script>
</head>
<body>
<div id="ani1" style="position:absolute;left:10;top:10">
Text ... on the go!
</div>
</body>
</html>
```

Finally, round off the example by using the `onLoad` event to trigger it—and you're done:

```
<html>
<head>
<title>A Simple Page</title>
<script language="JavaScript">
<!-- Cloaking device on!
function moveTxt()
{
if (document.ani1.left < 500)
{
document.ani1.left += 2;
setTimeout("moveTxt()", 50);
}
}
// Cloaking device off -->
</script>
</head>
<body onLoad="moveTxt()">
<div id="ani1" style="position:absolute;left:10;top:10">
Text ... on the go!
</div>
</body>
</html>
```

Load this example into Netscape Navigator 4 and see the results, which should look spookily like the Internet Explorer example (see Figure 13.24)!

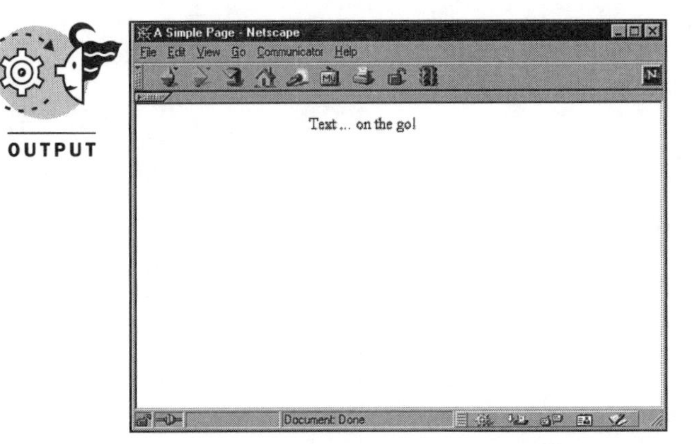

Figure 13.24: *Moving text... on the go in Netscape Navigator 4!*

Making It Work in Both Browsers!

Can it be done? Can these kinds of examples be made to work in two browsers? In fact, the answer is yes!

The key to this is realizing that you can use the differences. The difference you are going to use is the fact that in Internet Explorer an object known as `document.all` exists. So, if you use an `if` statement to test for this, you can find out whether you're dealing with Internet Explorer 5 or Netscape Navigator 4:

```
<script language="JavaScript">
<!-- Cloaking device on!
function someFunction()
{
if (document.all)
{
//Expression is true, so put IE5 statements here
}
else
//Expression is false, so put NN4 statements here
}
// Cloaking device off -->
</script>
```

Following this method, creating a super JavaScript that works in both browsers is just a matter of cutting out the sections from the separate scripts and popping them into this layout:

```
<html>
<head>
<title>A Simple Page</title>
```

```
<script language="JavaScript">
<!-- Cloaking device on!
function moveTxt()
{
if (document.all)
{
if (ani1.style.pixelLeft < 500)
{
ani1.style.pixelLeft += 2;
setTimeout("moveTxt()", 50);
}
}
else
if (document.ani1.left < 500)
{
document.ani1.left += 2;
setTimeout("moveTxt()", 50);
}
}
// Cloaking device off -->
</script>
</head>
<body onLoad="moveTxt()">
<div id="ani1" style="position:absolute;left:10;top:10">
Text ... on the go!
</div>
</body>
</html>
```

See how the separate Internet Explorer and Netscape Navigator scripts have been spliced together into this new `if` statement?

Load this into both browsers and see it in action.

EXERCISE

Work on modifying the previous example so the text moves in the opposite direction, from right to left. Remember, this involves changing the starting position and the point that the script stops at; in addition, instead of incrementing the number of pixels, you must decrement.

Ups and Downs

Want to go up and down instead of side to side? Easy! All you need to do is use the `pixelTop` attribute instead of `pixelLeft`.

Here is a simple modification of the Internet Explorer example to do just that:

```
<html>
<head>
<title>A Simple Page</title>
<script language="JavaScript">
<!-- Cloaking device on!
function moveTxt()
{
if (ani1.style.pixelTop < 500)
{
ani1.style.pixelTop += 2;
setTimeout("moveTxt()", 50);
}
}
// Cloaking device off -->
</script>
</head>
<body onLoad="moveTxt()">
<div id="ani1" style="position:absolute;left:10;top:10">
Text ... on the go!
</div>
</body>
</html>
```

Now, here's the same modification for the Netscape Navigator example. This substitutes the attribute `top` for `left`:

```
<html>
<head>
<title>A Simple Page</title>
<script language="JavaScript">
<!-- Cloaking device on!
function moveTxt()
{
if (document.ani1.top < 500)
{
document.ani1.top += 2;
setTimeout("moveTxt()", 50);
}
}
// Cloaking device off -->
</script>
</head>
<body onLoad="moveTxt()">
<div id="ani1" style="position:absolute;left:10;top:10">
Text ... on the go!
</div>
</body>
</html>
```

EXERCISE

Can you make these two examples into one that works in both browsers?

Want to Go Diagonally?

Going in a diagonal direction is just going both horizontally and vertically in one iteration. Here is an example that moves the text from the top-left to the bottom-right of the page.

First, here's the Internet Explorer 5 version:

```
<html>
<head>
<title>A Simple Page</title>
<script language="JavaScript">
<!-- Cloaking device on!
function moveTxt()
{
if (ani1.style.pixelTop < 500)
{
ani1.style.pixelTop += 2;
ani1.style.pixelLeft += 2;
setTimeout("moveTxt()", 50);
}
}
// Cloaking device off -->
</script>
</head>
<body onLoad="moveTxt()">
<div id="ani1" style="position:absolute;left:10;top:10">
Text ... on the go!
</div>
</body>
</html>
```

And here's the Netscape Navigator 4 version:

```
<html>
<head>
<title>A Simple Page</title>
<script language="JavaScript">
<!-- Cloaking device on!
function moveTxt()
{
if (document.ani1.top < 500)
{
```

```
document.ani1.top += 2;
document.ani1.left += 2;
setTimeout("moveTxt()", 50);
}
}
// Cloaking device off -->
</script>
</head>
<body onLoad="moveTxt()">
<div id="ani1" style="position:absolute;left:10;top:10">
Text ... on the go!
</div>
</body>
</html>
```

NOTE

You can use the value of either `top` or `left` for the controlling expression, which decides how far the object should move and is contained in the `if` statement.

EXERCISE

Now try your hand at making this an example that works in both browsers.

Back to JavaScript for a Moment...

Have you noticed how familiar the JavaScript you are using here feels? This is because, even though you might be combining one technology that you know (JavaScript) with one that you might not be so familiar with (CSS), you're still using the same JavaScript statements you learned earlier.

By having a good foundation in the scripting language and spending a lot of time on the basics, you're now able to apply those skills to other challenges. JavaScript is the glue that binds together all the various technologies that go into DHTML.

What's Next

You've seen how JavaScript interacts with CSS; next it's time to look at the Document Object Model. Find out what it is and how JavaScript can interact with it!

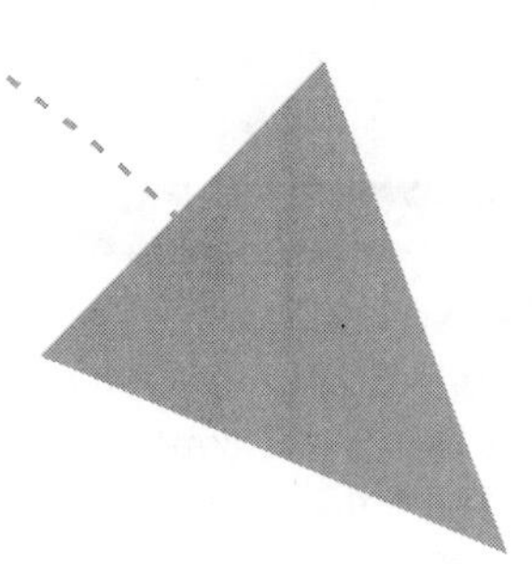

14

JavaScript and the Document Object Model

You've already looked at JavaScript objects, such as `Date`. Now it's time to look at the objects that make up the document itself. These browser objects form what is commonly known as the *Document Object Model* of the browser.

This chapter teaches you about the following:

- The Document Object Model
- Changing text on-the-fly using the Document Object Model
- The event model

An Introduction to the Document Object Model

"Document Object Model?" This was a phrase that struck fear into the hearts of Web developers when it started to appear with that other phrase "Dynamic HTML." What did it mean? What did it do? What could it be used for? These were just some of the hot questions of the time.

In fact, the Document Object Model (DOM) was at the time (when Internet Explorer 4 and Netscape Navigator 4 hit the world, although the Document Object Model actually predates both of these browsers) hailed as one of those "the next big thing in HTML," only this time it wasn't a change to the HTML itself. It was not a new tag (such as a color-changing `<blink>` tag that some people wanted!) or attribute to existing HTML tags; instead it provided a way to take control over all the existing tags on a Web page!

NOTE

In this chapter, the examples you look at are primarily aimed at Internet Explorer 5. This is no accident, because Internet Explorer has the most comprehensive and easily accessible DOM of all the browsers. Because you're here to learn how to use JavaScript, it's the best and easiest route to take.

The silver lining here is that a DOM standard specification has now been drawn up by the Web standards organization, W3C, for the Document Object Model. This means that over the next few months and years, the gulf between the major browsers will start to close.

As always, for the latest (and constantly changing) information on Internet Explorer, visit `http://msdn.microsoft.com/workshop`; for Netscape Navigator, visit `http://developer.netscape.com`.

How Much Power Does It Give Me?

The power the Document Object Model provides to the Web developer is huge. However, one problem does exist. One thing that Web developers need to leverage the Document Object Model is a good working knowledge of scripting, in particular, JavaScript.

This is because the Document Object Model is just a representation of the Web page itself, and in its own right it can't do anything by itself. It's very similar to variables. They hold some value or other, but without more JavaScript, they do nothing.

The latest incarnation of the Document Object Model provides four key innovations (or Web developer magical powers if you prefer):

- Access to all the elements on the page
- Instant page updating

- A full and comprehensive event model
- Changing the content of a page on-the-fly

There is one final key feature. Changes to the Web page can be made at any time! Before the page loads, during loading, and after loading, when the user presses a key, clicks the mouse, moves the mouse, when it's June 12, when it's midnight, midday, only when the visitor has a red desktop (yes, I'm serious!). Whenever. Total control!

With that awesome power in mind, let's take a look at how it works!

Access to Page Elements

During the days of Internet Explore 3.0 and Netscape Navigator 3.0 (no, not as long ago as it sounds!), Web developers could access some of the elements on a Web page using script. These select elements were elements such as `<a>` (the anchor tag), `<applet>` (the applet tag), and `<form>` (defines a form).

NOTE

Looking back, it's amazing to think what clever Web developers managed to do using this limited capability! There was a lot of great stuff on the Web even then!

However, limits to what you could do did exist. For example, even if you wanted to access a heading, you couldn't.

Until now. With the DOM this isn't the case any more. Every single element on the Web page is now accessible. The document features a collection called the `all` collection. This collection contains all the elements on the page, and you can index this collection by using the `name` and `id` attributes.

Simple Example of Accessing Page Elements

The following is an example. Want to check whether your page has an `<h1>` in it? Simple. Here is a simple page with one `<h1>` element:

```
<html>
<head>
<title>A Simple Page</title>
<script language="JavaScript">
<!-- Cloaking device on!

// Cloaking device off -->
</script>
</head>
<body>
<h1 id="head1">Heading One</h1>
</body>
</html>
```

You can detect the presence of this element using the `document.all` collection:

```
<html>
<head>
<title>A Simple Page</title>
<script language="JavaScript">
<!-- Cloaking device on!
function findhead1()
{
var detectElement;
detectElement = document.all("head1");
if (detectElement == head1)
{
alert("Element \'head1\' exists");
}
}

// Cloaking device off -->
</script>
</head>
<body onload="findhead1()">
<h1 id="head1">Heading One</h1>
</body>
</html>
```

Upon loading this page into the browser, you are faced with the alert box shown in Figure 14.1.

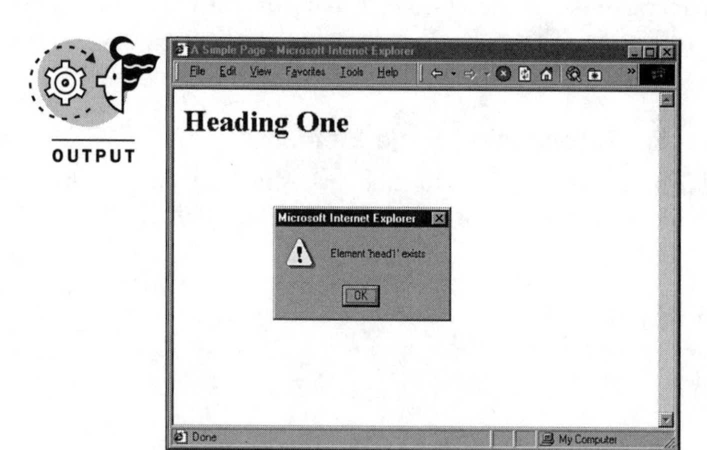

Figure 14.1: *Confirmation that the heading is present.*

You can build on this example to get the JavaScript to return all the elements on a page to you:

```
<html>
<head>
<title>A Simple Page</title>
<script language="JavaScript">
<!-- Cloaking device on!
function findhead1()
{
var tag, tags;
tags = "The tags in the page are:"
for(i = 0; i < document.all.length; i++)
{
tag = document.all(i).tagName;
tags = tags + "\r" + tag;
}
alert(tags);
}
// Cloaking device off -->
</script>
</head>
<body onload="findhead1()">
<h1>Heading One</h1>
</body>
</html>
```

Let's step through what this script does.

```
var tag, tags;
```

The first line of the script declares the variables you are going to be using here.

```
tags = "The tags in the page are:"
```

This next line assigns a value to the variable `tags`. This is done to avoid problems later in the script.

```
for(i = 0; i < document.all.length; i++)
{
tag = document.all(i).tagName;
tags = tags + "\r" + tag;
}
```

The next section of script is the `for` loop. The first line makes the `for` loop iterate through all the tags on the page by using the `length` property, iterating through the elements, starting at the first (`i = 0`, because the numbering of elements starts at 0 and not 1), and ending with the last (`i = document.all.length`), increasing the value of `i` by one each time (`i++`).

Each time the loop is iterated, the tag name is retrieved using the `tagName` method and stored in the variable `tag`. This is then passed to the `tags` variable, along with a carriage return (`\r`) to make the display readable. This is where the initial value of `tags` comes in. If this wasn't set in the first instance, the first item in the alert box would be `undefined`, which doesn't look good!

```
alert(tags);
```

Finally, all the collected tags are displayed in an alert box at the end (see Figure 14.2).

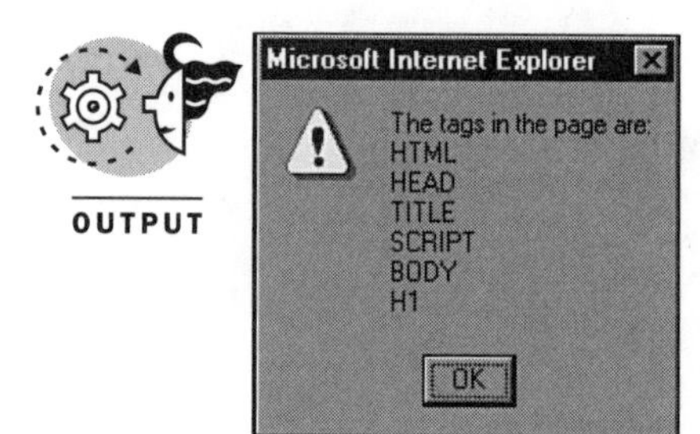

Figure 14.2: *All the tags on the page listed in the alert box.*

The More Elements the Better!

It doesn't matter how many tags you put on the page, the `all` collection can find them all. In this example, some tags (`<b>` and `<i>`) are nested inside other tags (the result is shown in Figure 14.3):

```
<html>
<head>
<title>A Simple Page</title>
<script language="JavaScript">
<!-- Cloaking device on!
function findhead1()
{
var tag, tags;
tags = "The tags in the page are:"
for(i = 0; i < document.all.length; i++)
{
tag = document.all(i).tagName;
tags = tags + "\r" + tag;
}
alert(tags);
}
// Cloaking device off -->
</script>
</head>
```

```
<body onload="findhead1()">
<h1>Heading One</h1>
<p>Some text</p>
<h2>Another heading</h2>
<p>More text and some <b>bold</b> text</p>
<h3>Another heading</h3>
<p>More text and some <i>italics</i> text</p>
</body>
</html>
```

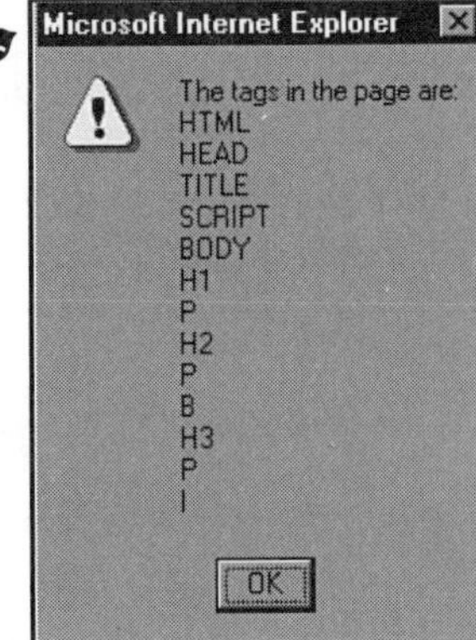

***Figure 14.3:** The tags can't even hide when nested inside other tags!*

Using `srcElement`

This ability to seek out new tags, wherever they are, is a powerful feature because it allows every element on a Web page, no matter how trivial, to become an active element. Consider the following example, which retrieves the name of the tag using `window.event.srcElement.tagName` and displays the tag in the status bar. `srcElement` refers to the source element—the element that caused the event in the first place. This enables you to easily pinpoint the element that generated the event. Here's the example:

```
<html>
<head>
<title>A Simple Page</title>
<script language="JavaScript">
<!-- Cloaking device on!
function tagInfo()
{
var tag;
tag = window.event.srcElement.tagName;
window.status = tag;
}
// Cloaking device off -->
```

```
</script>
</head>
<body onMouseover="tagInfo()">
<h1>Heading One</h1>
<p>Some text</p>
<h2>Another heading</h2>
<p>More text and some <b>bold</b> text</p>
<h3>Another heading</h3>
<p>More text and some <i>italics</i> text</p>
</body>
</html>
```

If you save this page and view it in the browser, you see that, as you move the mouse pointer over each element, the name of the tag is displayed in the status bar of the browser window (see Figure 14.4). (This is done by passing the variable `tag` to the `window.status` object.)

NOTE

More information on the `window.status` object is in Chapter 15, "Examples, Examples, Examples!"

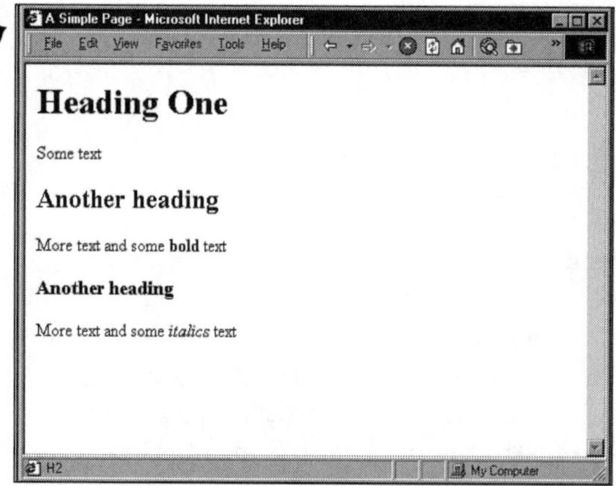

Figure 14.4: *The tag's name displayed in the browser's status bar.*

Adding `id`s

With a little modification, this example can be made to display the `id` of the tag in question (see Figure 14.5). To retrieve this, you use `window.event.srcElement.id`:

```
<html>
<head>
<title>A Simple Page</title>
<script language="JavaScript">
```

```
<!-- Cloaking device on!
function tagInfo()
{
var tag;
tag = "Element name: " + window.event.srcElement.tagName + " ID:
➥" + window.event.srcElement.id;
window.status = tag;
}
// Cloaking device off -->
</script>
</head>
<body onMouseover="tagInfo()" id="body1">
<h1 id="head1">Heading One</h1>
<p id="para1">Some text</p>
<h2 id="head2">Another heading</h2>
<p id="para2">More text and some <b id="bold1">bold</b> text</p>
<h3 id="head3">Another heading</h3>
<p id="para3">More text and some <i id="italics1">italics</i> text</p>
</body>
</html>
```

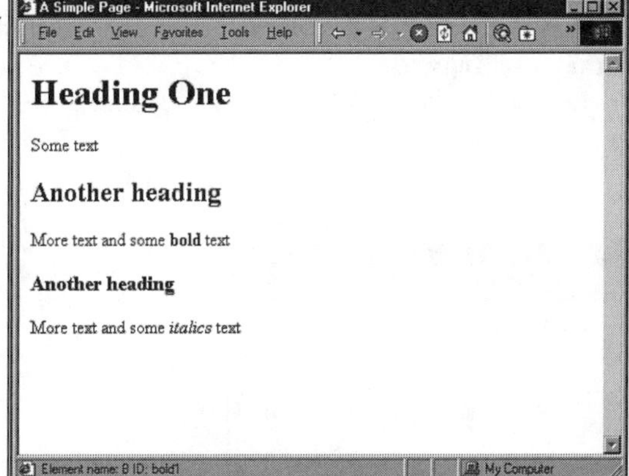

Figure 14.5: *The tag's name and* `id` *displayed in the browser's status bar.*

Parent Elements and Child Elements

A further enhancement (is there no end to what can be done?) is to be able to find out the parent element of an element. The *parent* element is the element in which the element is nested; the nested element is called a *child* element.

The following is an example of JavaScript that shows the parent element of any element on the page (see Figure 14.6):

```
<html>
<head>
<title>A Simple Page</title>
<script language="JavaScript">
<!-- Cloaking device on!
function tagInfo()
{
var tag;
tag = "Element name: " + window.event.srcElement.tagName + "
➥ID: " + window.event.srcElement.id + " Parent: " +
➥window.event.srcElement.parentElement.tagName;
window.status = tag;
}
// Cloaking device off -->
</script>
</head>
<body onMouseover="tagInfo()" id="body1">
<h1 id="head1">Heading One</h1>
<p id="para1">Some text</p>
<h2 id="head2">Another heading</h2>
<p id="para2">More text and some <b id="bold1">bold</b> text</p>
<h3 id="head3">Another heading</h3>
<p id="para3">More text and some <i id="italics1">italics</i> text</p>
</body>
</html>
```

OUTPUT

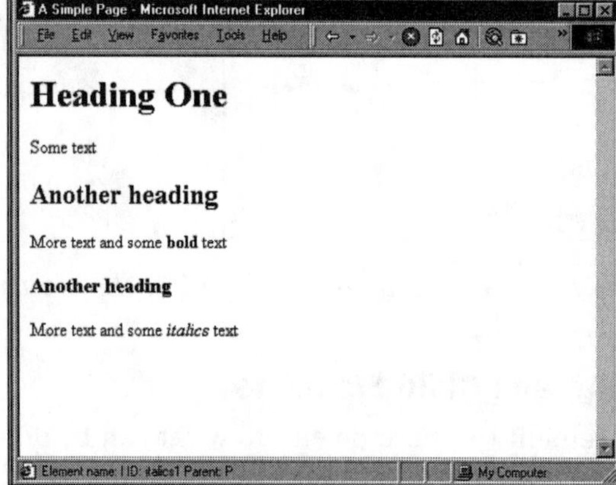

Figure 14.6: *The tag's name and* id *and the parent element displayed in the browser's status bar.*

The following is an example that places an underline automatically under all bold tags when the parent element is a <p> tag and when the mouse is moved over it (see Figure 14.7). The <b> tag whose parent element is the <h2> is not affected (see Figure 14.8). Here's the example:

```
<html>
<head>
<title>A Simple Page</title>
<script language="JavaScript">
<!-- Cloaking device on!
function checkBold()
{
var thistag, parentTag;
thistag = window.event.srcElement.tagName;
parentTag = window.event.srcElement.parentElement.tagName;
if (thistag == "B" && parentTag == "P")
{
window.event.srcElement.style.textDecoration = "underline";
}
}

function checkBoldOff()
{
var thistag, parentTag;
thistag = window.event.srcElement.tagName;
parentTag = window.event.srcElement.parentElement.tagName;
if (thistag == "B" && parentTag == "P")
{
window.event.srcElement.style.textDecoration = "none";
}
}
// Cloaking device off -->
</script>
</head>
<body onMouseover="checkBold()" onMouseout="checkBoldOff()" id="body1">
<h1 id="head1">Heading One</h1>
<p id="para1">Some text</p>
<h2 id="head2">Another heading</h2>
<p id="para2">More text and some <b id="bold1">bold</b> text</p>
<h3 id="head3">Another heading</h3>
<p id="para3">More text and some <i id="italics1">italics</i> text</p>
<h2><b>All bold!</b></h2>
</body>
</html>
```

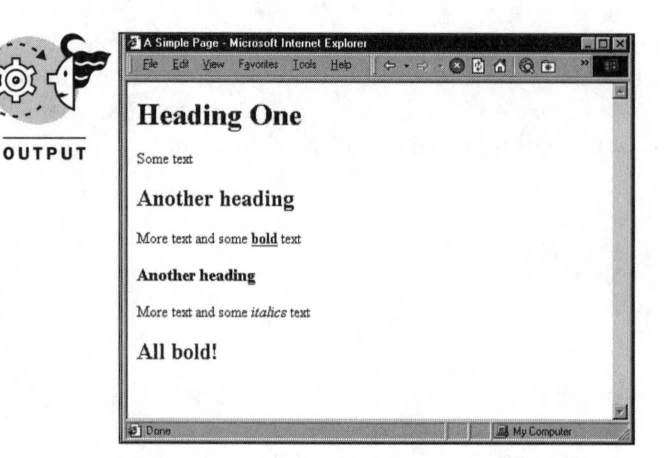

Figure 14.7: *The <b> tag whose parent element is a <p> tag is underlined.*

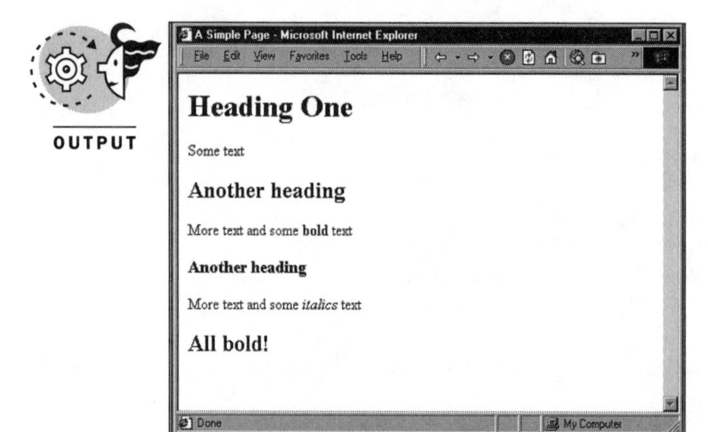

Figure 14.8: *The <b> tags without the <p> parent element are not underlined.*

This script is also sophisticated because there is a second function whose job it is to remove the underline as soon as the mouse pointer is moved off the appropriate tag.

WARNING

Tags are returned as uppercase letters, so when you're checking for them, remember to check against uppercase and not lowercase letters. Using lowercase letters instead will cause the script to fail.

Expanding-and-Collapsing Text Example

A useful function for this is in reducing the amount of text you have displayed onscreen at any one time. Using this method, you can reduce text information down to the headings and allow the reader to click the headings to expand them out to show the full text underneath.

To do this, you need to use a CSS attribute called `display`. This attribute has two values: `none` and blank (not the word "blank," but just nothing). When this is set to blank, the element is visible; when it's set to `none`, the element is completely hidden from view. Here's the code example (the Web page is shown in Figures 14.9 and 14.10):

```
<html>
<head>
<title>A Simple Page</title>
<script language="JavaScript">
<!-- Cloaking device on!
function clickEvent()
{
var thistag, parentTag;
thistag = window.event.srcElement.tagName;
parentTag = window.event.srcElement.parentElement.tagName;
if (thistag == "H1" && parentTag == "BODY")
{
if(document.all(window.event.srcElement.id + "p").style.
➥display == "none")
{
document.all(window.event.srcElement.id + "p").style.display = "";
}
else
{
document.all(window.event.srcElement.id + "p").style.display = "none";
}
}
}
// Cloaking device off -->
</script>
</head>
<body onclick="clickEvent()">
<h1 id="head1">Heading One</h1>
<p id="head1p" style="display:none">Lots and lots of interesting text
➥goes here ... Lots and lots of interesting text goes here ... Lots and
➥lots of interesting text goes here ... Lots and lots of interesting text
➥goes here ... Lots and lots of interesting text goes here ...</p>
<h1 id="head2">Heading Two</h1>
<p id="head2p" style="display:none">Lots and lots of interesting text
```

```
➥goes here ... Lots and lots of interesting text goes here ... Lots and
➥lots of interesting text goes here ... Lots and lots of interesting text
➥goes here ... Lots and lots of interesting text goes here ... </p>
<h1 id="head3">Heading Three</h1>
<p id="head3p" style="display:none">Lots and lots of interesting text
➥goes here ... Lots and lots of interesting text goes here ... Lots and
➥lots of interesting text goes here ... Lots and lots of interesting text
➥goes here ... Lots and lots of interesting text goes here ... </p>
</body>
</html>
```

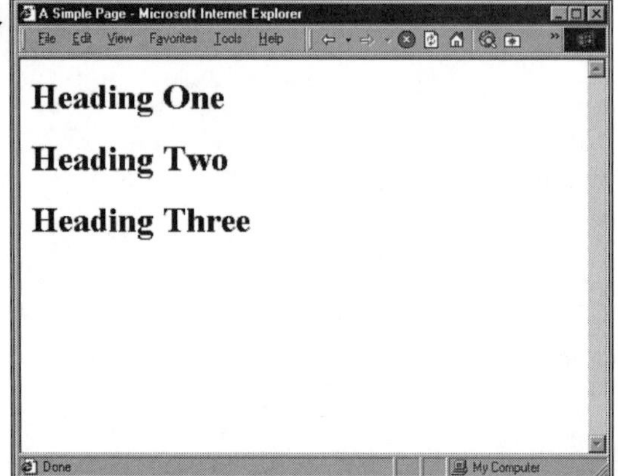

Figure 14.9: How the page appears initially.

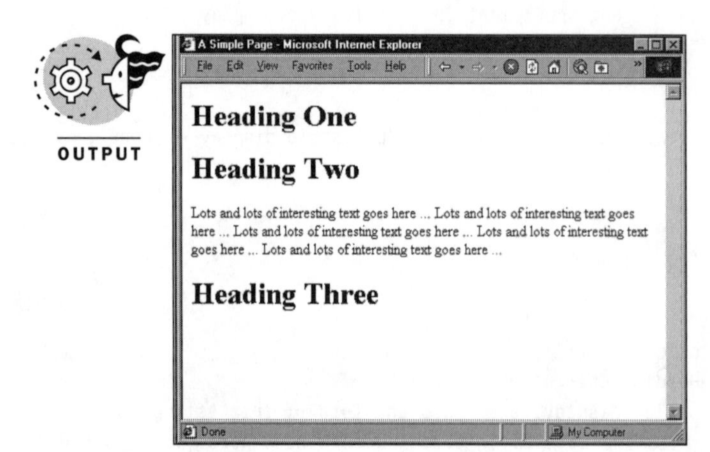

Figure 14.10: Clicking on the headings reveals text.

The JavaScript might seem complex at first (there are two `if` statements nested together here and a lot of curly brackets to keep track of), but the core of the script lies in these three statements:

```
...
if(document.all(window.event.srcElement.id + "p").style.
➥display == "none")
{
document.all(window.event.srcElement.id + "p").style.display = "";
}
else
{
document.all(window.event.srcElement.id + "p").style.display = "none";
...
```

The first statement is the condition, and if this condition is true, that is, the element with the `id` of `window.event.srcElement.id + "p"` is the default value of `"none"`, then concatenating the `id` of the source element with the letter `p` produces the `id` of the paragraph that lies below the heading. (You have to give careful thought to the `id`s you use when creating this kind of effect. However, once you have an example, you can always modify that until you become confident enough to create it from scratch yourself.) The text on the page is hidden initially and then made to appear by the next statement. If the condition is false (that is, the text isn't hidden), it's hidden for the user. This is how the text is made to disappear by the second click on the heading.

Table Cells Example

Sometimes it's useful to give the user a little bit of feedback when she is doing something. Here is a handy example to bear in mind, especially if you use a lot of tables. It changes the color of the cell the mouse pointer is in to a different color, which can be a real help when reading large tables.

The following example uses the `sourceIndex` property, which enables you to pinpoint a single element when in the middle of several others without having to assign `id`s to absolutely everything on the page. Again, from a JavaScript point of view, the script is just a modification of what you've already seen. All these scripts demonstrate how quick and easy accessing the Document Object Model is. The result of this example is shown in Figure 14.11:

```
<html>
<head>
<title>A Simple Page</title>
<script language="JavaScript">
<!-- Cloaking device on!
function chgColor()
```

```
{
var thistag, parentTag;
thistag = window.event.srcElement.tagName;
if (thistag == "TD")
{
document.all(window.event.srcElement.sourceIndex).bgColor =
➥"lemonchiffon"
}
}

function chgBack()
{
var thistag, parentTag;
thistag = window.event.srcElement.tagName;
if (thistag == "TD")
{
document.all(window.event.srcElement.sourceIndex).bgColor = ""
}
}
// Cloaking device off -->
</script>
</head>
<body onMouseover="chgColor()" onMouseout="chgBack()">
<table border="1" width="28%">
<tr>
<td width="25%"> </td>
<td width="25%"> </td>
<td width="25%"> </td>
<td width="25%"> </td>
</tr>
<tr>
<td width="25%"> </td>
<td width="25%"> </td>
<td width="25%"> </td>
<td width="25%"> </td>
</tr>
<tr>
<td width="25%"> </td>
<td width="25%"> </td>
<td width="25%"> </td>
<td width="25%"> </td>
</tr>
</table>
</body>
</html>
```

OUTPUT

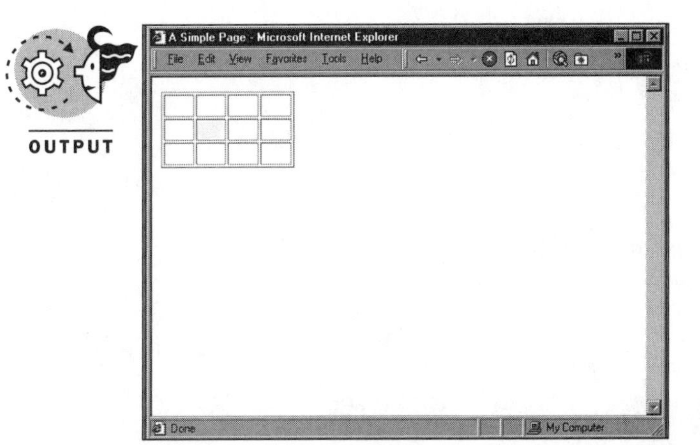

Figure 14.11: *Cells change color as the mouse moves over them.*

NOTE

All these effects occur without the need for the browser to communicate with the server at all. They will even work when the user is offline.

The Event Model

The event model supports a full range of user events. These events are ones the user can generate by mouse, keyboard, focus, and other specialist events.

The following sections discuss some of the events Internet Explorer 5.5 supports.

`onClick` Event

This event fires when the user clicks the left mouse button in the document.

`onContextmenu` Event

EXAMPLE

This event fires when the user clicks the right mouse button in the document area to open the context menu. Using this event enables you to run a script before the context menu pops up or to disable it completely (see Figure 14.12). You can cancel an event by using the `event.returnValue` property and setting this to `false`. This causes the default event, which should occur, to be lost. Here's an example:

```
<html>
<head>
<title>A Simple Page</title>
<script language="JavaScript">
<!-- Cloaking device on!
function menu()
```

```
{
alert("No context menu here!");
event.returnValue = false;
}
// Cloaking device off -->
</script>
</head>
<body onContextmenu="menu()">

</body>
</html>
```

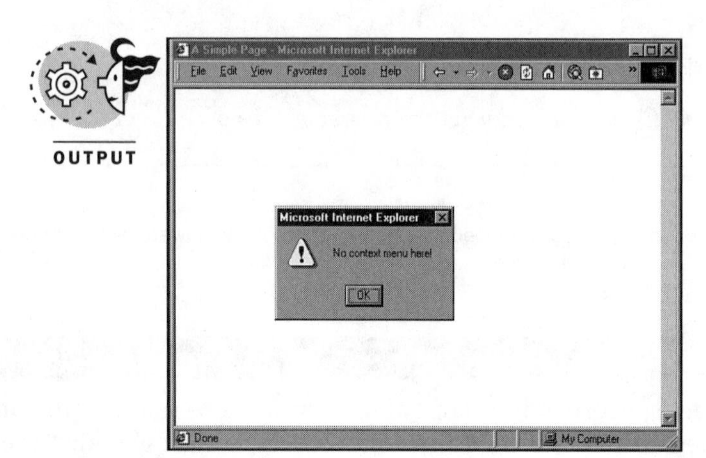

Figure 14.12: *The standard right-click context menu disabled.*

NOTE

A handy use of the previous example is to reduce unauthorized copying of images on your Web pages. It isn't foolproof, but it will fool many Web users!

`onDblclick` Event

This event fires when the user double-clicks in the document. Again, if you want to stop the standard help file being shown, you have to use the `event.returnValue` property.

`onHelp` Event

Providing additional help to your Web visitors is a great idea. You can override the standard Internet Explorer help files that appear when the user presses F1 by using the `onHelp` event.

CAUTION

It's unwise to do this sort of thing to your visitors on the Web, but on an intranet system it can be useful because you can provide the users with concise, applicable help.

This example displays a truly unhelpful alert box when the user asks for help (see Figure 14.13):

```
<html>
<head>
<title>A Simple Page</title>
<script language="JavaScript">
<!-- Cloaking device on!
function yourhelp()
{
alert("Hmmm, I don't know what you should do!");
event.returnValue = false;
}
// Cloaking device off -->
</script>
</head>
<body onHelp="yourhelp()">

</body>
</html>
```

OUTPUT

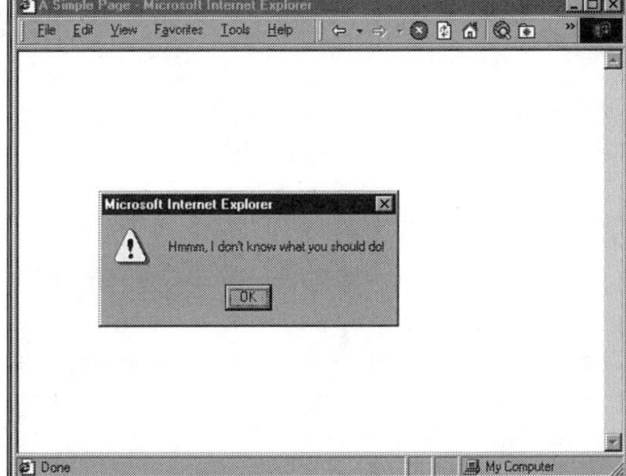

Figure 14.13: *Replace the existing help files with your own form of help!*

`onKeydown` Event

This event fires whenever the user presses a key.

As of Internet Explorer 5.0, the `onKeydown` event fires for the following keys:

Editing: DELETE, INSERT, BACKSPACE

Function: F1–F12

Letters: A–Z (uppercase and lowercase)

Navigation: HOME, END, LEFT ARROW, RIGHT ARROW, UP ARROW, DOWN ARROW, PAGE UP, PAGE DOWN

Numerals: 0–9

Symbols: !, @, #, $, %, ^, &, *, (,), _, -, +, =, <, [,], {, }, ., /, ?, \, |, ', `, ", ~, and ,

System: Esc, spacebar, Shift, Tab, Shift+Tab

Also, this event can be canceled for the following keys and key combinations by specifying `event.returnValue = false`:

Editing: Backspace, Delete

Letters: A–Z (uppercase and lowercase)

Navigation: PAGE UP, PAGE DOWN, END, HOME, LEFT ARROW, RIGHT ARROW, UP ARROW, DOWN ARROW

Numerals: 0–9

Symbols: !, @, #, $, %, ^, &, *, (,), _, -, +, =, <, [,], {, }, ., /, ?, \, |, ', `, ", ~, and ,

System: Spacebar, Esc, Tab, Shift+Tab

In the following example, the event is triggered as the key is pressed down and the character caught and changed from its standard Unicode format (numbers used to represent characters) to actual characters using `String.fromCharCode(event.keyCode)`. These are then displayed in an status bar. The result is shown in Figure 14.14:

```
<html>
<head>
<title>A Simple Page</title>
<script language="JavaScript">
<!-- Cloaking device on!
function press()
{
var char;
char = String.fromCharCode(event.keyCode);
```

```
window.status = "You pressed " + char;
}
// Cloaking device off -->
</script>
</head>
<body onkeydown="press()">

</body>
</html>
```

OUTPUT

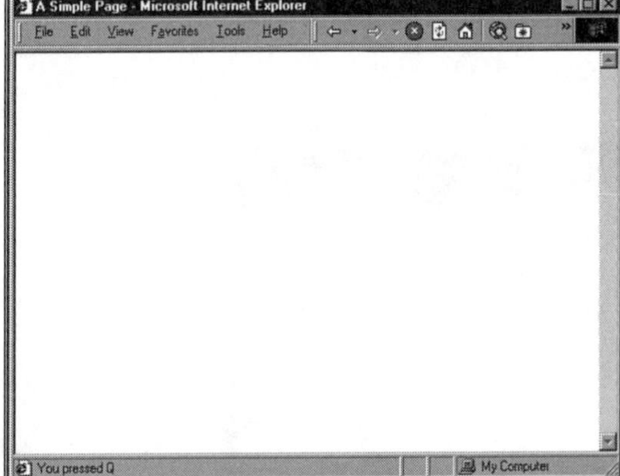

Figure 14.14: *Status bar displays character typed.*

onKeypress Event

This event fires when the user presses an alphanumeric key. It differs from `onKeydown` because this event isn't triggered until the key is fully pressed (as opposed to being on the way down).

onKeyup Event

This keyboard event also fires when the user releases a key. It is triggered when the key is released from the `onKeydown` position.

onMousedown Event

This event fires when the user clicks the document with either mouse button.

EXAMPLE

This example uses `event.x` and `event.y` to find the location of the event in the page and outputs this information to the status bar. Figure 14.15 shows the result:

```
<html>
<head>
<title>A Simple Page</title>
<script language="JavaScript">
```

```
<!-- Cloaking device on!
function clicked()
{
window.status = "You clicked at the coordinates: X = " + event.x + "
➥Y = " + event.y
}
// Cloaking device off -->
</script>
</head>
<body onmousedown="clicked()">

</body>
</html>
```

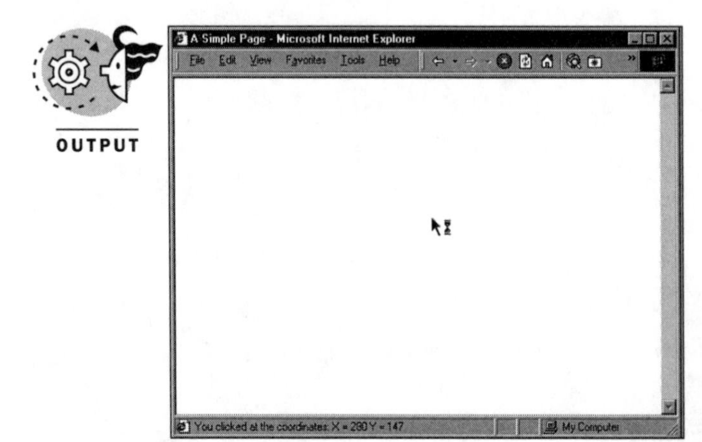

Figure 14.15: *Status bar displays click position.*

`onMousemove` Event

This is another mouse event that fires when the user moves the mouse over the document. This example keeps track of the user's mouse pointer the whole time, with the text also keeping track of it. See Figure 14.16 for the result:

```
<html>
<head>
<title>A Simple Page</title>
<script language="JavaScript">
<!-- Cloaking device on!
function moved()
{
window.status = "Current mouse coordinates: X = " + event.x + " Y =
➥" + event.y
follower.style.pixelTop = event.y
```

```
follower.style.pixelLeft = event.x
}
// Cloaking device off -->
</script>
</head>
<body onmousemove="moved()">
<p id="follower" style="position:absolute">Squeak!</p>
</body>
</html>
```

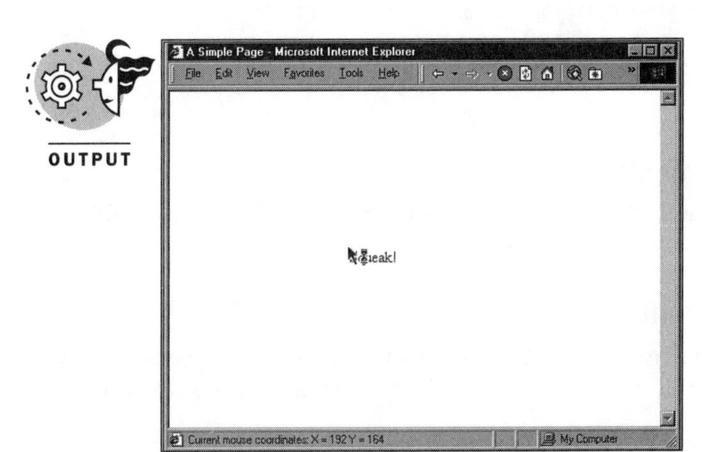

Figure 14.16: *Status bar displays the position of the mouse pointer.*

`onMouseout` Event

This mouse event fires when the user moves the mouse pointer outside the boundaries of the document. This includes moving into another element.

In this example, when the mouse moves outside the document, a message is displayed. The same message is also displayed when the pointer quickly moves toward the text. This is because the user can move the pointer more quickly than the text can move, so in effect it's moving into another element and triggering the event. Here's the example:

```
<html>
<head>
<title>A Simple Page</title>
<script language="JavaScript">
<!-- Cloaking device on!
function moved()
{
window.status = "Current mouse coordinates: X = " + event.x + " Y =
➥" + event.y
follower.style.pixelTop = event.y
follower.style.pixelLeft = event.x
```

```
}

function outofbounds()
{
alert("Hey, come back!  I can't follow you there!");
}
// Cloaking device off -->
</script>
</head>
<body onmousemove="moved()" onmouseout="outofbounds()">
<p id="follower" style="position:absolute">Squeak!</p>
</body>
</html>
```

onMouseover Event

This mouse event responds when the user moves the mouse pointer into the document.

onMouseup Event

The onMouseup event fires when the user releases a mouse button while the mouse is over the document. It is the event that occurs after the onClick event.

onStop Event

This is the final event you're going to look at here. This one fires when the user clicks the Stop button in the browser or leaves the Web page for another one:

```
<html>
<head>
<title>A Simple Page</title>
<script language="JavaScript">
<!-- Cloaking device on!
function stopped()
{
alert("Hey, don't go");
}
// Cloaking device off -->
</script>
</head>
<body onstop="stopped()">

</body>
</html>
```

TIP

This example is probably one of the least irritating uses of the `onStop` event. On a Web page, don't use it to keep visitors penned in your site or fire up loads of warnings about leaving—these things are irritating to users!

A good use for this event is on intranet pages (perhaps to keep a kiosk open) or if you are developing something such as an online game (to warn the visitors that leaving would affect their score or something).

JavaScript Power

This chapter doesn't pretend to be a comprehensive coverage of the Document Object Model; this would be a very thick book indeed just for one browser! The plan has been to give you a flavor of the things you can do with examples for you to follow to get the idea of how they're done. The examples are things you can modify easily and set to work to do something useful on your Web site.

As has been said before, browsers are continually changing, and the best source of information about them is the manufacturers, which have vast online resources cataloging the features of their browsers. The Microsoft Web Workshop site alone has hundreds (maybe even thousands) of pages detailing its browser. What stays the same is how you can use JavaScript to use the tools the browsers place at your disposal. Learn JavaScript and the rest is easy, and it's even easier now because both Microsoft and Netscape provide copious JavaScript examples. These examples should be very useful now that you know not only how to write JavaScript but how to read it, too!

What's Next

Congratulations! You've made it to the end! JavaScript is no longer something you just wish you could learn to use; instead, it's a serious, powerful tool you have at your disposal. In the next chapter, you take a tour through some of the most common uses for JavaScript on the Web today.

See you there!

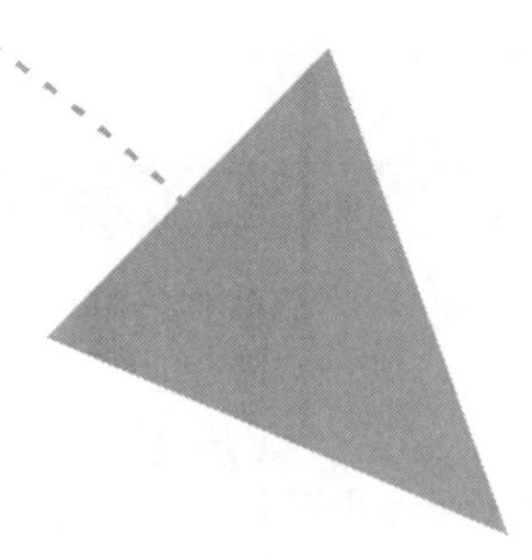

15

Examples, Examples, Examples!

This chapter is filled with examples, in which you will see how some of the most common JavaScript effects on the Web are accomplished. You also learn the scripts and the know-how to modify them for use on your own Web site.

This chapter teaches you about the following:

- Adding last modified dates to Web pages
- Adding a simple clock
- Adding a countdown counter
- Simple form validation
- Creating rollovers
- Creating a scrolling status bar message
- Controlling cookies

Example 1—Adding Last Modified Dates to Web Pages

Of the examples in this chapter, this one is probably the simplest and the one that needs the least code for accomplishing the effect.

Adding a last modified date to a Web page enables your visitors to know when the page last changed, which in turn helps them decide whether they want to read the page. It's a great example and really easy to use. Here it is in action:

```
<html>
<head>
<title>A Simple Page</title>
</head>
<body>
<script language = "JavaScript">
<!-- Cloaking device on!
document.write("Page last updated: " + document.lastModified)
// Cloaking device off -->
</script>
</body>
</html>
```

This example uses one method and one property of the document object. It uses the lastModified property to retrieve the date on which the page was last saved, and it uses the write() method to write the whole string to the actual Web page (see Figure 15.1).

Because you want this to write the last modified date onto the page, you have to move the script block from the <head> of the page down to the body. You can place this anywhere in the body that suits your page.

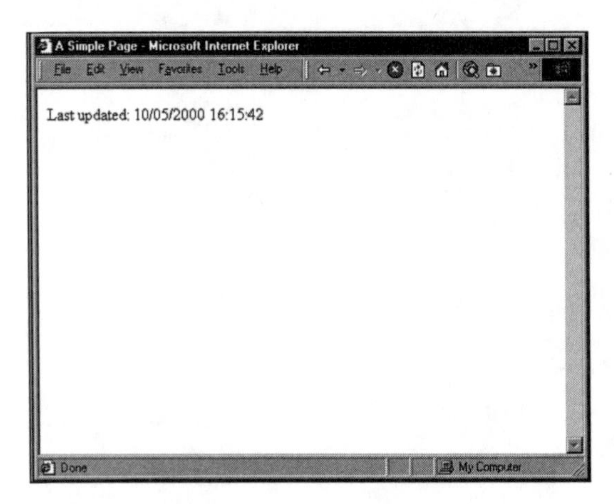

Figure 15.1: *The last modified date and time printed in the page.*

Modifications

No modifications are possible.

Example 2—Simple Clock

A clock is a favorite of many Web developers, who use it to add a little bit of dynamic content to a Web page. In this example (which works in both Internet Explorer and Netscape Navigator), the time is displayed in the input box (see Figure 15.2):

```
<html>
<head>
<title>A Simple Page</title>
<script language="JavaScript">
<!-- Cloaking device on!
function gettime() {
var date= new Date();
var hr = date.getHours();
var m = date.getMinutes();
var s = date.getSeconds();
var ampm = "AM";
if (hr > 11)
{
ampm = "PM"
}
if (hr > 12)
{
hr -= 12
}
if(m < 10)
{
m = "0" + m
}
if(s < 10)
{
s = "0" + s
}
document.clockform.clock.value = hr + ":" + m + ":" + s + " " +ampm;
setTimeout("gettime()",100)
}
// Cloaking device off -->
</script>
</head>
<body onload="gettime()">
<form name="clockform">
<input type="text" name="clock">
</form>
</body>
</html>
```

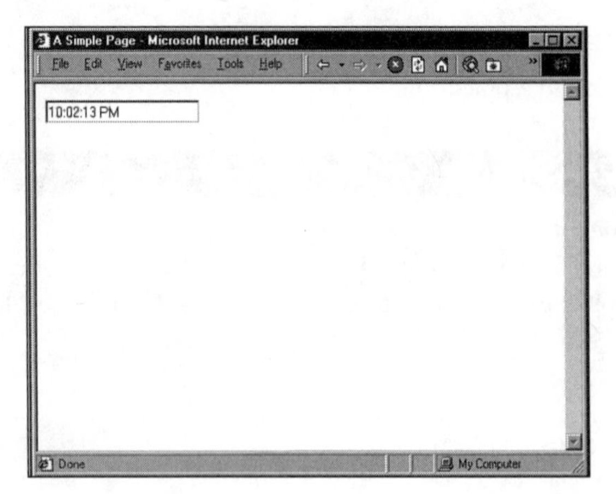

Figure 15.2: *A clock on the Web page.*

Modifications

If you cut out a little of the code (the references to `AM` and `PM` and the `if` statement that takes 12 away from the hour if it is greater than 12), the clock becomes a military (or 24-hour) clock (see Figure 15.3):

```
<html>
<head>
<title>A Simple Page</title>
<script language="JavaScript">
<!-- Cloaking device on!
function gettime() {
var date= new Date();
var hr = date.getHours();
var m = date.getMinutes();
var s = date.getSeconds();
if(m < 10)
{
m = "0" + m
}
if(s < 10)
{
s = "0" + s
}
document.clockform.clock.value = hr + ":" + m + ":" + s;
setTimeout("gettime()",100)
}
// Cloaking device off -->
</script>
</head>
<body onload="gettime()">
```

```
<form name="clockform">
<input type="text" name="clock">
</form>
</body>
</html>
```

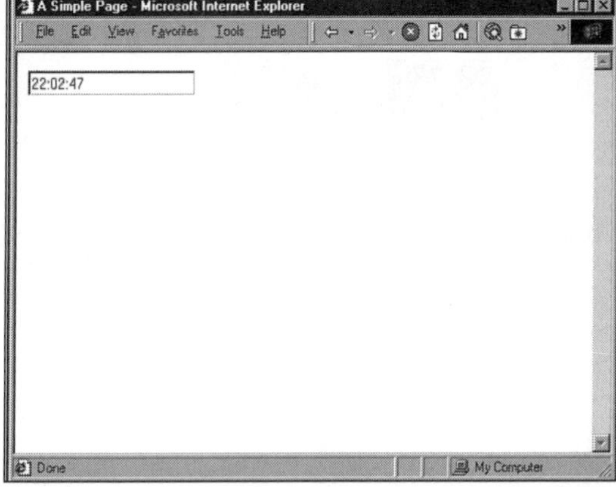

Figure 15.3: *A clock displaying military time on the Web page.*

Example 3—Simple Countdown Counter

This is a really handy script if you want to have a counter on the page. A counter can be handy for things such as showing when a page or image might refresh if you have, say, a Web cam that updates an image on a regular basis. The actual page change can be done by a meta tag refresher (which appears following the title tag).

Here is a simple example, the results of which are shown in Figure 15.4:

```
<html>
<head>
<title>A Simple Page</title>
<meta http-equiv="refresh" content="30">
<script language="JavaScript">
<!-- Cloaking device on!
var x=30;
var y=1;
function startClock(){
x=x-y;
document.form1.clock.value = x;
timerID=setTimeout("startClock()", 1000);
}
// Cloaking device off -->
</script>
```

```
</head>
<body onload="startClock()">
<form name="form1">
<input type="text" name="clock">
</form>
</body>
</html>
```

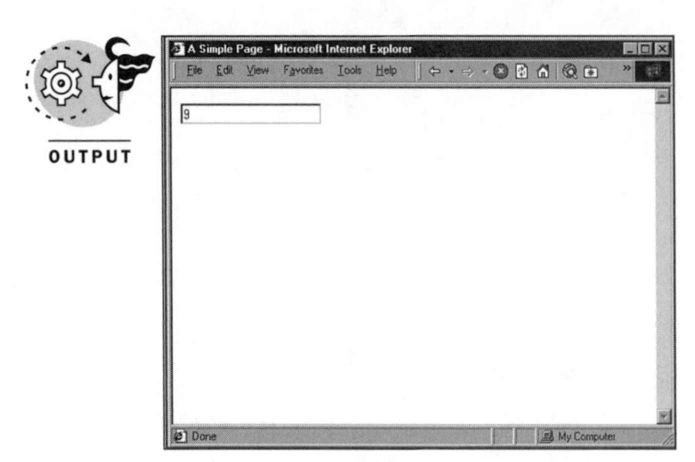

Figure 15.4: *A countdown in action.*

Modifications

You can make a few modifications to this counter. You can change the starting point of the counter (by changing the value of the variable x), or you can change the interval (by changing the value of the variable y).

Example 4—Simple Form Validation

If you have a form of any kind on your Web site, you will probably want to reduce the amount of junk or inaccurate information you receive. One of the quickest ways to do this is by having a script that validates the information sent to you.

Here is a simple example that validates one input box that is expecting to receive some text. If it is empty, it refuses to submit the form and tells the user to enter text (see Figure 15.5):

```
<html>
<head>
<title>A Simple Page</title>
<script language="JavaScript">
<!-- Cloaking device on!
```

```
function sendMe()
{
return confirm("Do you want to continue the submission?");
}

function chkForm()
{
if (form1.inp1.value == "")
{
alert("Please fill in the text box");
form1.inp1.focus();
return false;
}
}
// Cloaking device off -->
</script>
</head>
<body>
<form name="form1" method="POST" action="someCGI.cgi" onSubmit="return sendMe()">
<p><input type="text" name="inp1">
<input type="submit" value="Submit" onClick="return chkForm()">
<input type="reset" value="Reset"></p>
</form>
</body>
</html>
```

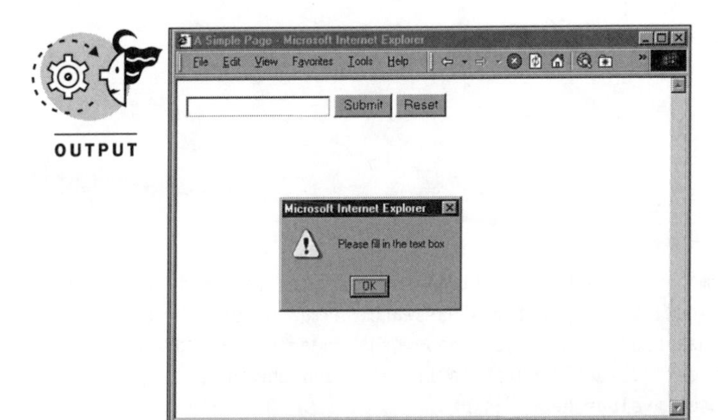

Figure 15.5: *An alert box is displayed if no text is typed into the input box.*

Using this kind of script prevents a user from submitting a form with a blank field. The script is also clever enough to put the cursor back in the input box by using the `form1.inp1.focus` method.

Modifications

Many modifications are possible on the form verification theme—so many in fact that the whole book could have been devoted to the subject. However, here is another useful example. This one is used to verify that the user has set his password correctly by getting him to type it in twice. If the two strings don't match, the user made a mistake, and it's better he find out about it before trying to use his password next time! Here's the example, with the resulting alert box shown in Figure 15.6:

```
<html>
<head>
<title>A Simple Page</title>
<script language="JavaScript">
<!-- Cloaking device on!
function sendMe()
{
return confirm("Do you want to continue the submission?");
}

function chkForm()
{
if (form1.pass1.value != form1.pass2.value)
{
alert("Please re-enter your password");
form1.pass1.value = "";
form1.pass2.value = "";
form1.pass1.focus();
return false;
}
}
// Cloaking device off -->
</script>
</head>
<body>
<form name="form1" method="POST" action="someCGI.cgi" onSubmit="return sendMe()">
<p>Enter your password: <input type="password" name="pass1"><br>
Re-enter your password: <input type="password" name="pass2"><br>
<input type="submit" value="Submit" onClick="return chkForm()">
<input type="reset" value="Reset"></p>
</form>
</body>
</html>
```

If the two entries aren't the same, it clears both of them and places the cursor in the first input box, which is ready for new inputs from the user. If the passwords do match, the form is submitted normally.

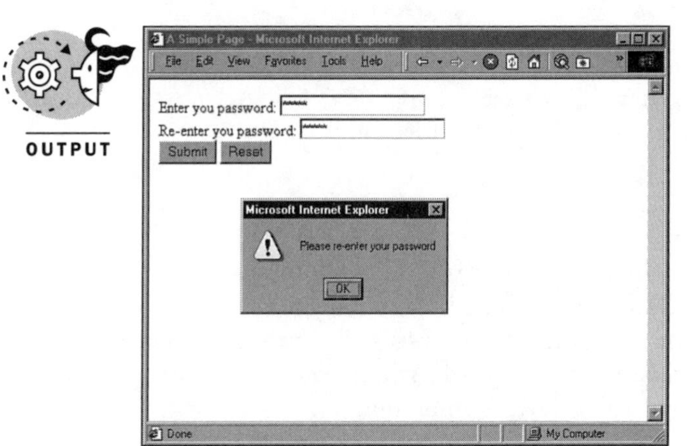

Figure 15.6: *The two passwords entered must match.*

Example 5—Rollovers

A *rollover* is an effect in which one image is replaced for another when the user moves the mouse pointer over it. Often, this is used only with images that host hyperlinks, but that isn't necessarily a rollover's only use. The following is an example:

```
<html>
<head>
<title>A Simple Page</title>
<script language="JavaScript">
<!-- Cloaking device on!
if (document.images)
{
img1 = new Image;
img2 = new Image;
img1.src = "img1.gif";
img2.src = "img2.gif";
}
else
{
img1 = "";
img2 = "";
document.imgSwap = "";
}
// Cloaking device off -->
</script>
</head>
```

```
<body>
<a href="moveon.htm" onMouseover="document.imgSwap.src = img2.src"
➥onMouseout="document.imgSwap.src = img1.src">
<img src="img1.gif" name="imgSwap" border="0">
</a>
</body>
</html>
```

The reason for the `if` statement is to exclude browsers that don't understand what `document.images` means but that might understand JavaScript. This single tactic prevents any browsers that are not at least JavaScript 1.1 compliant from using the script—in which case this script wouldn't work. Figure 15.7 shows the rollovers in action.

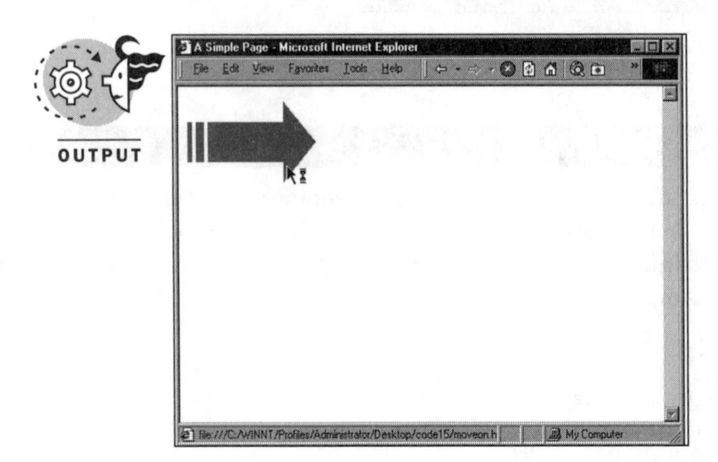

***Figure 15.7:** Rollovers in action.*

Modifications

Again, many modifications to rollovers are possible, but they really all center around the same theme. You can add more rollovers on different images, make the images larger, make them smaller, and so on.

Example 6—Scrolling Status Bar Message

Another common JavaScript-powered effect is the scrolling message in the status bar of the browser. It's a great way to pass small amounts of information to the visitor without having to resort to alert boxes. Even though the status bar is small and unobtrusive, it is still effective.

Here is a simple example that places a little information in the status bar when the user moves the mouse over an image hyperlink:

```
<html>
<head>
<title>A Simple Page</title>
<script language="JavaScript">
<!-- Cloaking device on!
function addMsg()
{
window.status="Sample image";
return true;
}
// Cloaking device off -->
</script>
</head>
<body>
<a href="moveon.htm" onMouseover="window.status='Sample image';
➥return true" onMouseout="window.status='';return true">
<img src="img1.gif" border="0">
</a>
</body>
</html>
```

Moving the mouse pointer over the image or hyperlink causes the message to be displayed in the status bar of the browser (see Figure 15.8).

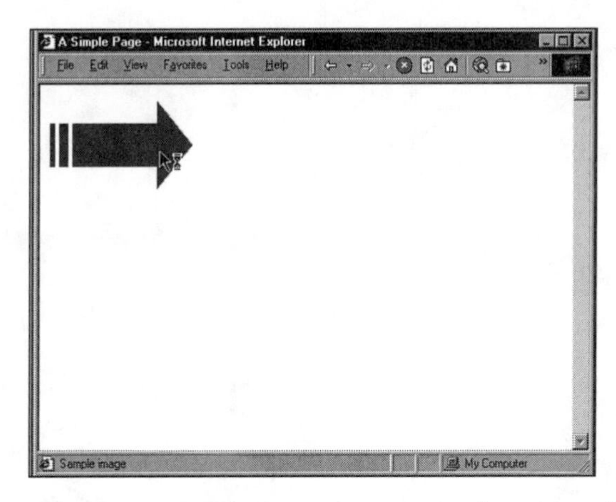

Figure 15.8: *The test message in the status bar.*

NOTE

`return true` is required in the code to make it work.

Modifications

One of the most popular modifications to the status bar message is to upgrade the JavaScript so that you have a scrolling message instead of a static one. Here is an example (shown in action in Figure 15.9) that does just that:

```
<html>
<head>
<title>A Simple Page</title>
<script language="JavaScript">
<!-- Cloaking device on!
var msg = "Thanks for visiting our Web site! ... ";
function scrollMsg()
{
window.status = msg;
msg = msg.substring(1,msg.length) + msg.substring(0,1);
setTimeout("scrollMsg()",150);
}
// Cloaking device off -->
</script>
</head>
<body onload="scrollMsg()">

</body>
</html>
```

Figure 15.9: *A scrolling status bar message.*

The controlling part of this JavaScript is this statement:

```
msg = msg.substring(1,msg.length) + msg.substring(0,1)
```

The first of these statements is the part of the script that actually does the chopping of the initial message held in the variable msg. The part of the statement on the right side of the equal sign represents the original message. The left side is the chopped-up version, which, on each run of the script, takes the first character of the message that's displayed and places it at the end—giving the illusion that the message is scrolling. In fact, all that is happening is that the string is being rearranged—the first character is being moved to the end.

So let's break it down:

- `msg`—This is the current string.
- `msg.substring(1, msg.length)`—This is the whole string apart from the first character (because numbering starts at 0).
- `msg.substring(0, 1)`—This is the first character, which is then taken from the front and glued onto the end of the part of the string represented by `msg.substring(1, msg.length)`.

So, at each run of the script (controlled by the statement `setTimeout("showMsg()",150)`, which appears on the next line), this process is repeated—with the letter that's at the beginning of the string being moved to the end. The script is rerun every 150 milliseconds. This is an arbitrary value, and you're free to change this to suit your needs.

More Modifications

Having the scrolling text there all the time might annoy some users, so why not reduce it to running just once? To do this, keep count of the number of times you've performed the front-character–to–back-character swap and stop after you've done them all. This example has 39 characters, so after you have gone from 0 to 38, it's time to stop:

```
<html>
<head>
<title>A Simple Page</title>
<script language="JavaScript">
<!-- Cloaking device on!
var counter = 0
var msg = "Thanks for visiting our Web site! ... ";
function scrollMsg()
{
if (counter < 38)
{
window.status = msg;
msg = msg.substring(1,msg.length) + msg.substring(0,1);
setTimeout("scrollMsg()",150);
counter += 1
```

```
}
else
{
window.status = "";
}
}
// Cloaking device off -->
</script>
</head>
<body onload="scrollMsg()">

</body>
</html>
```

TIP

Don't have a continuous scrolling message on the status bar because it can annoy users, especially if they want to use the status bar to see where your hyperlinks are taking them. Instead, go for one that stops after one or two runs.

Example 7—Controlling Cookies

The final example here looks at how you can take control over cookies with JavaScript. Cookies are more widely used on the Web now than ever before to personalize Web content for frequent visitors (not to mention the tracking capability cookies provide, which is useful for marketing and sales purposes!).

Cookies are unique pieces of information a Web site gives the browser. The next time the browser goes to that site, invariably the information contained in that cookie is read. This enables the Web site to remember that you've been there before.

NOTE

The individual bits of information contained in a cookie are, not surprisingly, called *crumbs*!

JavaScript lets you do some clever things with cookies. They can let you remember your visitors' usernames and passwords, preferences, and much more.

EXAMPLE

Let's begin with a Web page with one input box on it for the user's username. The link on the page will take the user to the next page, which will be used to display the contents of the cookie:

```
<html>
<head>
<title>Page 1</title>
```

```
<script language="JavaScript">
<!-- Cloaking device on!

// Cloaking device off -->
</script>
</head>
<body>
<form name="form1">
<p>Username: <input type="text" name="user1"><br>
<a href="page2.htm">continue ...</a></p>
</form>
</body>
</html>
```

To create cookies, the first thing you must do is create a new `Date` object called `expireAt`, which will be used to pick a date three months from the date the cookie is activated:

```
<html>
<head>
<title>Page 1</title>
<script language="JavaScript">
<!-- Cloaking device on!
expireAt = new Date;
expireAt.setMonth(expireAt.getMonth() + 3);
// Cloaking device off -->
</script>
</head>
<body>
<form name="form1">
<p>Username: <input type="text" name="user1"><br>
<a href="page2.htm">continue ...</a></p>
</form>
</body>
</html>
```

Next, you create an empty variable called `username`:

```
<html>
<head>
<title>Page 1</title>
<script language="JavaScript">
<!-- Cloaking device on!
expireAt = new Date;
expireAt.setMonth(expireAt.getMonth() + 3);
username = "";
// Cloaking device off -->
</script>
```

```
</head>
<body>
<form name="form1">
<p>Username: <input type="text" name="user1"><br>
<a href="page2.htm">continue ...</a></p>
</form>
</body>
</html>
```

Next, write the function that creates the cookie. The function to do this comprises two statements:

```
<html>
<head>
<title>Page 1</title>
<script language="JavaScript">
<!-- Cloaking device on!
expireAt = new Date;
expireAt.setMonth(expireAt.getMonth() + 3);
username = "";

function makeCookie()
{
username = document.form1.user1.value
document.cookie = "name=" + username + ";expires=" + expireAt.toGMTString()
}
// Cloaking device off -->
</script>
</head>
<body>
<form name="form1">
<p>Username: <input type="text" name="user1"><br>
<a href="page2.htm">continue ...</a></p>
</form>
</body>
</html>
```

The first statement of the function reads the contents of the input box, and the second line creates the cookie. The cookie consists of two parts. The first part (`"name=" + username`) takes the value of `username` and concatenates it with a chosen pseudovariable (not really a variable, but more like a name assigned to the data) for the value (here `name` has been chosen). Make sure you don't enter inadvertent spaces into the string you are creating; otherwise, things won't go as expected. The second part (`";expires=" + expireAt.toGMTString()`) sets when the cookie will expire (in other words, when it stops working). This is a date three months from when it was created. This time format needs to be in GMT format, so the `expireAt.toGMTString()` method is used.

The final thing to do on this page is to use the `onclick` event on the hyperlink to trigger the function `makeCookie()`:

```
<html>
<head>
<title>Page 1</title>
<script language="JavaScript">
<!-- Cloaking device on!
expireAt = new Date;
expireAt.setMonth(expireAt.getMonth() + 3);
username = "";

function makeCookie()
{
username = document.form1.user1.value
document.cookie = "name=" + username + ";expires=" + expireAt.toGMTString()
}
// Cloaking device off -->
</script>
</head>
<body>
<form name="form1">
<p>Username: <input type="text" name="user1"><br>
<a href="page2.htm" onclick="makeCookie()">continue ...</a></p>
</form>
</body>
</html>
```

This page is now finished. All that needs to be done now is to create a second page (called `page2.htm`) that reads the cookie. Here is a page to do just that:

```
<html>
<head>
<title>Page 2</title>
<script language="JavaScript">
<!-- Cloaking device on!
function fillIn()
{
if (document.cookie != "")
{
cookieCrumb = document.cookie.split("=")[1];
document.form1.read1.value = cookieCrumb;
}
else
{
document.form1.read1.value = "Cookie empty!";
```

```
}
}
// Cloaking device off -->
</script>
</head>
<body onload="fillIn()">
<form name="form1">
<p>The username you entered was: <input type="text" name="read1"></p>
</form>
</body>
</html>
```

This function, `fillIn()`, is run by the `onload` event when the page is loaded. The `if` statement first checks to see whether the cookie is blank (that is, doesn't exist for this page). If the cookie doesn't exist then the input box is filled with the string `Cookie Empty`. If it does exist then the next statement splits the cookie string at the `=` sign, and the second part (defined by the `[1]` at the end because the first part would be `[0]`) is assigned to the variable `cookieCrumb`. This crumb is finally passed to the input box for display.

With both pages saved, you can try the example. Open the first page and type something into the input box (see Figure 15.10).

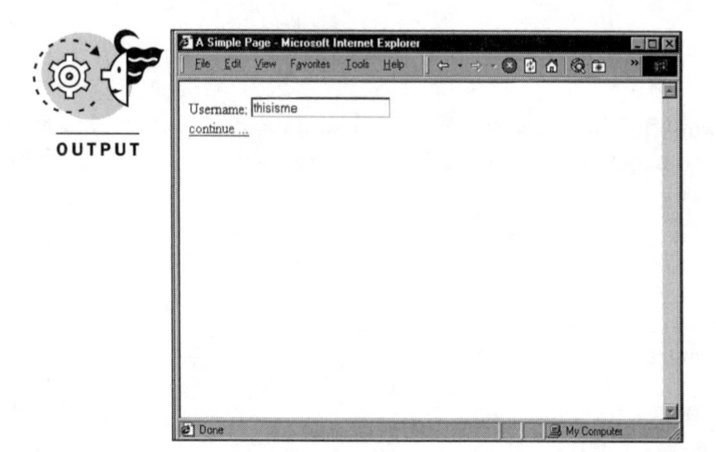

Figure 15.10: *Type some text into the input box.*

Then, click the hyperlink at the bottom of the page to load the second page, and the contents of the cookie are displayed in the input box (see Figure 15.11).

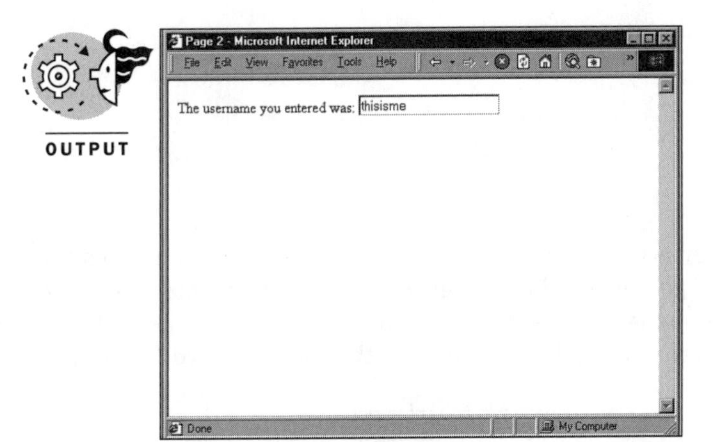

Figure 15.11: *The contents of the cookie are placed in the input box on the second page.*

Modifications

You can do a great many things with cookies. You can save almost any type of small data in cookies (even things such as CSS attribute values), so the scope of them is broad. One thing you will probably want to do with cookies at some point is to give the user a way to delete them. Deleting a cookie (or making them *stale*, as it's sometimes called) is a simple process of changing the expiration date of the cookie to a date that has passed.

Here is a function that deletes the cookie you have created by changing its expiration date to a month prior to the current system date:

```
<html>
<head>
<title>A Simple Page</title>
<script language="JavaScript">
<!-- Cloaking device on!
expireAt = new Date;
expireAt.setMonth(expireAt.getMonth() - 1);

if (document.cookie != "")
{
if (confirm("Are you sure you want to delete the cookies from this Web site?"));
{
crumbs = document.cookie.split("; ");
for(i=0; i < crumbs.length; i++)
{
crumbName = crumbs[i].split("=")[0];
document.cookie = crumbName + "=;expires=" + expireAt.toGMTString();
}
}
}
```

```
// Cloaking device off -->
</script>
</head>
<body>

</body>
</html>
```

This is actually a very nice way to delete cookies because it gives the user a chance to change her mind (see Figure 15.12). In addition, it also lets you delete all the cookies your site has given the user by using the `length` property to iterate through all the cookies in the cookie record for your Web site.

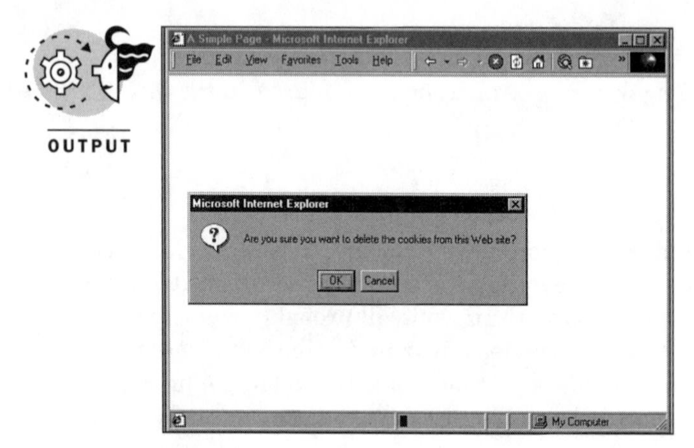

Figure 15.12: *The option of whether to proceed with the cookie clearance.*

You can check to see whether the cookie has been loaded by loading the second page from the cookie set and showing the previous series (called `page2.htm`). Figure 15.13 shows that no cookies exist.

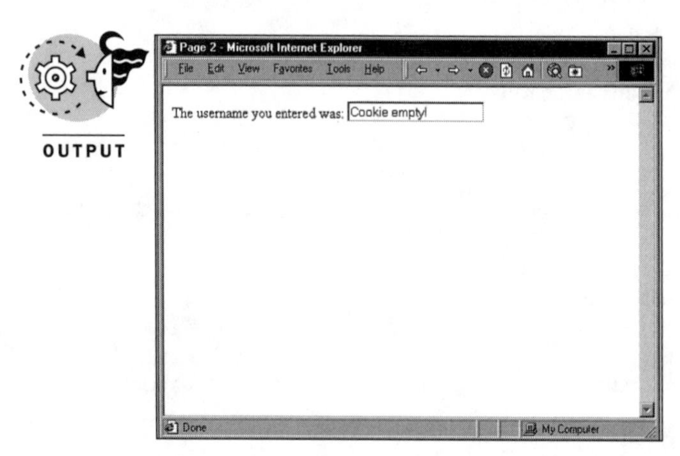

Figure 15.13: *No cookies are used after the clearance.*

What's Next

Well, nothing more in the book! All that is left for you to do is to take your newfound JavaScript skills out into cyberspace and make fine use of this great and versatile technology!

Good luck and have fun!

Kathie and Adrian

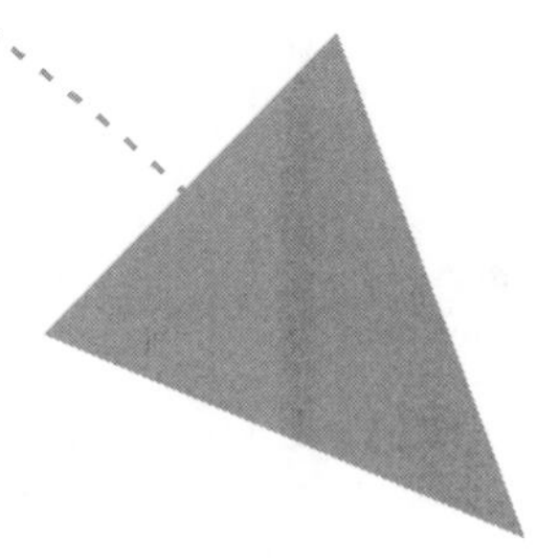

Index

E

F

N

O

P-Q

W-Z